ADWALTON MOOR 1643

The Battle that Changed a War

by

David Johnson

BLACKTHORN PRESS

Blackthorn Press, Blackthorn House
Middleton Rd, Pickering YO18 8AL
United Kingdom

www.blackthornpress.com

ISBN 0 9540535 8 3

The cover photograph is a detail of "Cromwell After the Battle of Marston Moor" by Ernest Crofts.

Printed and bound by Antony Rowe Ltd, Eastbourne

Dedication

It was originally intended to dedicate this book to the memory of those who fought at the battle of Adwalton Moor. This intention has however been overtaken by events, and while the dedication to the soldiers of 1643 still stands, it is now accompanied by a tribute to Dr P.R.Newman who died in January 2003.

Peter Newman was quite simply a remarkable man. Since the completion in 1978 of his doctoral research into the northern Royalist army of William Cavendish, earl of Newcastle, Newman's published work has established and confirmed his position and reputation as a leading historian of the English Civil Wars. Many readers will be familiar, for example, with his pioneering work on the battle of Marston Moor, and his exhaustive research into the careers and backgrounds of English and Welsh Royalist colonels. Newman's work is characterized throughout by a meticulous scholarship allied to a penetrating intellect. It is impossible to read Peter Newman without a profound sense that one is in the presence of a master craftsman.

It was my great privilege, in the final year of his life, to not only make Peter Newman's acquaintance but also to become his friend. What I discovered, in addition to Peter's obvious prowess as a formidable historian, was an amusing, charming and incredibly generous man. My work on Adwalton Moor, originally inspired by Newman's early battlefield investigations at Marston Moor, has benefited enormously from his invaluable advice and close scrutiny. I can only hope that the publication of this book will go some way to repaying that debt.

Peter Newman's work has extended our knowledge and understanding, he serves as an inspiration and an example; this is indeed a legacy of which any one of us would be justifiably proud.

Acknowledgements

This book started life in 1998 as a thesis submitted, two years later, in part fulfillment of the course requirements for an MA in Historical Research at the University of Hull. Over the five years of research and writing, during which the project developed from thesis proposal to published book, I have had the good fortune to become acquainted with a number of people who have provided valuable assistance and advice, and to whom I offer my sincere thanks. Of special note are the following:

Professor Glenn Burgess and Dr Julian Haseldine, Department of History, University of Hull; Dave Cooke, Yorkshire Branch of the Battlefields Trust; Dr Andrew Hopper, University of East Anglia; Glenn Foard, former County Archaeologist for Northamptonshire and currently Projects Officer for the Battlefields Trust; Clive McManus of Leeds; Ronnie Barnes, Drighlington local historian; David Atkinson of Morley; Ian Sanderson and Vince Devine, West Yorkshire Archaeology Service (Wakefield); David Neelon, USA; Dr Andrew Brown, English Heritage; Walter Brown of East Ardsley; my publisher at the Blackthorn Press, Alan Avery; and finally my dear wife Wendy.

As is customary on these occasions, I accept complete responsibility for any errors that may be contained in the following pages.

CONTENTS

MAPS & ILLUSTRATIONS

Maps

Illustrations

INTRODUCTION

THE BATTLE THAT CHANGED A WAR

On Friday 30th June 1643, across a barren ridge of West Yorkshire moorland five miles south east of Bradford, the earl of Newcastle's northern Royalist army completely destroyed General Ferdinando Lord Fairfax's northern Parliamentary forces. The battle of Adwalton Moor brought a hard and fluctuating seven-month campaign for military control of Yorkshire to a decisive conclusion. The victorious Royalists held control of virtually the entire county, leaving the shattered remnants of Fairfax's army to take refuge within the one remaining Parliamentary garrison: the walled port of Hull. Historians, as a consequence, have invariably accorded the battle a regional rather than a national significance. Yet it is the purpose of this introduction to demonstrate that Adwalton Moor changed the course of the English Civil War. It will be argued here that the magnitude of the Royalist victory was such that it forced Parliament into a religious and military alliance with Scotland: The Solemn League and Covenant. The Covenant created a new balance of power which led directly to the critical Parliamentary victory at Marston Moor in July 1644. In this analysis both the regional and national significance of Adwalton Moor are recognized for the first time. In addition, it will be argued that the battle itself came much closer than is generally appreciated to producing an 'against all odds' Parliamentarian victory.

At the onset of the Civil War in the summer of 1642 it was widely believed that the first large scale military confrontation would settle the issue one way or the other. When, however, the armies of King and Parliament fought to a standstill at Edgehill on 23rd October and subsequently faced each other without coming to blows at Turnham Green on 13th November, it became apparent that an indeterminate period of warfare lay ahead. Thereafter, in 1643, the situation quickly deteriorated into a series of largely separate regional contests in which the possession of territory and the acquisition of garrisons became the overriding consideration.

In this to some extent disjointed war, the northern theatre was the first in which a decisive victory - Adwalton Moor - threatened to bring the wider Civil War to some sort of conclusion. The defeat of Lord Fairfax's Yorkshire army on 30th June 1643 provided the earl of Newcastle with an opportunity to march against London, creating the very real possibility of an outright Royalist military victory or a total Parliamentarian surrender. However, because the advantage was squandered in a futile siege of Hull - the war in the north continuing for another year until finally and famously decided by the crushing Parliamentary victory at Marston Moor in July 1644 - historians, as a result, have understandably considered Marston Moor to be the critical moment of the northern conflict. This, in turn, has significantly reduced the perceived (but not the real) importance of Adwalton Moor, rendering the battle peripheral - both in terms of geography and effect. Consequently, it is in this relatively narrow

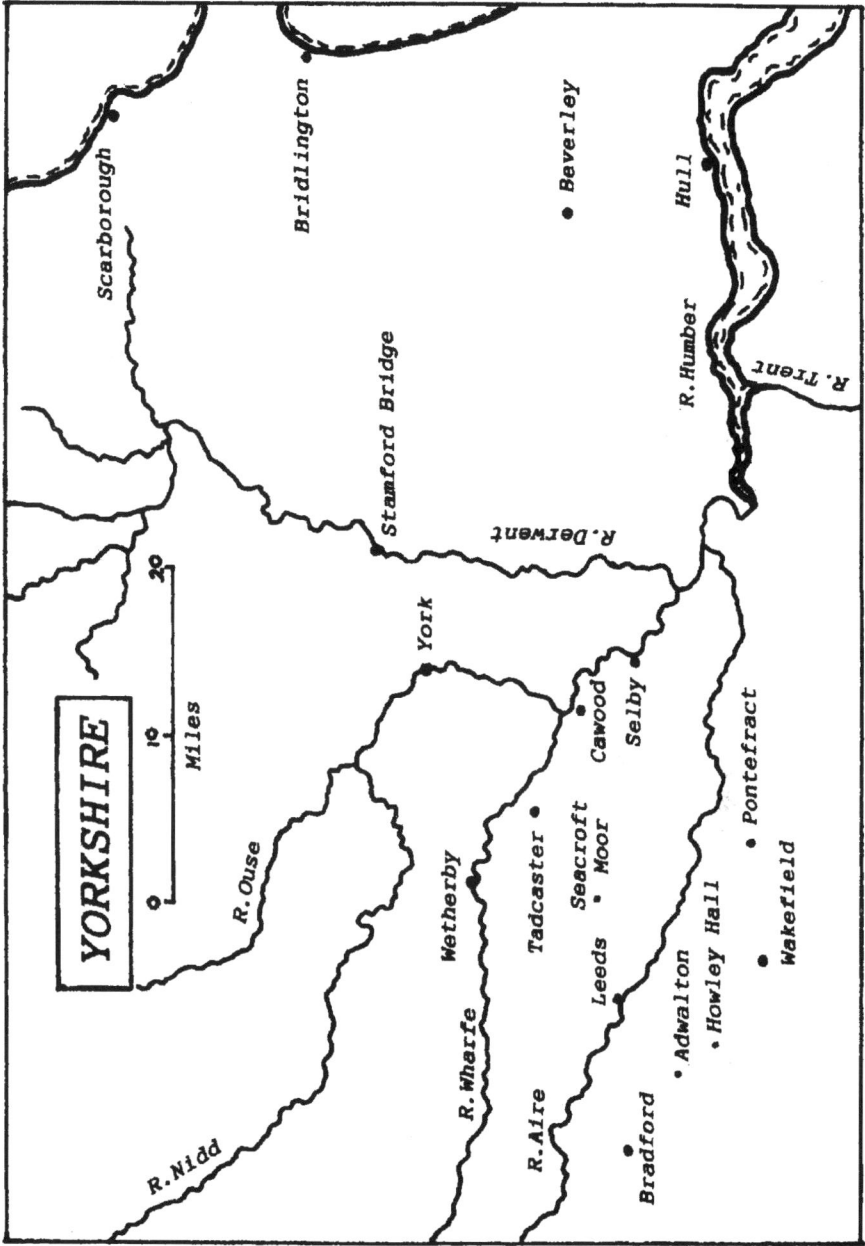

regional context that the significance of Adwalton Moor is generally seen to lie, providing the Royalist cause with a temporary domination of the north that can all too readily be seen to have lasted for no more than a mere six months. However, to contemporary opinion in July 1643 the battle appeared to have decided the northern war, leaving Parliament in crisis as the victorious earl of Newcastle threatened to march his triumphant army southwards.

Yet it was, in fact, the principal consequence of Adwalton Moor - the Scottish alliance - that provided Parliament with final victory in the north. The invasion of Northumberland in January 1644 by a Scottish army of over 20,000 men shifted the balance of military power firmly in favour of Parliament. The loss of the north at Marston Moor in July 1644 was a decisive blow to Royalist hopes, one, moreover, from which the King's cause never recovered:

> This fatal blow, which so much changed the King's condition that till then was very hopeful.[1]

Thus it was Adwalton Moor that changed the course of the war. The Solemn League and Covenant represented the only means by which the catastrophe of 30th June 1643 could be reversed. From January 1644 it is clearly evident that the military advantage, held by the King for the greater part of 1643, was lost to Parliament. Yet the hostility with which many members of Parliament regarded the conditions imposed by the Scots for a military alliance - the introduction of Presbyterianism into England and the financial cost of supporting the Scottish army - meant that only a disaster of unprecedented proportions - one that threatened outright defeat - could have persuaded both the Lords and the Commons of the need for Scottish assistance. To those assembled at Westminster during the early days of July 1643, Adwalton Moor was precisely that disaster.

To properly disentangle the real significance of the battle, it is necessary to understand the way in which Adwalton Moor was submerged and overtaken by the course of the wider Civil War during the second half of 1643. This requires a consideration of three particular issues. Firstly, the way in which a series of Royalist victories during the summer of 1643 resulted in an escalating Parliamentarian crisis that obscured the real relationship between Adwalton Moor and the Scottish alliance. Secondly, the way in which the importance of the military advantage won by the Royalist army at Adwalton Moor was subsequently diminished by the unsuccessful exploitation of that advantage. And thirdly, the way in which the defeat at Adwalton Moor broke Parliament's resistance to Scottish pressure for a direct military role in the war in England.

The Parliament's Crisis of July 1643

The earl of Newcastle's victory at Adwalton Moor on 30th June was only the first in a series of major Parliamentarian setbacks that threatened to end the war by the close of 1643. Two weeks later on 13th July the army of Parliament's Western Association, commanded by Sir William Waller, was destroyed at the battle of Roundway Down by a combined force of west country Royalists and hastily despatched cavalry from the King's Oxford army. This was followed by the catastrophic loss of Bristol, England's second port and Parliament's most important western garrison, to Prince Rupert on 26th July. Added to these alarms were the Royalist rising in Kent and the disintegration as an effective fighting force of the main Parliamentary field army commanded by the earl of Essex. The Kent revolt, on the very doorstep of the capital, began on 18th July and lasted for almost a week, while the army of the earl of Essex, operating against the King's Oxford army in the Thames valley, was wasted by camp fever and incompetent leadership. Everywhere the King's forces were gaining ground. By the end of July the failure, one by one, of Parliament's armies threatened total defeat. The only issue appeared to be the means by which the final blow would be delivered, be it by Royalist military force or a negotiated peace that would almost certainly amount to a complete Parliamentarian surrender.

To John Pym, unofficial leader of the House of Commons and pre-eminent amongst those opposed to a restoration of the King's authority, the crisis offered only one solution: an alliance with Scotland. Though both the Lords and Commons resolved to open negotiations with all possible speed, the protracted nature of the negotiation process itself obscured and marginalized the causal impact of Adwalton Moor. The Solemn League and Covenant wasn't agreed in Edinburgh until 17th August - and then not finally ratified by Parliament until 25th September - and because the military details of the treaty were not signed until 29th November, the Scottish army did not cross the border into England until 19th January 1644. As a result historians have tended to portray the whole series of dramatic Royalist successes during the month of July 1643 as a cumulative process, creating a mounting military crisis in which the Scottish alliance with the English Parliament became inescapable. S.R.Gardiner claimed that it was the combination of defeats at Adwalton Moor and Roundway Down that produced the need for an alliance.[2] Less specifically J.H. Hexter described the midst of the July panic as the point at which military assistance was requested from north of the border.[3] C.V.Wedgwood, despite failing to mention Adwalton Moor, nevertheless came closer to the truth by stating that it was the defeat of Lord Fairfax's northern army which produced the necessity for an alliance.[4] A.Woolrych simply identified the July crisis,[5] while J. Jones stated that it was the whole series of defeats and alarms that were responsible.[6] P.Haythornthwaite suggested that it was, once again, the combined weight of Royalist successes, rather than the outcome of a single battle, that forced Pym's hand.[7] M.Bennet stated that in the summer of 1643 it was the distinct possibility of a Royalist victory that compelled the English and Scots to unite.[8] L.Kaplan described a combination of factors, of which Adwalton Moor was only one.[9]

However, an examination of the sources reveals that it was in fact the battle of Adwalton Moor, and no other battle or combination of military reverses that compelled Parliament to seek Scottish assistance. The *Journal of the House of Commons*, the *Journal of the House of Lords*, the propaganda newsbook *Parliament Scout*, and the earl of Clarendon's *History of the Rebellion*, demonstrate clearly the precise link between the battle and the creation of the Solemn League and Covenant.

Officially at least, Parliament was first informed of the situation in Yorkshire on 5th July 1643, five days after Adwalton Moor. The *Journal of the House of Commons* records:

> A letter from Mr Stockdale to Mr White, agent for the northern parts, of the First of July, desiring relief in all sorts of succours, was this day read.[10]

This somewhat ambiguous report was in fact a reference to Thomas Stockdale's eyewitness account of Adwalton Moor written from Halifax the day after the battle. Stockdale, a close confidant of Yorkshire's Parliamentary general, Ferdinando Lord Fairfax, provided a graphic and dramatic description of the aftermath:

> our loss of prisoners taken by the enemy was great, but the number is not equal to the fear and distraction it hath begotten in the country......The country is wasted and exhausted and tired out with the weight of the troubles continually falling upon this part of Yorkshire, the soldiers want pay, and which is worse, arms and powder and other ammunition, and are over-charged with the most potent strength that opposeth the Parliament; insomuch as the soldiers disband and desert the service, and the country overawed cannot longer assist the army; and if speedy supply be not sent with some considerable succour of men, the Lord General will be constrained to accept of some dishonourable conditions from the enemy.[11]

Fortunately for Parliament, a plot to deliver the port of Hull to the King was discovered and had been foiled the day before Adwalton Moor. General Ferdinando Lord Fairfax, together with the bedraggled remains of his Yorkshire army, took refuge within the port walls, narrowly avoiding the disaster of having to surrender. Even so, the situation described by Stockdale was indeed desperate. The defeat at Adwalton Moor was all the more shocking because of the tenacious way Lord Fairfax and his son, Sir Thomas Fairfax, had held the Royalists at bay for over six months. Now, however, all that counted for nothing. Hundreds of Parliamentary soldiers had been captured, many had deserted, the West Riding was exhausted, the populace fearful of Royalist reprisals. Most shocking of all, the earl of Newcastle's victorious army stood poised to march against London. Parliament was only too well aware that the successful execution of such a strategy would in all probability win the war for Charles. The King recognized that victory, if it were to be comprehensive and without complication, depended upon the capitulation of the capital. Adwalton Moor presented an opportunity to bring the conflict to a relatively swift conclusion.

The reaction of Parliament was both immediate and decisive. As soon as Stockdale's letter had been read to the Commons it was at once resolved that:

> the Scotts Nation shall be forthwith desired to send in Aid and Assistance for the Preservation and Maintenance of the Religion and Liberties of the Kingdom; and that the Lords Concurrence be desired herein.......Ordered, That the Letter from Mr Stockdale be shewed to the Lords......Ordered, That the Committee appointed to prepare instructions do meet this afternoon, and forthwith prepare instructions for the Committees to be sent into Scotland, and to bring them in with all speed.[12]

The reaction of the Upper House to Stockdale's letter was equally decisive. *The Journal of the House of Lords* records:

> Ordered, That this house will send Two Lords, as Committees, into Scotland, by this day sevennight, *or sooner if they can be ready;* and do concur with the House of Commons, that one of their instructions shall be, to desire the Aid and Assistance of the Scotts nation against papists and others, now in arms, to destroy the Protestant Religion, and the Liberty of this Kingdom[13] [Author's italics]

The seriousness of the situation facing Parliament is emphasized by the urgent desire of the Lords to despatch negotiators to Scotland within the week. This is significant. The decision to solicit Scottish assistance represented the victory of John Pym and his allies - prepared to prosecute the war to a military victory - over those Parliamentarians who believed a negotiated settlement to be possible and preferable. Adwalton Moor convinced many members of both houses that the King possessed the forces with which to fight the war to a finish. The decision of Parliament to act quickly and radically underlines the precariousness of the military situation. Having lost the northern army, and by implication uncertain of the effectiveness with which the forces of the Eastern Association could oppose the earl of Newcastle, Parliament desperately required a new army with which to continue the war.

As news of Adwalton Moor reached the capital it promptly became common knowledge that Lords and Commons were actively seeking military assistance from Scotland. The 29th June to 6th July issue of the London newsbook *Parliament Scout* described clearly the intentions of Parliament:

> the consideration of this unhappy accident [Adwalton Moor] hath put the House of Commons to a serious consideration of the business of supply from Scotland (whose late Declaration shows them true friends to the parliament of England) and thereupon they sent to the Lords that they should join, for the sending Commissioners forthwith to call in the Scots.[14]

Further evidence is provided by the vitally important contemporary testimony of Edward Hyde, later earl of Clarendon. In the Long Parliament - convened in November 1640 - Hyde was elected MP for Saltash, successfully concerning himself with reform of the administration of the law. Although initially opposed to the King on a number of questions, Hyde had no sympathy for the increasingly radical reform of religion proposed by Pym and others. Making excuses for his health, Hyde left Westminster in May 1642 to join the King at York. Spending much of the war at Charles' side, Hyde became famous as the author of *The History of the Rebellion*, the most important of the contemporary accounts of the Civil War. Although *The History* does not mention Adwalton Moor by name, Hyde states categorically that the battle prompted the opening of negotiations with the Scots:

> Upon news of the Lord Fairfax's being defeated in the north, they [Parliament] resolved presently to send a committee of the two Houses into Scotland, to desire their brethren of that kingdom presently to advance with an army for their relief.[15]

Clearly, therefore, the weight of evidence demonstrates that the ramifications of Adwalton Moor were such that Parliament could no longer remain confident of its ability to wage war, let alone win it. The acquisition, by alliance with Scotland, of a new army was, it appeared, the only realistic way forward. The urgency of the crisis was, of course, heightened during the subsequent weeks of July 1643 by the defeat at Roundway Down, the fall of Bristol, the rising in Kent, and the continued ineffectiveness of the earl of Essex. However, these important developments occurred *after* the decisions taken on 5th July by the House of Lords and the House of Commons. It was the earl of Newcastle's victory at Adwalton Moor, and the threat to the capital consequent upon that victory, that forced a panic stricken Parliament into the arms of the Scots.

Royalist Military Strategy 1643

Having established the true relationship between Adwalton Moor and the Scottish alliance, it is necessary to examine the battle in a wider military context: that of a national Royalist strategy. Newcastle's victory on 30th June 1643 provided the King with a strategic breakthrough, one, however, that Charles was ultimately unable to take advantage of. The military exploitation of Adwalton Moor, therefore, is of such profound importance, both for the prosecution of the Royalist war effort and the significance with which the battle has subsequently been viewed, that it must be examined in some detail.

It has been noted that following the failure of either King or Parliament to win outright victory at Edgehill or Turnham Green in 1642, the Civil War developed into a number of apparently uncoordinated regional contests. However, some historians have argued that during 1643 Charles devised an alternative strategy by which three separate Royalist armies would combine to force the surrender of the capital. S.R.Gardiner described a plan in which the earl of Newcastle would forge south through East Anglia to blockade London from the Essex bank of the Thames, the King's Oxford army would hold the earl of Essex at bay in the Thames valley, while, finally, Sir Ralph Hopton's west country Royalists would advance through the southern counties to blockade London from the Kent bank of the Thames. Once in position, Gardiner continued, the armies of Newcastle and Hopton would:

> find no difficulty in stopping the passage of shipping on the river, and by the annihilation of its commerce, the great city, and with it the Parliamentary army, would be starved into submission.[16]

Although the existence of such an elaborate strategy is contested in some quarters for lack of evidence,[17] there is absolutely no doubt that Newcastle was acutely aware of the impatience with which the King desired the northern army to move south. The Queen wrote to the earl on 18th June to convey her husband's command that the northern army march to him.[18] Although such an undertaking was impractical at the time, the Yorkshire Parliamentarians were not defeated until 30th June, the letter is nevertheless important in establishing that Newcastle was aware of the King's strategy *before* Adwalton Moor was fought. However, there is no evidence that the earl acted with any urgency once Yorkshire was finally secured. According to the biography written by Newcastle's second wife - Margaret, duchess of Newcastle - the earl returned to York, leaving a force of cavalry in the East Riding to keep watch over Lord Fairfax at Hull. It was only news of a Parliamentary incursion into Lincolnshire - Gainsborough fell to Lord Willoughby on 16th July - that prompted Newcastle to order the invasion of the county with reinforcements under the command of Lieutenant General James King. However, perhaps at last conscious of the urgency of the situation, further procrastination being impossible, Newcastle finally elected to follow General King into Lincolnshire with the bulk of the army.[19] By the end of July the Royalists had retaken Gainsborough, garrisoned Lincoln, and forced the remaining Parliamentarian forces into Boston. With the enemy in retreat, it appeared that nothing could prevent Newcastle's continued progress towards the Thames. Yet in August the earl returned to Yorkshire to begin, on 2nd September, the second Royalist attempt of the Civil War to reduce Hull by siege.

At so critical a point in the campaign, it is hardly surprising that Newcastle's apparently counterproductive and contradictory conduct should become the subject of a heated controversy. His successes in Yorkshire and Lincolnshire, in accordance with the King's wishes, had opened a path to the capital, the earl was poised to deal the enemy a mortal blow. S.R.Gardiner was convinced that the northern Royalist army had within its power an almost inevitable victory had it reached Essex:

> That Newcastle if he had pushed on would have brought the civil war to an end

in favour of the King, is as nearly certain as any hypothetical conclusion can be.[20]

C.H.Firth came to a similar if slightly less certain conclusion:

> The combined movement on London planned by the King might have changed the fortune of the war, for at the end of July the Parliament had no army capable of keeping the field.[21]

And perhaps most significantly, because the information came in all probability from the earl himself, the duchess of Newcastle wrote of the intended march south:

> if it had taken effect, would doubtless have made an end to the war.[22]

That Newcastle can have been in no doubt as to the King's strategic intentions is evidenced by the way in which Charles continued to summon the earl south after Adwalton Moor and the belated move into Lincolnshire. Clarendon asserts that following the fall of Bristol to Prince Rupert on 26th July, the King sent a messenger to the earl ordering an advance into Norfolk, Suffolk, Cambridgeshire and Essex; to be carried out as part of a pincer movement in conjunction with a march towards the capital by the Oxford army. As the Oxford army approached the Parliamentary garrison of Gloucester the messenger returned with news that Newcastle could not obey the King's orders.[23] It was only upon receipt of this communication that Charles, led to believe that the town would fall in a matter of days, began the unsuccessful siege of Gloucester on 10th August. Had Newcastle marched south as the King required, the siege of Gloucester would not have taken place and a two pronged advance on London would have been underway. Undeterred Charles instructed the Queen, who wrote on 13th August, to send word that Newcastle was to march into Suffolk, Norfolk or Huntingdonshire.[24] Sir Philip Warwick, the King's messenger, then embarked on a second fruitless attempt to order the earl south, this time arriving during Newcastle's disastrous and wasteful autumn siege of the impregnable walled port of Hull.[25]

How it was that one of England's most loyal and devoted noblemen should find it impossible to comply with the commands of his King when obedience would, the evidence suggests, have led only to greater personal glory and final triumph remains an issue of unresolved controversy. Sir Philip Warwick, the messenger previously referred to, claimed that Newcastle feared the loss of his independent command should the northern Royalist army become involved in any combined operation with the King's Oxford army. According to Warwick, Newcastle was unwilling to accept a subordinate position to Prince Rupert, whom the earl feared would assume overall command of the King's forces.[26] The difficult relationship with Rupert was to prove disastrous a year later when the failure of both men to properly co-ordinate their respective armies played a material part in the catastrophic Royalist defeat at Marston Moor. The duchess of Newcastle, however, claimed that it was the increasingly desperate appeals of Yorkshire's Royalist gentry, alarmed by Sir Thomas Fairfax's raids into the East Riding, that compelled her husband to return to the county in order to deal finally with Hull.[27] Similarly Clarendon stated that Newcastle had declined to accede to Sir Philip Warwick's first attempt to persuade the earl to march south because:

> the gentlemen of the country who had the best regiments, and were among the best officers, utterly refused to march except Hull were taken first; and that he had not strength enough to march and to leave Hull securely blocked up.[28]

However, Warwick went on to claim that the Yorkshire officers would have been content to deal with Hull themselves, leaving the earl to advance south with that portion of his army raised in Northumberland and County Durham, and that Newcastle himself was intent on recruiting in Lincolnshire to increase his strength further.[29] On this particular point it is perhaps revealing to note that in January 1644, when Newcastle was confronted with the Scottish invasion of Northumberland, the earl commanded his Yorkshire forces to remain in their native county – in order to contain the Fairfaxes – while advancing towards the Scots with his north country recruits.

This is clearly a difficult question. Newcastle's explanation that any mobilization was impossible while Hull remained in Parliament's hands was, at the very least, partly true. An abiding characteristic of the Civil War was the extreme difficulty, and often impossibility, of persuading armies to fight outside their areas of recruitment. Though the parochialism of the Yorkshiremen was undoubtedly a very real consideration, 'there is little doubt', according to C.H.Firth, that its employment as an excuse to justify continued operations in the north coincided with Newcastle's 'own inclinations'.[30] P.R.Newman, however, takes the view that the earl's inviolable loyalty gives greater credence to the argument for Yorkshire intransigence:

> This factor, Yorkshire Royalism's inherent local preoccupations, may be the factor which prevented any follow-up to Adwalton. It is far more likely than is the idea that Newcastle was afraid to submerge himself and his army in any general fusion of forces directed against London. He was too loyal to let that matter to him.[31]

Clarendon, despite his admiration for Newcastle as a gentleman, castigated the earl for a lack of urgency at critical moments in the campaign, for downright negligence in respect of the King's orders, and for an almost narcissistic obsession with the superiority of Prince Rupert's rank.[32] At a time when the course of the Civil War was possibly moving too slowly in the King's favour, it was imperative that Newcastle should capitalize upon his advantage with all speed. With greater financial resources, command of the Navy, and, following Adwalton Moor, the impending Scottish invasion, Parliament's cause had to be defeated before its advantage in money, men, and ships could prove decisive. Clarendon clearly believed that Newcastle was in part responsible for the subsequent demise of Royalism in the north and, by implication, for the King's ultimate defeat in the wider Civil War. Yet whatever the real truth of the matter may be, the essential point here is that Newcastle's failure allowed the contemporary significance of Adwalton Moor to be dissipated and lost.

The Solemn League and Covenant

The point has often been made that the English Civil War should more properly be known as the *British Wars* or the *War of the Three Kingdoms*.[33] Any examination of the Solemn League and Covenant will naturally emphasize the inter-connected nature of politics, religion, and warfare during the late 1630s and 1640s. Before fighting broke out in England during the summer of 1642, the English and the Scots had already contested the so-called Bishops Wars of 1639 and 1640, and, in addition, the Irish Rebellion of 1641 had drawn in English and Scottish forces. By the time King Charles I declared war on his Parliament in August 1642 fighting in all three Kingdoms had taken place. The Solemn League and Covenant of 1643 was itself inextricably linked with the earlier Bishops Wars. Scottish interest in an alliance with the English Parliament was, from the outset, motivated by a desperation to safeguard the religious autonomy won at the King's expense during 1639 and 1640.

By the end of 1643 the failure of Newcastle to march south against London, and the failure of the King's Oxford army to take Gloucester by siege or to defeat the earl of Essex at the battle of Newbury on 20th September, gave Parliament a badly needed breathing space in which the Solemn League and Covenant could be concluded. The summer of Royalist victories had come to an end and the greatly feared advance on London had not materialized. As the King's forces lost momentum the Scottish invasion of England in January 1644 began the process by which Charles I would ultimately be defeated.

Though the Scottish army was not to be as successful as it's predecessor of 1640, the invasion nevertheless opened up a vital second front in northern England. The consequent division of Newcastle's army into two distinct forces - to simultaneously fight the Scots in Northumberland and the Parliamentarians in Yorkshire - set in chain a sequence of events in which Newcastle's gains of 1643 were lost and the divided Royalist army defeated at Selby in April 1644 and Marston Moor in July 1644.

It is clear that the Solemn League and Covenant marked the turn of the military tide. The reversal of Royalist fortune was paradoxically born in the destruction of the northern Parliamentary army at Adwalton Moor and subsequently exacerbated by the inability of the King's forces to successfully pursue that advantage. But what is not appreciated, however, is that while Adwalton Moor shocked Parliament as a whole into a process of negotiation with the Scots, the battle also marked the point at which those working for an alliance in both Scotland and England since the summer of 1642 finally gained a dominant position. The Scottish war party had managed to engineer sufficient political and religious support for its policy of military intervention before Adwalton Moor, and had applied diplomatic pressure to underline the sincerity and urgency of its cause.[34] However, in England, it was news of Adwalton Moor, rather than the increasingly desperate and explicit pressure of the Scots, that finally persuaded those Parliamentarians opposed to Scottish intervention that an alliance was the only viable course of action.

The Bishops Wars of 1639 and 1640 had persuaded the Kirk that only unity of church worship and church government in both England and Scotland could guarantee the long term security of Scottish Presbyterianism. Once the Civil War in England had broken out in the summer of 1642 the Kirk pursued a policy of military intervention. A Royalist victory in England would provide the battle hardened soldiers and the financial resources with which the King would inevitably seek to avenge the defeats of 1639 and 1640. Charles and his advisers would then be free to re-impose the Book of Common Prayer and other planned reforms. Therefore, not only was military intervention by means of an English alliance to be the device by which the King would be defeated, it was also to be the means by which the English Parliament - as part payment for Scottish assistance - would be compelled to commit itself to the introduction of Scottish Presbyterianism.

Though the Kirk exerted a significant influence in Scottish politics, it was not in a position in 1642 to command widespread support for a military alliance with Parliament. Opposition to the Kirk - and its principal secular supporter Archibald Campbell, earl of Argyll - centred around the King's special adviser on Scotland, James, duke of Hamilton. Hamilton, unable to galvanize military support for the Crown in Scotland because of the unpopularity of the King, attempted to defeat the interventionist designs of the Kirk by adopting a policy of neutrality. This he proposed to strengthen, in the autumn of 1642, by offering to mediate in the dispute between King and Parliament. Though Charles ignored Hamilton's suggestion, the plan was resurrected by Argyll in January 1643 and approved by the Scottish Privy Council. This was a masterstroke. Argyll and the Kirk cleverly included a number of proposals that were bound to prove unacceptable to the King. Sure enough, once the Scottish delegation had arrived at Oxford in March, the King not only rejected the treaty but also insulted the Scots by claiming that they had no right to interfere in English affairs and that they could not hope to understand the complexity of those affairs.[35]

The outright rejection of the Scottish proposals, and the discourtesy with which the delegates felt they had been treated, convinced many Scots that the King did not wish to conclude the war by negotiation. Argyll and the Kirk, consequently, gained support for their military policy at the expense of Hamilton's neutral party. The King's damaged reputation was finally destroyed on 6th June when the discovery of the so-called "Antrim Plot" revealed:

a Royalist attempt to seek a cease-fire between the Irish rebels and the English soldiers in Ireland. These troops were then to surprise the Isles and the Highlands and set up a fortress for twenty thousand men at Carlisle, from which point they would lay waste the south of Scotland.[36]

Distrust of the King and an increasing fear for Scottish security enabled the war party to persuade the Privy Council of the immediate need to convene a Convention of Estates. This, it was argued, was the only body fit to discuss the gravity of the threat facing Scotland. The Convention, which began its work on 22nd June, was seen by Argyll and the Kirk as the proper institution to approve what was believed to be an imminent request for military assistance from the English Parliament. That this request did not materialize as the Scots anticipated - despite the firm belief that the Convention of Estates was certain to be interpreted in England as unequivocal proof of Scottish willingness to fight Charles - is entirely due to the timing and impact of Adwalton Moor.

When, to the dismay of Argyll and his supporters, the Convention failed to attract any representation from London, it is recorded that:

> There were letters sent from the States in Scotland to the Parliament in England, Declaring that they having sent a petition to his Majestie by way of a Remonstrance, wherein their greivances were expressed, and can receive no answer thereof, and in respect that they are in danger in their own country if the Earl of Newcastle should prevail in the north, they to prevent the same, and obtain their inst [?] defences, are resolved once again to come into England with an army of 10,000 men, under conduct of the Earl of Argyll, with which to their powers, they will be assistant to the Parliament.[37]

Evidence that supports L.Kaplan's argument that 'even without an alliance the Scots might have been forced to intervene.'[38] Eventually, on 14th July, Miles Corbett, a member of Parliament, reached Edinburgh with news that properly appointed commissioners would be despatched as soon as possible. Anxious and disappointed that Corbett did not have the power to negotiate, the Scots were becoming daily more concerned, particularly once news of Adwalton Moor reached the Scottish capital. Finally, on 7th August, to palpable Scottish relief, a delegation of Parliamentary commissioners led by Sir Henry Vane arrived in Edinburgh.

According to L. Kaplan, why 'the delegates had taken so long to arrive has never been adequately explained.'[39] The Convention of Estates was convened on 22nd June, Miles Corbett did not arrive until 14th July, and Sir Henry Vane not until 7th August - an interval of six and a half weeks. Kaplan has suggested that the death of leading Parliamentarian John Hampden on 24th June, compounded by the subsequent conduct of the earl of Essex, so disrupted John Pym's normally assured supervision of the House of Commons that control was lost for about a month. It was only when Pym, architect of the Scottish alliance, re-established a guiding influence that attention could once again turn to the Scots. However, this puzzling delay becomes more intelligible once Adwalton Moor is added to the equation.

The battle was fought on 30th June, followed on 5th July by the decision of Parliament to negotiate an alliance with Scotland. If, as Kaplan suggests, Pym lost control from late June onwards, the decision of 5th July can only be interpreted as so sudden and complete a recognition of impending doom that it did not require Pym's ability to manipulate Commons and Lords. In short, the news from Adwalton Moor was so calamitous in itself that nothing else was required to persuade a previously hostile Parliament of the need for Scottish help. That the impact of Adwalton Moor was decisive is demonstrated by the interval of only nine days before Miles Corbett arrived in Edinburgh on 14th July. The fact that Sir William Waller's Parliamentary army of the west was destroyed at Roundway Down on 13th July means that Corbett must have left for Edinburgh *before* news of the battle could have reached Westminster. Therefore, the decisions of 5th July, followed by the despatch of Corbett to reassure the Scots, were clearly measures driven by Adwalton Moor and Adwalton Moor alone. That Sir Henry Vane and his delegation did not reach the Scottish capital until 7th August was probably due firstly to the delicacy of the deliberations by which Parliament's negotiating strategy was agreed, and secondly to the fact that by the beginning of August Newcastle had gained almost complete control of Lincolnshire. The consequent threat to the Eastern Association was such that the opening of negotiations could, in all probability, no longer be delayed.

It is evident that the battle of Adwalton Moor changed the course of the English Civil War. From the Royalist point of view it delivered Yorkshire, except for the garrison port of Hull, into the King's hands, thereby offering the earl of Newcastle the opportunity to advance through Lincolnshire towards London. From the point of view of Parliament it compelled the negotiation of the Solemn League and Covenant, an alliance which brought Scottish soldiers onto English soil with decisive results. Adwalton Moor offered the King the prospect of victory and Parliament the promise of defeat. The King proved incapable of capitalizing upon his advantage, but Parliament took the necessary measures to avoid disaster. Adwalton Moor signalled the end of the beginning for Parliament, and the beginning of the end for the King.

Reconstructing Adwalton Moor

It is a commonplace of military historiography that the most significant battles in any war or campaign are described and analysed individually and in detail. For example, the three most famous battles of the English Civil War - Edgehill, Marston Moor and Naseby - have been extensively researched and the results widely published. The battle of Edgehill because it was the first large scale encounter of the war; Marston Moor – probably the largest battle fought on English soil - because it resulted in the defeat of armed Royalism in the north of England; and the battle of Naseby because it witnessed the destruction of the

King's main field army. Adwalton Moor, by comparison, has been almost completely ignored. Almost because, as previously demonstrated, the battle is at least acknowledged to have had a regional importance. This, however, has done no more than grant Adwalton Moor the status of one military event among the many military events that constitute the English Civil War. Much has been made in this introduction of the real significance and importance of the battle. If one accepts the argument for that significance and importance then it becomes appropriate to reconstruct the fighting of Adwalton Moor in the kind of detail that identifies the battle as a major event. It is that reconstruction that forms the core of this book.

If placing a battle in its political and military context - by describing the causes and effects of the fighting - constitutes the means by which the importance of the battle is to be determined, why, one might ask, is it therefore necessary to provide any account of the combat itself? If the actual battle of Adwalton Moor is subordinate to its origin and outcome, why pause to describe the fighting? Many reasons suggest themselves, but two in particular are of concern here. Firstly, the act of battle is the result of a conscious decision to fight. Either willingly or unwillingly soldiers place themselves in mortal danger; by any definition of human behaviour this represents a very specific form of activity. One, moreover, that is worthy of the historian's attention. Secondly, by the analysis of first-hand accounts; by the acquisition of an intimate knowledge of the battlefield terrain; and by an examination of the weapons and tactics employed; it may be possible to gain some idea of what it was actually like to take part in battle. Historians are of course aware that the past cannot be recreated, but the traces left behind can give an indication of what the past was like. The picture may not be complete, but it is a recognizable picture nevertheless.

Of course, the reconstruction of any battle is only properly comprehensible when placed in context. This introduction has attempted to establish the significance of Adwalton Moor by describing the battle's political and military repercussions. With reference to the fighting itself, the authors of the eyewitness and contemporary accounts (known as primary sources) are examined in chapter one, together with a history of the way in which historians have subsequently used, or not used, those sources to describe the battle (secondary sources). This kind of survey is in fact a useful indicator of the perceived importance of Adwalton Moor. Brief biographies of the eyewitness and contemporary account authors are combined with textual histories of the documents themselves to illuminate the circumstances in which the sources were created and to offer a preliminary assessment of any factors which might compromise their reliability. The military background is described in chapter two. Following a brief explanation of the national context in which the Civil War in the north was fought, the Yorkshire campaign of December 1642 to June 1643 - which resulted in the battle of Adwalton Moor - is traced in some detail. No battle can be properly understood unless the ground over which the fighting took place is investigated and examined. The battlefield terrain of 30th June 1643 is therefore discussed in chapter three. Based on the fieldwork undertaken by English Heritage, the study combines the testimony of the primary sources, the findings of local 19th century antiquarians, the evidence of non military documents such as Tithe Awards and historic maps, plus the results of personal observation, to build a picture of the terrain as it appeared over 350 years ago. The battle itself is reconstructed in chapter four. Resting upon the topographical work of the previous chapter, the testimony of the primary sources will be evaluated, where necessary, against the interpretations of previous writers and an understanding of 17th century military practice. Central to this chapter is an attempt to unravel the process by which an apparently ordered Royalist withdrawal became a sweeping and emphatic Royalist victory. It will be argued that at Adwalton Moor the margin between success and failure was so small that the day in all probability turned on the conduct of a single Royalist officer. Finally, in chapter five, the immediate aftermath of the fighting is examined along with events leading to the Parliamentary retreat to Hull.

The study of battles and battlefields has developed significantly in recent years; the result of an acknowledgement that the detailed consideration of both terrain and battle debris are absolutely fundamental to any understanding of the events under examination. There are three battle studies in particular, in each of which the investigation of the battlefield landscape is paramount, that have directly influenced the present work. The result of all three has been, by virtue of a detailed examination and interpretation of the battlefield topography, to substantially alter existing ideas.

The first, P.R. Newman's *Marston Moor, 2 July 1644: The Sources and the Site* (1978), demonstrated that a neglect of both fieldwork and the recovery of battlefield artefacts had produced not only a misunderstanding of the terrain itself but also a consequent misinterpretation of the disposition of the rival armies and the course of the subsequent fighting. Newman's *Battle of Marston Moor* (1981) further developed and expanded the earlier research to produce a full and detailed battle narrative. Interestingly, Newman's work on Marston Moor has been revised in collaboration with and in the light of new archaeological evidence painstakingly gathered and recorded by P.R. Roberts. *Marston Moor 1644: The Battle of the Five Armies* (2003) represents the latest development in battlefield writing; a reconciliation of documentary and archaeological evidence creating a more complete and accurate battle account. The second battle study to have influenced the present work was in fact a precursor of the Newman/Roberts collaboration. G. Foard's *Naseby: The Decisive Campaign* (1995) demonstrated that the careful and systematic mapping of archaeological finds provided, with reference to the documentary sources, new evidence for a reinterpretation and relocation of the final stages of the fighting. The final study, *The Field of Redemore: The Battle of Bosworth* (1990) by P.Foss, provided a radically new interpretation of the battlefield site by virtue of an interdisciplinary examination of a whole range of apparently diverse sources that enabled the reconstruction of a landscape for which reliable evidence was believed to be severely limited.

Despite the passage of time and the inevitable encroachment of modern development Marston Moor, Naseby and Bosworth remain essentially rural battlefield sites. This, of course, is of enormous benefit when one is attempting to reconstruct a landscape that existed hundreds of years ago. At Adwalton Moor, by contrast, roughly fifty percent of the old moorland and hedged enclosures have been lost. The construction of industrial buildings, railway embankments, new roads and modern houses have produced a new landscape, one that the combatants of 1643 would scarcely recognize. Given the architecture of the older buildings that surround the moor today, it is apparent that the development of the site began in the second half of the 19th century. This is confirmed by John Ryley Robinson who visited the battlefield in 1887:

> It was with feelings of considerable interest, irrespective of its historic associations, that I noticed the great alterations which had taken place in the neighbourhood, above thirty-five years having elapsed since my last visit; and what was then an almost uninhabited district, a wide expanse of barren moor, with here and there a few cottages of humble character, but little known and rarely visited, is now to a great extent built upon; large numbers of houses erected, with mill property of considerable value, and what at that time would have been thought most unlikely ever to exist in that locality - a railway station almost on the moor itself.[40]

While it is quite possible that a definitive reconstruction of Adwalton Moor battlefield may always remain elusive, it is nevertheless possible, by the application of the principles described, to extrapolate a landscape that convincingly reconciles the remaining topographical evidence with the testimony of the surviving documentation. An attempt to reconstruct the 17th century terrain is, of course, absolutely fundamental to any understanding of the battle. Even a superficial examination of the existing accounts of Adwalton Moor will show how confusing many writers have found the battle to be. A confusion that is almost entirely due to the difficulty of understanding a lost landscape.

Though the armies that fought at Adwalton Moor consisted in total of perhaps no more than 15,000 men, the battle was, in the context of the Civil War in mid 1643, a huge confrontation. But what is not generally recognized is that at the time Adwalton Moor was fought, the battle was in fact the second largest of the war - only Edgehill had exceeded it in terms of numbers of combatants. Thus not only was Adwalton Moor a critical event in terms of the subsequent military and political course of the English Civil War, it was also a large and bloody battle in its own right.

CHAPTER 1

HISTORIANS AND SOURCES

It is possible to reconstruct the battle of Adwalton Moor because a number of eyewitness and contemporary accounts of the fighting have survived and are known to historians. Over the last couple of centuries a variety of writers have used these documents to produce a succession of battle descriptions. Some have used only one source while others have taken geat pains to examine all the available documentation. Historians, while of course taking care to properly scrutinize the testimony of each account, need also to know something of the author and the circumstances in which the document was created. In addition the means by which the manuscript has survived and the way in which the content has been preserved and passed down is also relevant and of concern. The historian has to evaluate the quality and reliability of each individual source so that where accounts differ, or directly contradict one another, the historian is able to make an informed interpretation and lucid judgement of the evidence.

In the case of Adwalton Moor only a relatively small number of sources are known to exist, certainly far fewer than for the larger and more famous English Civil War battles of Edgehill, Marston Moor and Naseby. Nevertheless the quantity and quality remain sufficient to reconstruct in considerable detail the events of 30th June 1643. There are, of course, areas where additional information would help to illuminate difficult questions, and these will naturally be examined and discussed as appropriate. Yet despite the inevitable problems that attend any process of historical research it is still possible - it will be demonstrated here - to successfully account for the Royalist victory at Adwalton Moor by recourse to the known sources.

However, the reliance upon no more than the *known* sources need not impose a constraint on the historian's work. For where the discovery of new documentation is unlikely or has not taken place for a considerable period of time, the re-interpretation of existing sources becomes the means by which historical inquiry is advanced. The present account of Adwalton Moor, in the absence of new eyewitness or contemporary reports, is therefore to be based upon the process of re-interpretation. This particular chapter will initially discuss the authors of the principal Adwalton Moor sources - in order to throw light on an accompanying consideration of the textual histories of the documents themselves - and will be followed by an examination of the way in which historians have chosen to use these sources to research and write about the battle. It has already been noted that this kind of survey is a useful indicator of the perceived significance of the battle at a particular point in time. Consequently, it is the purpose of the present writer to construct an account that will provide an unequivocal indication of the true importance of Adwalton Moor.

Sir Thomas Fairfax's Account[41]

Commander of horse in the northern Parliamentary army and second in overall command to his father General Lord Ferdinando Fairfax, Sir Thomas led the right wing at Adwalton Moor. Though Fairfax claims to have been detached from much of the fighting in the centre and Parliamentarian left, his statement is nevertheless a crucial piece of eyewitness evidence. The description of the preliminary exchanges and the subsequent development of the fighting on his flank is, perhaps, the best known and most widely used account of the battle. Controversially Sir Thomas pins the blame for defeat at Adwalton Moor on a fellow Parliamentarian officer, Major General Gifford, whom Fairfax accuses of treachery. As will be discussed, accusations of treachery were not confined to Sir Thomas.

Fairfax's recollection of Adwalton Moor is taken from one of two memorials written during the final years of his life. The first, *A Short Memoriall Of The Northern Actions During The War There, From The Yeare 1642 Till 1644*, is an invaluable source of military detail for the entire Yorkshire campaign. Two copies of the manuscripts, in the author's own hand, are held at Leeds Castle. A much altered version of the Memorials, designed not to offend Royalist sensibilities, was first published in 1699. Just over a century later, in 1808, a complete and faithful copy was printed in Volume III of the *Antiquarian Repertory* by Edmund Lodge.[42] In 1884 a transcription of the original manuscript taken by Fairfax's nephew, Thomas Hutton, was published by Francis Collins in the *Yorkshire Archaeological Journal*.[43] This version is almost identical to that reproduced in the *Antiquarian Repertory* - the accounts of Adwalton Moor for example differ by one word only. It is Hutton's published transcription that will be used here.

Sir Thomas died in 1671 at the age of fifty nine. According to C.R.Markham the Memorials were not written until the final two years of his life.[44] Fairfax's account of Adwalton Moor, therefore, did not see the light of day until almost thirty years after the event. Although Sir Thomas is most certainly an eyewitness, his recollection of the battle is not a 'contemporary' source in the strictest sense of the word.

Thomas Stockdale's Account[45]

The threat to the established social order posed by the arming and organization of politically and religiously motivated lower order groups ran as an undercurrent throughout the Civil War. Royalist and Parliamentarian gentry alike were alarmed and fearful that a rebellion provoked by a breakdown in the relationship between Parliament and King would be overtaken by a revolution

Sir Thomas Fairfax

that not only threatened the political elite but also the structure within which that elite operated. To many gentlemen on both sides of the war, Thomas Stockdale personified the terrifying spectre of social upheaval.[46]

Committed to a radical exploitation of sub-gentry support for the northern Parliamentary war effort, Thomas Stockdale exercised a significant influence over Ferdinando Lord Fairfax throughout the Yorkshire campaign. A close friend and professional associate of the Lord General, he performed a kind of 'staff officer' role at Adwalton Moor:

> Stockdale who stood at my Lord Fairfax's elbow, adviseth my Lord...[47]

From his position in the centre of the Parliamentarian order of battle, Stockdale broadly corroborated the sequence of events outlined by Sir Thomas Fairfax. However, the principal value of the account lies firstly in its detailed description of the strength and deployment of the Parliamentary army and, secondly, in the vital fact that the document was written the day after the battle, in the form of a letter, to William Lenthall, Speaker of the House of Commons. This is a 'contemporary' source in the strictest sense.

As previously demonstrated, the reading of Stockdale's account to Lords and Commons on 5th July 1643 proved to be a turning point in the Civil War. In the absence of any known report of Adwalton Moor written by the Lord General Ferdinando Fairfax, Stockdale's letter, composed in his capacity as secretary to Fairfax, must be regarded as the official Parliamentarian despatch.

Stockdale's account is one of many seventeenth century documents transcribed by the Rev. John Nalson, Rector of Doddington and Canon of Ely. Nalson (1637-1685) was permitted virtually unrestricted access to the papers in the office of the Clerk of the Parliament. The resulting collection of original manuscripts and transcriptions, amounting to twenty two volumes, was discovered in a cupboard in the duke of Portland's library at Welbeck Abbey. A Calendar of the documents was published by the Historical Manuscripts Commission in 1891. Stockdale's letter is one of several transcriptions for which the original document has not been traced. All of these were written between 1 April and 1 July 1643, prompting speculation that the originals may have been lost or destroyed as a bundle. This sub-collection of transcriptions is presented as an appendix to the Calendar.[48]

The authenticity of Stockdale's account is thus dependent upon the accuracy of Nalson's transcription. However, where the original documents have been located, no disparagement is cast upon the quality of Nalson's work by the editor of the Historical Manuscripts Commission.

The Cavendish Accounts

Commander-in-chief of the northern Royalist army from the summer of 1642 until the battle of Marston Moor two years later, William Cavendish, earl

William Cavendish, earl of Newcastle

of Newcastle, led the King's forces at Adwalton Moor. Cavendish, together with his chief adviser Lieutenant General James King, not only directed the Royalist army in the field, but appears to have taken an active part in the fighting itself.[49] Clearly, therefore, any account of the battle attributable to the Commander-in-chief would be of the utmost importance. However, despite the survival of two eyewitness reports, ostensibly emanating from Cavendish himself, a precise attribution of provenance remains problematic.

The first account occurs in a biography of the earl, subsequently marquis then duke, written by Margaret Lucas his second wife.[50] Perhaps conscious of a general perception amongst the elite of Restoration society that her husband's somewhat precipitate flight into exile following the disaster at Marston Moor had not cast the earl in the most favourable light, Margaret's biography reads as an extended contribution to an on-going polemic.[51] As the couple were not married until 1645, Margaret was unable to provide her own account of Newcastle's military participation in the Civil War. Instead she relied upon the eyewitness recollections of Newcastle's secretary John Rolleston.[52] C.H.Firth, editor of the 1906 edition of the biography, bemoans the fact that:

> Rolleston had filled a position which must have enabled him to know the truth on many doubtful points, and to explain, had he thought fit, the causes which determined the strategy of his General. It is therefore much to be regretted that so meagre an account is given of many important incidents and resolutions during the Yorkshire campaigns.[53]

It is also possible, and perhaps even probable, that during the interval of twenty or so years between Margaret's marriage to the earl and the point at which she began to write her biography, Newcastle revealed to her some details of his military campaigns. The account of the Yorkshire war, reliant for the most part on Rolleston, must surely have included the odd snippet of information that was provided by the Commander-in-chief himself.

Margaret's *Life of the Duke of Newcastle* was first published in 1667. Before the duke's death in 1676 two further versions appeared in print. The first, a Latin translation, was published in 1668, followed by a second English edition in 1675. As Firth pointed out:

> The three editions published during the lifetime of the subject testify to the popularity of the book at a time when the events recorded in it were still fresh in the memories of those who read it.[54]

The account of Adwalton Moor contains a valuable description of the battlefield topography plus a useful chronology of the fighting itself. What is particularly frustrating however is the almost total absence of any attempt to detail the structure and numerical strength of the Royalist army. This clearly represents one of Firth's *regrettable* instances in which Rolleston could have provided much additional and invaluable information.

The second Cavendish account, *An Express Relation of the Passages and Proceedings of his Majesty's Army, under the Command of his Excellence the Earl of Newcastle, against the Rebels under the Command of the Lord Fairfax and his Adherents*, has been printed as an appendix to Firth's 1906 edition of Margaret's biography.[55] Firth attributes this anonymous pamphlet to William Cavendish on the grounds, firstly, of a stylistic similarity to another of the earl's despatches and, secondly, to the distinct possibility that it was printed at Oxford in 1643.[56] The original pamphlet is not part of the British Library's *Thomason Tract* collection, and, frustratingly, Firth does not provide further information.

The pamphlet is a contemporary source while Margaret's description of the battle is more than twenty years old. The pamphlet confirms the view of the biography that the Royalists came unexpectedly upon the Parliamentarian army. Each details the advantageous deployment of Fairfax's musketeers amongst a series of hedged enclosures, and stresses the less than satisfactory placing of the Royalist horse amid a cluster of old coal pits. In addition, both make reference to a large ditch dividing the rival forces which, it is claimed, nullified the numerical superiority of the Royalist cavalry. Finally, each makes a point of noting the superior firepower of the Parliamentarian foot and the decisive combination, once Newcastle's dispositions had been completed, of the Royalist pike, horse and cannon. Set against these considerable similarities are only one or two differences. The biography refers to Adwalton as 'Atherton' while the pamphlet renders it 'Adderton'.[57] Margaret also mentions, in addition to the ditch, a 'high bank' as an obstruction to the Royalist horse. This observation is absent from the pamphlet.

Taken together the two accounts offer a largely convergent view of the fighting and the impact of the terrain as a significant hindrance to Royalist battlefield operations. It has been demonstrated that John Rolleston provided the account of Adwalton Moor for the biography while Newcastle, according to Firth, was the probable author of the despatch. As the biography provides slightly more detail than the pamphlet, it is possible that, as Newcastle's secretary, Rolleston may have retained a copy of the despatch, adding to it some of his own first hand recollections for the biography. Reading Margaret's account it is difficult not to come to the conclusion that the author's primary concern was to disguise the real difficulty with which her husband's forces overcame a much smaller Parliamentarian army. This will be returned to in chapter four.

Sir Henry Slingsby's Account [58]

A leading member of Yorkshire's Royalist gentry, Sir Henry Slingsby was forty years old at the outbreak of the Civil War. Member for Knaresborough in each of the parliaments summoned in 1640, Slingsby was commissioned during the King's visit to York in the summer of 1642 to take command of the

Sir Henry Slingsby

city regiment of trained bands. When the earl of Newcastle invaded the county in December 1642 Slingsby received a second commission, this time to raise a volunteer regiment of foot.[59] Regarded as a man of honour and integrity, Slingsby, in the view of Clarendon, was also a stoic:

> Sir H.Slingsby.....was in the first rank of the gentlemen of Yorkshire....of good understanding, but of very few words....joined with the first who took up arms for the King. And when the war was ended, he remained still in his own house, prepared and disposed to run the fortune of the Crown in any other attempt....[60]

Slingsby's interest to students of the Civil War is twofold. Firstly, as a colonel in the King's northern army, Sir Henry commands the attention of those who have sought to shed light on the conflict by means of a detailed study of gentry allegiance.[61] Secondly, and perhaps more importantly, as the author of a diary concerned principally with the Civil War years in Yorkshire, Slingsby provides a priceless view of the politics, personalities and campaigns of the day. The diary covers the decade from 1638 to 1648: the author revealing that the composition of the document took the form of a hobby, to be written as and when inclination permitted, rather than as a meticulous day to day record of events.[62] Tentatively, therefore, the Diary may be regarded as a contemporary account. What is not in doubt, however, is its importance as a record of military events.

The Diary has twice been published. Firstly, in an abridged form, by Sir Walter Scott in 1806 and, secondly, by the Reverend Daniel Parsons in 1836. However, Parsons was compelled to use a copy of the Diary made in 1715 by Sir Saville Slingsby. The original manuscript, thought in the nineteenth century to have been lost, has since resurfaced amongst the collections of the Manuscript Department of the University of Nottingham. The principal difference between this and Parsons' transcription is that the manuscript contains a fuller account of the diseases suffered by Slingsby and his wife.[63] As for Slingsby's description of Adwalton Moor, the fundamental question concerns Sir Henry's whereabouts at the time of the battle. P.R. Newman believes Slingsby to have been an eyewitness, commenting that his account is:

> important because it is evident that he was there.[64]

It is possible that the tenor of Sir Henry's account, written in a style that may suggest eyewitness testimony, has convinced Newman of Slingsby's presence. J. Jones offers no opinion either way, other than to comment that the treatment of Adwalton Moor must be handled with care as the document was composed some years after the event.[65] Dr Andrew Brown, the former English Heritage Inspector of Ancient Monuments for the area in which the battlefield is to be found, believes Slingsby to have been engaged elsewhere:

> Sir Henry Slingsby's diary gives a close second-hand account of the battle from the Royalists' perspective. He knew several of those present at the battle and, as a regiment commander, he relays their accounts in summary fashion from the soldier's viewpoint.[66]

This is a difficult problem. Sir Henry's style, even when dealing with events he is known to have participated in, is often dispassionate and business like. His account of Adwalton Moor, as with so much of the Diary, is composed in this almost objective fashion. Slingsby, if he were present, makes no reference whatever to any part played either by himself or those under his command. However, Slingsby reports that around 5th May 1643 he took command of the garrison at York. Here he remained for eight weeks until ordered to march out.[67] Eight weeks from 5th May takes the chronology to 30th June - the day of the battle itself. As the Royalist army fighting at Adwalton Moor advanced from Howley Hall, having secured the building several days earlier, Slingsby and his regiment would have been on garrison duty at York when this action took place. Therefore, even allowing for any discrepancy in Slingsby's recollection of time and date, the location of both Newcastle's army and Sir Henry's regiment in the period immediately before Adwalton Moor would appear to preclude his presence on the battlefield. Sir Henry's account is most probably a report of perhaps several conversations he later recorded with those who had fought at Adwalton Moor.

John Rushworth's Account[68]

For the student of seventeenth century Britain, John Rushworth's *Historical Collections* are as synonymous with the English Civil War as Clarendon's *Rebellion*. Although described by Firth as an 'historian',[69] P.R. Newman makes the point that Rushworth's work is essentially that of a Parliamentarian scribe and should be regarded as such.[70] Though not, of course, an eyewitness to the events of 30th June 1643, the account of Adwalton Moor assumes some importance as a consequence of the position held by Rushworth at Westminster during this period of the Civil War.

Despite his training as a lawyer, affairs of state appear to have held a far greater fascination for Rushworth than his chosen profession. The turbulent politics of the 1630's prompted the collection of information concerning the dramatic upheavals of the day:

> I did personally attend and observe all occurrences of moment during that interval in the Star Chamber, Court of Honour, and Exchequer Chamber, when all the Judges of England met there upon extraordinary cases; at the Council-table when great cases were heard before the king and council. And when matters were agitated at a greater distance, I was there also, and went on purpose out of a curiosity to see and observe the passages of the camp at Berwick, at the fight at Newburn, at the treaty of Ripon, at the great council at York, and at the meeting of the Long Parliament, and present every day at the trial of the Earl of Strafford.[71]

On 25 April 1640, while still in his twenties, Rushworth was appointed clerk-assistant to the House of Commons.[72] It is Firth's contention that Rushworth did not enjoy privileged access to the official documentation thrown up by the Civil War, but was instead compelled to rely upon the innumerable propaganda newsbooks and pamphlets.[73] Rushworth, however, in the preface to the first volume, declares that he was:

> employed as an agent in and entrusted with affairs of weightiest concernment; privy also to the debates in Parliament and to the most secret results of councils of war in times of action[74]

The third part of *Historical Collections*, dealing with the period 1640-1644, was first published in 1692. Following the publication of the fourth and final part in 1701 an abridged version was printed in 1703, before a full second edition appeared in 1721.

Rushworth's account of Adwalton Moor, although brief, contains all the pertinent detail required for a rudimentary understanding of the course of the fighting. As one might expect from someone in Rushworth's position, the report reads like a distillation of the various accounts of Adwalton Moor that would have been available in the late 17th century. Certainly, there are one or two striking similarities with the narrative provided by the duchess of Newcastle's biography of William Cavendish. Perhaps the brevity of the account is due to the inauspicious outcome of the battle, particularly as Rushworth goes on to describe in greater detail the perilous but ultimately successful retreat of Sir Thomas Fairfax to Hull.[75]

Sir Philip Warwick's Account[76]

Elected member for Radnor in the Long Parliament, Warwick, without commission, fought as a gentleman volunteer in the King's army at Edgehill. Thereafter, he became increasingly useful to Charles as an emissary and much trusted secretary.[77] Warwick's memoir, for which he is chiefly remembered, is important for its often intimate portrayal of the King and his entourage. The manuscript, composed between 1675 and 1677, is claimed to have been faithfully reproduced when published in 1701.[78]

The principal value of Warwick's memoir derives from his close proximity to the King. Yet the account of Adwalton Moor, though the author was not himself present at the battle, is possibly more important than one might expect. During 1643, in the capacity of Royal messenger, Warwick twice visited the earl of Newcastle, creating the distinct possibility that the account of Adwalton Moor was provided by the earl himself. Indeed, rather than describe the whole battle, Warwick simply concentrated upon the sequence of events that won the day. The account has about it the air of a longer conversation from which a particularly memorable part has been recorded. While one must allow for the passage of more than thirty years between event and documentation, the circumstances nevertheless lend an unexpected significance to Warwick's report.

Newsbooks and Pamphlets

The Civil War years witnessed an unprecedented explosion of what may be termed 'popular journalism'. The weekly newsbooks and pamphlets, rushing from the printing presses of London, Oxford and York, disseminated without compunction the wanton propaganda of King and Parliament to an eager readership. Those published in London were almost wholly Parliamentarian while those emanating from Oxford and York, where the King established printing presses, were entirely Royalist. George Thomason, a 17th century London bookseller, diligently collected the newsbooks and pamphlets circulating in the capital. Known as the *Thomason Tracts* the resulting collection, now part of the British Library, constitutes - despite its obvious partiality - an invaluable primary source for the whole of the Civil War period. The battle of Adwalton Moor, major news during the first weeks of July 1643, is reported in three separate newsbook titles.

The first account appears in an edition of the *Parliament Scout* dated Thursday 29th June to Thursday 6th July 1643.[79] Despite its anti-Royalist orientation the report clearly indicates a Parliamentarian reverse of some significance. This is attributed to the gallant rashness of Lord Fairfax's heroic army combined with a quite heinous act of betrayal. Though the passage includes some useful references to the course of the fighting, the author declines, as one might expect, to record the true gravity of the defeat.

The second Adwalton Moor account occurs in the Royalist newsbook *Mercurius Aulicus* dated Monday 3rd July 1643.[80] With scarcely concealed delight, the report describes a sweeping Royalist victory in which the verdict of the Almighty was clearly evident. Despite the hyperbole, however, the document includes the important claim that victory was snatched from the jaws of defeat by the personal conduct and valour of the earl of Newcastle. S.R. Gardiner generally considered *Mercurius Aulicus* to be somewhat untrustworthy:

> Birkenhead, its writer, composes his attacks on the enemy under no sense of responsibility, and with the sole end of making Puritans and Parliamentarians ridiculous, though even in his work are sometimes included reports or despatches of Royalist commanders which add something to our knowledge.[81]

The account of Adwalton Moor, describing the heroics of Newcastle, could therefore be one such occasion where the usually unreliable reporting of news included some factual material.

The third and final battle account occurs in the 3rd July to 10th July 1643 issue of *Certaine Informations*.[82] Of Parliamentarian authorship, the report confines itself to a brief matter of fact account in which only a reverse of fortune is intimated. Nowhere is the full scale of the disaster even alluded to. Interestingly Lord Fairfax's army is given as 1000 horse and up to 6000 foot. Both Sir Thomas Fairfax and Thomas Stockdale, eyewitness authors of the principal Parliamentarian accounts, provide considerably smaller estimates. The discrepancy is possibly a product of the unquantifiable number of West Yorkshire Clubmen that accompanied Lord Fairfax's army.

Historians and Histories

Having discussed the principal eyewitness and contemporary accounts of Adwalton Moor it is appropriate to consider the most significant of the secondary sources. Almost without exception the existing published accounts of the battle consist of only a few pages of text, and form no more than a small part of the much larger work in which they are contained. If one were to exclude the present book, there is only one other published account devoted solely to the battle of Adwalton Moor.[83]

If historians of the Civil War have by and large overlooked the significance of Adwalton Moor as an historical event in its own right, it is hardly surprising therefore to discover that the battle has similarly failed to attract widespread attention as a military event. The recent position has, however, to some extent improved. Not because the political significance of the battle has finally been recognized, but because the volume of military literature devoted to the Civil War has increased, and because a growing concern for environmental issues, allied to a continuing development of the 'Heritage Industry', has raised to new levels the public profile of battlefield sites. The historiography of Adwalton Moor - that is the history of the way in which the battle has been investigated and written about - is, therefore, not only an important source of information concerning the battlefield and the fighting, but also, as has been noted, a revealing indicator of the battle's perceived significance over a period of time.

Broadly speaking the historiography of Adwalton Moor breaks down into two quite distinct periods. The first, roughly covering the century up to World War One, is characterized by the local historian and the local antiquarian - the later concerned to describe the battle as one event among many in a compilation of historic incidents and anecdotes. However, the importance of these accounts should not be underestimated. They provide a significant description of the nineteenth century landscape and an often vital identification of unearthed battlefield artefacts. The second period, from the late 1950's onwards, is characterized by the professional historian writing for a national audience. Although Adwalton Moor becomes more widely covered, it is the result of an increasing general interest in the English Civil War rather than a particular recognition of the battle itself.

The first, and perhaps the most important attempt to recount Adwalton Moor and the terrain over which it was fought, was published in 1830 by the West Riding antiquary Norrisson Scatcherd.[84] Scatcherd, a man of pronounced Parliamentarian sympathies, relied exclusively on Sir Thomas Fairfax's eyewitness account of the battle for his description of the fighting. The value of

Norrisson Scatcherd

the work, however, lies in Scatcherd's attempt to reconcile Fairfax's recollections with the battlefield terrain of 1830 - important for the description it provided of the still rural early 19th century topography. In addition to critical information concerning the location and identification of battlefield finds, Scatcherd relates a useful account of the many traditions of local folklore that surround the fighting itself.

A decade later John James included a short description of the battle in his history of Bradford.[85] Following in Scatcherd's footsteps and using Scatcherd's account, James twice visited the battlefield, making a small but important addition to the information provided by his predecessor. In 1866 James published a revised and updated history of the town. The description of Adwalton Moor was extended to include the minor contemporary account of Joseph Lister, a native of Bradford, and an abridged version of the duchess of Newcastle's account. It is also evident that James consulted Rushworth in order to determine the date upon which the town fell to the Royalist siege that followed the battle.[86]

The best researched nineteenth century description of Adwalton Moor appeared in Clement Markham's biography of Sir Thomas Fairfax.[87] Markham, writing for a national rather than a local audience, based his account of the battle on the seven primary sources known to him. Only Thomas Stockdale's letter to Parliament and the anonymous account attributed to the earl of Newcastle - neither published until after the biography – remained unused by Markham. Confirming, by virtue of his own observation, the topographical account given in Scatcherd, Markham made a workmanlike and occasionally colourful attempt to understand the battle and to discuss some of the problems of interpretation. Interestingly, in a footnote, Markham made the observation that Clarendon's failure to mention Adwalton Moor by name may be accounted for by two blank pages in the manuscript that was first published in 1849. Markham inferred that these pages were intended to contain an account of the battle - an account, of course, that Clarendon never completed. It is perhaps not unreasonable to suggest that had Clarendon put pen to paper, the battle of Adwalton Moor would surely have acquired a far greater prominence in the accounts of the Civil War that followed the publication of the *History of the Rebellion*.

In 1887 the publishers of a series of papers concerned with the history of the North of England produced, under the authorship of John Ryley Robinson, an account of Adwalton Moor.[88] Though in essence an assimilation of Markham, Fairfax, and Scatcherd, the narrative nevertheless included a valuable description of the way in which the terrain had altered and been developed during the 19th century. An equally important reference to the discovery of various types of battlefield artefact was also included. The northern theme was continued only four years later when Edward Lamplough published a history of Yorkshire battles.[89] The four pages devoted to Adwalton Moor, however, disappointingly amounted to no more than a brief paraphrasing of Markham. Predictably perhaps, Markham's erroneous assertion that the Royalist army arrived at

Adwalton Moor on the evening of the 29th June was unfortunately repeated by Lamplough. This important point will be returned to below.

In the early years of the twentieth century James Parker published a local history/walkers guide to the area of the West Riding in which Adwalton Moor was fought.[90] The description of the battle, following Scatcherd's example, was that provided by Sir Thomas Fairfax, while an explanation of the disposition of the Parliamentarian forces appears also to be based upon Scatcherd. Throughout the narrative Parker litters his work with a succession of local traditions, derived largely from either Scatcherd or James. Interestingly, one or two are presented for the first time; the most important being a claim that many of the dead were buried at a site adjacent to the Crown Point Grounds. Unlike several others, this anecdote has to be taken seriously. The position of the Crown Point Grounds is precisely that in which the Parliamentarian left wing was routed. Hence the distinct possibility of a burial pit and mass grave.

A few years later Hugh Kendall, in successive issues of the *Transactions of the Halifax Antiquarian Society*, published three lectures concerning the Civil War in Halifax and its immediate vicinity. Kendall's account of Adwalton Moor,[91] relatively brief because of the principal concern with Halifax, appears to have been taken from Markham's biography of Sir Thomas Fairfax. Kendall, directly contradicting one of the many local traditions recounted by Parker, claimed that Hodgson Lane - a track running along the south western fringe of Tong Moor and Adwalton Moor - was not in fact named after Captain Hodgson, a local Parliamentarian soldier who reputedly fought at the battle. Kendall's first paper, describing the Civil War in the West Riding up to Adwalton Moor, contains a useful reference to the spread of cottage based clothiers onto moorland areas in the early years of the 17th century. It is evident from Thomas Stockdale's eyewitness account that dwellings of this type were the scene of fierce close range fighting.

By the eve of the First World War, therefore, only Markham's narrative had been based on the full range of published sources. The rest, unlike Markham, had written specifically for a local audience, to whom Sir Thomas Fairfax was the figure of greatest interest and, conveniently, the author of the best known eyewitness account. However, the late 19th century publication of Thomas Stockdale's letter and the anonymous despatch attributed to Newcastle meant that a more detailed and extensive account of the battle had become possible. It is indicative of the contemporary obscurity of Adwalton Moor that it was not until a decade after the end of the Second World War that a new attempt was made to recount the battle.

In 1959 A.H.Burne and P.Young published a military history of the 1642-1646 Civil War in which a fairly detailed attempt was made to describe Adwalton Moor.[92] By principal reference to Fairfax and Stockdale, complimented by a methodical attempt to understand both the terrain and the disposition of the rival armies, Burne and Young successfully constructed a broadly coherent battle narrative. The work included a brief reference to the possible identity of the Royalist officer arguably responsible for the battle's dramatic conclusion. Disappointingly, however, the authors side-stepped some of the detailed problems of interpretation that would necessarily have arisen from a more exhaustive examination of the sources. To be fair, it is probable that the scope of the work did not permit such an undertaking, especially when one considers the low status of the battle. The Adwalton Moor narrative was reprinted, word for word, in a later and expanded military history that included all three Civil Wars.[93]

Two decades after Burne and Young, P.R.Newman completed a Doctoral Thesis examining the Northern Royalist Army in the First Civil War.[94] Newman's monumental study not only provided a detailed picture of those who took up arms on the King's behalf, but in addition subjected, for the first time, the whole northern conflict to the kind of comprehensive scrutiny hitherto reserved for other theatres of the Civil War. Presenting each of the principal Adwalton Moor sources in turn, Newman constructed the most detailed survey of the battle to date. The anonymous source attributed by Firth to Newcastle was discussed for the first time along with the possibility that the personal conduct of the earl may have made a material contribution to the Royalist victory. Among a number of thought provoking conclusions, including the difficult task of estimating the size of the rival armies, Newman painted a less than favourable picture of Sir Thomas Fairfax's contribution to the battle.

Published a decade after Newman in 1989, Ivan Broadhead's guide to Yorkshire battlefields perhaps surprisingly included a brief account of Adwalton Moor.[95] Surprising because the modern proliferation of battlefield literature has not always included Adwalton Moor. However, by firmly locating the battle in its military and political context, Broadhead produced a concise and pertinent outline of the fighting. In addition, for those interested in visiting the battlefield itself, the author included motorway directions plus an Ordnance Survey grid reference. Broadhead's work, though clearly aimed at the general reader, nevertheless reflects a growing public interest in, and awareness of, the battlefield as both tourist attraction and historic monument.

The leisure theme was continued the following year when Martyn Bennett published a *Traveller's Guide to the Battlefields of the English Civil War*.[96] Successfully dividing the work by chronology and location Bennett provided a lucid account of Newcastle's Yorkshire campaign against the Fairfaxes. The narrative is augmented by illuminating profiles of the leading personalities; in the case of Yorkshire, Sir Thomas Fairfax and the earl of Newcastle. The description of Adwalton Moor is notable for the fact that it included the first published attempt to locate the rival armies by means of a rudimentary battlefield map.

J. Jones' 1991 Doctoral Thesis examining the Northern Parliamentary Army was clearly intended as a reply to Newman's earlier work on the Northern Royalist Army.[97] It is clear that Jones wrote as an advocate for the Parliamentarian army in much the same way that Newman had examined the northern war from a Royalist perspective. However, whereas Newman had constructed an account of Adwalton Moor that was based on a one by one assessment of the primary sources, Jones took the process a stage further by synthesizing the first hand and contemporary accounts into a chronologically shaped description of the battle. In addition to methodical attempts to calculate the size of the rival forces, and to describe the importance of the battlefield terrain, Jones also provided a detailed consideration of the factors that had compelled the Fairfaxes to take the field against a numerically superior enemy. It is probable that the battle would have attracted a greater interest had the research of either Newman or Jones not remained unpublished.

In 1995 Adwalton Moor finally received what it had been waiting over 350 years for: The English Heritage *Register of Historic Battlefields.*[98] The document, which identified 43 sites of national importance, was primarily intended to define - for the purposes of protection and conservation - the physical extent of each battlefield area. As a consequence English Heritage produced 43 detailed battlefield reports, each based on the archaeological technique of landscape interpretation, in which the careful analysis and reconstruction of the terrain became *the* essential component of the battle story. This was particularly important in the case of Adwalton Moor, where the obliteration of much of the 17th century battlefield must surely, on perhaps numerous occasions, have acted as a deterrent to potential researchers and writers. Though the result has been the production of, in some respects, a controversial report, the intervention of English Heritage has at least provided the first step towards a more thorough archaeological examination of the site. In addition English Heritage have published a glossy and colourful history of British battles, in which a brief account of Adwalton Moor forms part of a large section devoted to the principal battles of the English Civil War.[99]

A year later D.Cooke, in conjunction with the recently established Yorkshire Battlefields Society, published the first work devoted solely to Adwalton Moor.[100] Cooke's study is in fact a complete campaign history, tracing the Yorkshire War from the intervention of the earl of Newcastle in December 1642 to the confinement, following the defeat at Adwalton Moor, of the remaining Parliamentarian forces within the walls of Hull. Though primarily concerned to describe events in a military context, Cooke, in discussing the historic neglect of the battle, alludes to the connection between Adwalton Moor, the Scottish alliance, and the battle of Marston Moor. Also included are two useful appendices in which a brief visitor guide to the battlefield area is preceded by a reproduction of the relevant sections of the principal contemporary accounts.

Finally, in 1998, Stuart Reid published a military history of the entire Civil War period: 1642-1651.[101] While the book was well received by Civil War enthusiasts, Reid's account of Adwalton Moor appeared to be slightly confused. Correctly stating that the opposing armies mobilized on the morning of 30th June, Reid understandably misunderstood the initial engagement of the respective forlorn hopes so that it then became difficult to reconcile the subsequent narrative with the contemporary sources and the battlefield topography. However, Reid made a commendable attempt to reconstruct the deployment of Lord Fairfax's army and to calculate the size of Newcastle's Royalist forces. What all this illustrates is the extreme difficulty of unravelling such a complicated story without first conducting a detailed reconstruction of the battlefield terrain. In the absence of such research any account of Adwalton Moor will inevitably fail to properly understand the difficult, and at times contradictory, testimony of the primary sources.

However, there remains one further and less conventional piece of historiography to consider. In 1999 the environmental charity Groundwork Leeds, together with a local Drighlington company, Plasticisers Fibres, erected five commemorative information plaques. The first, attached to an exterior wall of the village library, consists of a detailed battle description supplemented by maps and illustrations of Civil War soldiers. The four remaining plaques, constructed of metal and secured to large rocks situated at various points around the moor, describe the location of the armies and the course of the fighting. While not, perhaps, as impressive as a larger monument - such as that to be found at Marston Moor for example - these relatively simple commemorative devices nevertheless mark part of the battlefield site and importantly describe something of the fighting that helped to shape the course of the English Civil War.

CHAPTER 2

CIVIL WAR IN YORKSHIRE
December 1642 to June 1643

The campaign that led to the battle of Adwalton Moor effectively began on 1st December 1642 when William Cavendish, earl of Newcastle, invaded Yorkshire with a Royalist army raised in County Durham and Northumberland. Aged fifty at the outbreak of the Civil War, Newcastle had become by 1640/1641 an influential figure at the Caroline court. A staunch supporter of the King, the earl's loyalty and personal wealth had secured royal patronage in the form of membership of the Privy Council and governorship of the Prince of Wales. When, in the summer of 1642, Charles set about raising an army, Cavendish was ordered to Newcastle-upon-Tyne as governor of the town and commander of the four northern counties: Cumberland, Westmorland, Northumberland, and Durham. Though devoid of any military experience - by reputation and instinct a dilettante - the earl's authority was nevertheless to be totally independent. Assuming complete responsibility for the Royalist war effort in the north, Newcastle was to fight a wholly separate conflict to that of the King until the summer of 1644.[102]

With the strategic fortress of Hull in Parliamentary hands it was imperative, for communications with the continent, that Charles secured a strong and defensible port on the North Sea coast. Newcastle-upon-Tyne was ideally situated to facilitate such a passage, particularly for Her Majesty, then engaged in raising men, money, and munitions in Denmark and Holland. Having imposed his authority upon the town and the counties for which he was responsible, Newcastle set about recruiting an army with the specific intention of marching the forces thus raised to the assistance of the King. Charles, delighted by Newcastle's initiative, sent the earl:

> commissions for that purpose, to constitute him General of all the forces raised in all the parts of the kingdom, Trent-North, and moreover in the several counties of Lincoln, Nottingham, Derby, Lancashire, Cheshire, Leicester, Rutland, Cambridge, Huntingdon, Norfolk, Suffolk, and Essex, and Commander-in-Chief for the same; as also to empower and authorise him to confer the honour of knighthood upon such persons as he should conceive deserved it, and to coin money and print whensoever he saw occasion for it.[103]

It may be deduced at this early stage that Newcastle did not simply envisage a relatively passive commission controlling the territory over which the King's writ had given him jurisdiction, but instead an active command in which

Henry Clifford, earl of Cumberland

Ferdinando Lord Fairfax

the earl would lead men to directly confront the rebels. The extent to which Charles vested power in Newcastle is a clear indication of the King's intent that an advance towards the capital was to be an essential part of the process by which military victory would be secured. Margaret, describing the formation of an army of no less than 8000 men, claimed that by the beginning of November 1642 the earl was set to march this substantial force southward.[104] If true, the execution of such a plan would in all probability have afforded Charles the necessary reinforcements with which to fight a pitched battle for London around the middle of November. Unfortunately for the King the rapidly deteriorating military situation in Yorkshire was set to foil this grand design, compelling Newcastle to remain in the north until the middle of 1643.

Having joined Charles at York in May 1642, Henry Clifford, earl of Cumberland, had been appointed commander-in-chief of Royalist forces in the county, while Sir Thomas Glemham - a soldier of some experience - had been created Governor of the city. The choice of Cumberland, as Clarendon records, was to prove a dangerous and ill-advised appointment:

> the earl of Cumberland being at that time (though of entire affection to the King) much decayed in the vigour of his body and his mind, and unfit for that activity which the season required.[105]

Once Captain John Hotham's capture by force of the Archbishop of York's castle at Cawood on 4th October 1642 had effectively shattered Ferdinando Lord Fairfax's attempts to negotiate a pact of neutrality in Yorkshire, the earl of Cumberland's ineffectual command of the Yorkshire Royalists meant that the more energetic Parliamentarians were soon closing in on York itself. Though Cumberland had garrisoned Pontefract and Knaresborough, Sir John Hotham held Hull for the Parliament, Sir Hugh Cholmley - Governor of Scarborough castle - opposed Cumberland from Stamford Bridge, while Captain John Hotham ranged almost unchallenged from Cawood Castle. In addition Ferdinando Lord Fairfax, approved by Westminster in September 1642 to take overall command of Yorkshire's Parliamentarian forces, threatened, with the support of his son Sir Thomas Fairfax, the security of York from Tadcaster and Wetherby respectively.

Not surprisingly perhaps, and as early as September 1642, the county's leading Royalist gentry had begun a process of negotiation by which the intervention of Newcastle's northern army was to be requested. For his part the earl was at pains to secure an agreement that not only safeguarded the financial and material well-being of his forces, but in addition publicly justified the controversial recruitment of recusant Roman Catholics into the northern Royalist army.[106] Having successfully concluded the terms of his engagement, Newcastle set out for Yorkshire at the end of November 1642.

Though York had remained safely in Royalist hands throughout the period of alarm and negotiation, the earl's invasion was to have a dramatic and

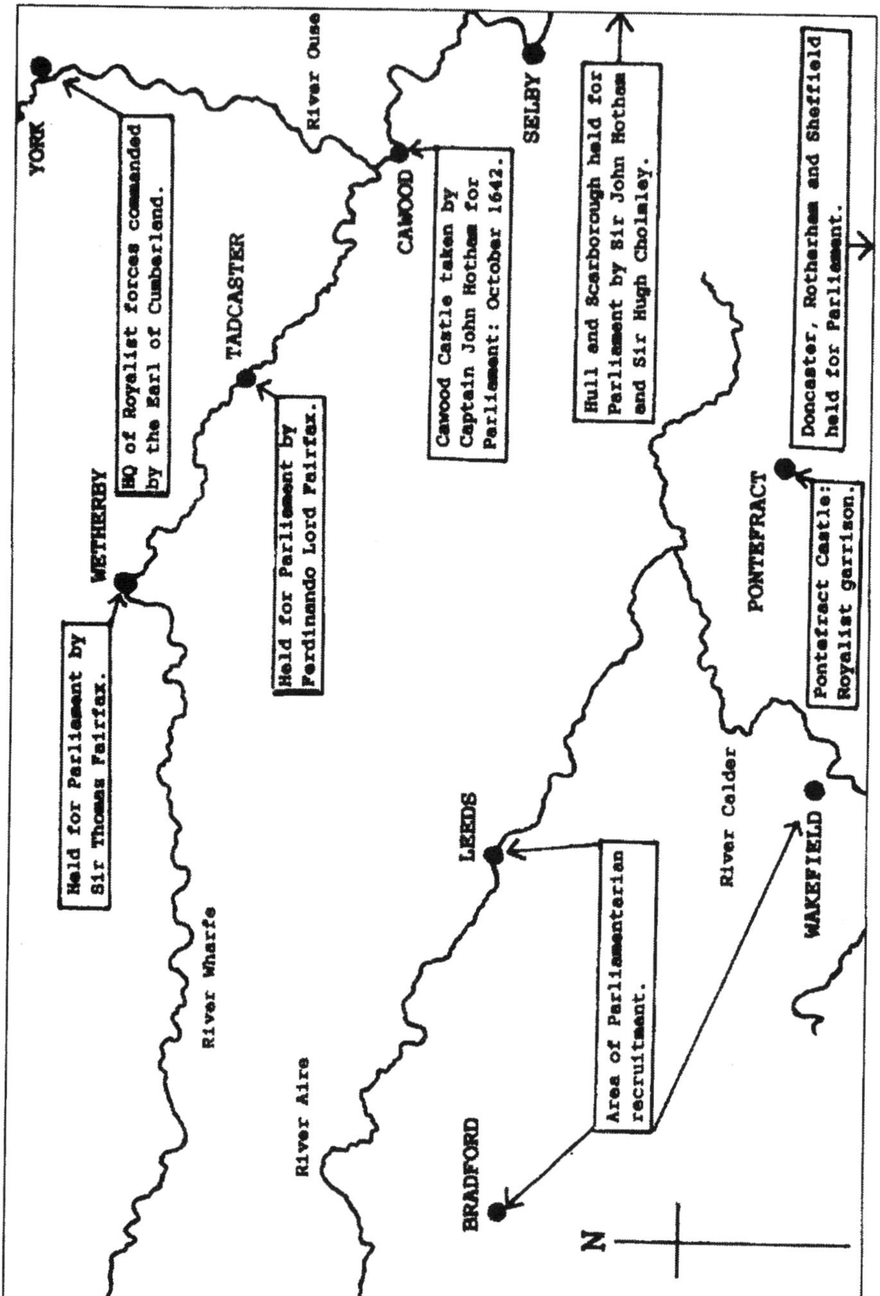
YORK
HQ of Royalist forces commanded by the Earl of Cumberland.
River Ouse
SELBY
CAWOOD
Cawood Castle taken by Captain John Hotham for Parliament: October 1642.
Hull and Scarborough held for Parliament by Sir John Hotham and Sir Hugh Cholmley.
Doncaster, Rotherham and Sheffield held for Parliament.
TADCASTER
Held for Parliament by Ferdinando Lord Fairfax.
WETHERBY
Held for Parliament by Sir Thomas Fairfax.
PONTEFRACT
Pontefract Castle: Royalist garrison.
River Calder
WAKEFIELD
LEEDS
Area of Parliamentarian recruitment.
River Wharfe
River Aire
BRADFORD
N

YORKSHIRE, November 1642

immediate impact upon the war in Yorkshire:

> With the advent of the earl of Newcastle, to whom the earl of Cumberland had reluctantly yielded up the command, matters took a turn less favourable to the Parliamentary forces. Sir Edward Loftus with all the Richmondshire troops, and Sir Henry Anderson with the men of Cleveland and the North Riding, to the number of one thousand, abandoned the struggle; Sir Hugh Cholmley drew off his 700 men from Stamford Bridge to garrison Scarborough, and Colonel Boynton with another 800 was sent to strengthen Hull.[107]

Facing a Royalist army of 8000 men Ferdinando Lord Fairfax commanded approximately 2500 horse and foot divided between the Parliamentarian garrisons at Wetherby, Tadcaster, Cawood, and Selby.[108] The situation was desperate. Not only did Newcastle substantially outnumber Fairfax, but in addition, a complicated series of personal rivalries with the Hotham's at Hull and Sir Hugh Cholmley at Scarborough meant that the Parliamentarian General was never able to rely upon the kind of support that he had probably anticipated.[109] However, Ferdinando and his son Sir Thomas - appointed second-in-command to his father and General of the Yorkshire horse - possessed between them a modicum of military training and experience that was to prove a significant advantage in the difficult months to come. Recruiting an enthusiastic and remarkably effective army in and around the Puritan cloth towns of the West Riding, the Fairfaxes were able to wage a form of guerrilla warfare until sheer weight of numbers finally contributed to disaster at Adwalton Moor on 30th June 1643. Even the arch-Royalist Clarendon was compelled to concede that:

> the enemy in those parts, with whom the earl of Newcastle was to contend, in courage, vigilance, and insuperable industry, was not inferior to any who disquieted his majesty in any part of his dominions, and who pursued any advantage he got farther, and recovered any loss he underwent sooner, than any other in the kingdom: so that there were more sharp skirmishes and more notable battles in that one county of York than in all the kingdom besides, and less alteration upon them than could be expected; the Lord Fairfax and his son with incredible activity reducing towns when they had an army, and when they were defeated in the field out of small towns recovering new armies.[110]

Given Clarendon's less than favourable opinion of Newcastle as a military commander it is not impossible to detect in his admiration for the Fairfaxes a frustrated sense of 'what might have been' had, perhaps, the earl demonstrated a similar tenacity to that which was to distinguish the way in which the Fairfaxes confronted the adversity of war.

Newcastle's Yorkshire Campaign

Though in fact praised by Clarendon for the decisive manner in which his intervention saved York,[111] Newcastle has nevertheless been censured for an overly cautious approach to a numerically inferior enemy.[112] The earl's prosecution of the Yorkshire campaign has attracted understandable, if perhaps slightly unfair criticism:

> Considering the great superiority of his forces, Newcastle's operations against Lord Fairfax, which commenced in December 1642, can hardly be considered very creditable to his military talents. It required three separate attacks to expel the Fairfaxes from the West Riding[113]

One must, however, remain mindful of the fact that the earl's appointment as Commander-in-chief was primarily intended to reflect social standing. The civilian world of 17th century society was to be replicated in the military organization of both Royalist and Parliamentarian forces. As a figure head for the King's cause in the north, Newcastle was compelled to depend upon the expertise and advice of those gentlemen appointed to his service as a consequence of their military talent and experience. Any criticism of Newcastle as commander, therefore, must reflect to a lesser or greater extent upon the counsel of others.

Initially, Newcastle dealt successfully and efficiently with the immediate threat posed by the Parliamentarian army gathering around York. Crossing the border into Yorkshire at Piercebridge on 1st December 1642, the Royalists quickly routed a small enemy force of 1500 under the command of Captain John Hotham. Moving swiftly to secure the county town, and assuming command of Yorkshire in the stead of the earl of Cumberland, Newcastle began to plan the campaign - which was to have three incarnations - by which the Fairfaxes would be defeated and evicted from the West Riding.

Newcastle's First Attack: December 1642-January 1643

Against the earl of Cumberland, General Ferdinando Lord Fairfax had attempted to defend the line of the River Wharfe south of York.[114] The arrival of Newcastle's large and concentrated army, however, had radically altered the once favourable balance of power. Having but recently posed a real threat to the Royalist HQ at York, the Parliamentarians under the Lord General's command now found themselves dangerously dispersed and exposed. Recalling Captain Hotham's garrison troops from Wetherby, Fairfax attempted to strengthen his principal position at Tadcaster. A major concern was the need to safeguard both access to his supplies in the West Riding cloth towns and communications with the Parliamentary garrison at Hull on the Humber estuary. From a fall back line in which Selby was to be at the centre, Fairfax reasoned that he would have the flexibility to manoeuvre either east or west as the situation demanded.

Having secured York, Newcastle had before him a series of military objectives that until successfully accomplished would prevent a march south to join the King. His first concern was to bring to battle and defeat the Fairfaxes,

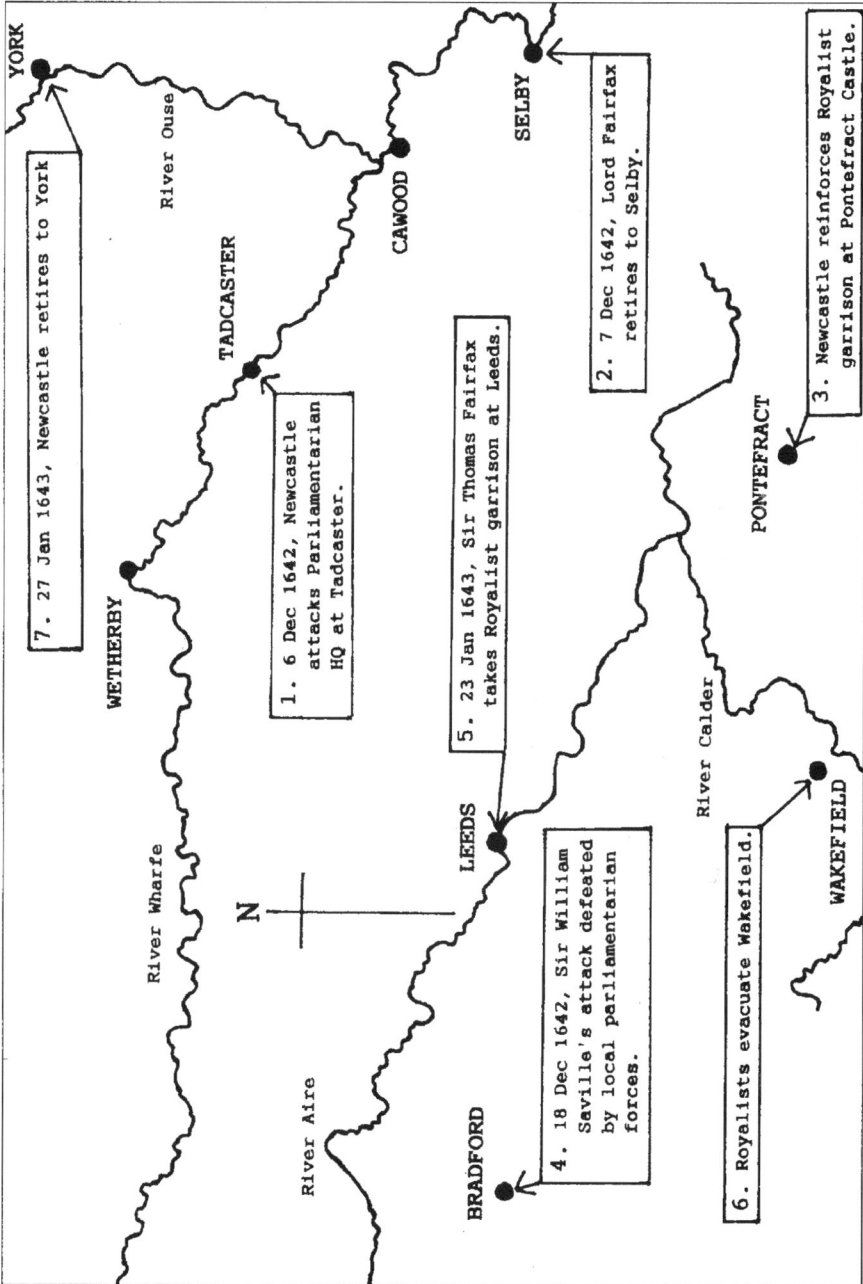

1. 6 Dec 1642, Newcastle attacks Parliamentarian HQ at Tadcaster.

2. 7 Dec 1642, Lord Fairfax retires to Selby.

3. Newcastle reinforces Royalist garrison at Pontefract Castle.

4. 18 Dec 1642, Sir William Saville's attack defeated by local parliamentarian forces.

5. 23 Jan 1643, Sir Thomas Fairfax takes Royalist garrison at Leeds.

6. Royalists evacuate Wakefield.

7. 27 Jan 1643, Newcastle retires to York

YORK

River Ouse

TADCASTER

CAWOOD

SELBY

WETHERBY

PONTEFRACT

River Wharfe

River Calder

N

LEEDS

WAKEFIELD

River Aire

BRADFORD

YORKSHIRE, Dec 1642 – Jan 1643

his second to establish control of the road south from York through Pontefract to Newark, and his third to prepare for the landing of the Queen and military supplies from the continent. Without a secure route from the east coast to the midlands neither Newcastle, Her Majesty, or the priceless supply of arms and ammunition could safely reach Charles at Oxford.

Taking the offensive, Newcastle marched to attack the Fairfaxes at Tadcaster on 6th December 1642. Having, as part of his strategy, detached a body of horse under the command of the Lieutenant General, the earl of Newport, via Wetherby to encircle Fairfax's army, Newcastle pushed the Parliamentarians back into the town. Only the fierce resistance of Fairfax's heavily outnumbered musketeers and the non-appearance of Newport's out-flanking cavalry enabled the Lord General to make a controlled withdrawal to Selby under the cover of darkness.

Though he had not for the moment defeated the enemy, Newcastle moved quickly to strengthen his position by re-establishing a strong force at Pontefract Castle and garrisoning the vital staging post of Newark. Having taken the decision to withdraw to Selby, Newcastle's drive south had effectively cut off Lord Fairfax's lines of communication with his power base in the West Riding cloth towns. Directing operations from Pontefract Castle, Newcastle despatched Sir William Saville to strike at the heart of Puritan territory by attacking Leeds, Wakefield, and Bradford. Though Leeds and Wakefield acquiesced without resistance, the Parliamentarian forces in Bradford - for the most part hastily assembled townsfolk - nevertheless repulsed the Royalist advance on 18th December. Sir Thomas Fairfax quickly reinforced the town and began to recruit an army with which to strike back. In this Sir Thomas was heavily influenced by the desperation of the local populace - the West Riding's trade having been severely disrupted by Newcastle's garrisoning of Leeds with 1500 men and Wakefield with 1200.[115] While the willingness of Sir Thomas Fairfax and Thomas Stockdale to harness the fighting vigour of the lower orders provided a welcome source of additional manpower, it served only to deepen divisions with the Hothams and Cholmley. This in turn forced the Fairfaxes into an absolute dependence upon the Parliamentarian sympathies of the West Riding.

Though the tenacity with which the enemy had resisted at Tadcaster and Bradford may have surprised Newcastle, the earl had at least the satisfaction that his occupation of Northumberland and County Durham had placed the north east coal trade in the hands of the King. Charles offered to continue to supply the capital at greatly inflated prices. Parliament, not unnaturally perhaps, steadfastly refused to sanction what would have constituted an indirect contribution to Royalist war finances. As a consequence London's morale, and Parliament's popularity in the capital, was to be tested by a long and cold winter devoid of adequate heating.[116]

It would appear that as Christmas passed Newcastle was unable to launch a fresh offensive until re-supplied with ammunition. This not only presented Sir Thomas Fairfax with a breathing space in which to prepare his embryonic force at Bradford, but also enabled Sir Hugh Cholmley to demonstrate the danger of underestimating Parliamentarian ability to fight a rearguard campaign. On 16th January 1643 a Royalist supply convoy from Newcastle-upon-Tyne was intercepted and destroyed at Guisborough in North Yorkshire by troops from Cholmley's Scarborough garrison.[117] Effectively immobilized as an offensive force by the want of munitions, Newcastle was then shocked into hasty retreat by the unexpected loss of Leeds on 23rd January. Having completed the recruitment of a small force of approximately 1200 men, Sir Thomas Fairfax launched an attack upon the refusal of the governor, Sir William Saville, to surrender the town. After two hours of bitter fighting the Royalists were forced to withdraw, leaving behind a large quantity of precious ammunition. The earl of Newcastle, no doubt shattered by events, abandoned Pontefract, ordered the complete evacuation of Wakefield, and marched his remaining army back to York on 27th January 1643.

A somewhat dramatic response perhaps, but Newcastle may in all probability have been left with no alternative course of action. It seems possible, even likely, that he had received important intelligence concerning the Queen's proposed landing on the Yorkshire coast. His primary considerations at this stage of the campaign were clearly those of Her Majesty's personal safety and, of course, the invaluable shipment of munitions and money that accompanied her. The problem of the Fairfaxes would simply have to wait.

Newcastle's Second Attack: March - May 1643

Frustrated thus far by an inability to engage the enemy in a conventional battle situation, in which superior numbers would undoubtedly tell, Newcastle instead provoked a war of words with Lord Fairfax. The earl, among other things, challenged the Parliamentarians as a matter of honour to take the field against the Royalist army. This would have amounted to suicide for Fairfax who, not surprisingly, offered to give battle wherever and whenever a suitable opportunity presented itself.[118]

While the Royalist withdrawal to York had restored Parliamentarian control in the West Riding, opening up communications with the Lord General at Selby, Fairfax knew only too well that the day of reckoning had merely been postponed. Through February and March, though Newcastle had not yet completed his preparations for a new offensive, the situation with which the Fairfaxes had to contend steadily declined. On 1st February Sir Hugh Cholmley's attempt to intercept another Royalist arms convoy bound for York ended in total defeat at Yarm Bridge on the North Yorkshire border. Not only was the convoy a significant development in terms of the supply of Newcastle's army, it was, more importantly perhaps, led by the Scottish General James King. King (created Lord Eythin on 28th March 1643), a veteran of continental warfare in the service of the King of Sweden, had been persuaded to return to England by the Queen. Although an able commander, as demonstrated at

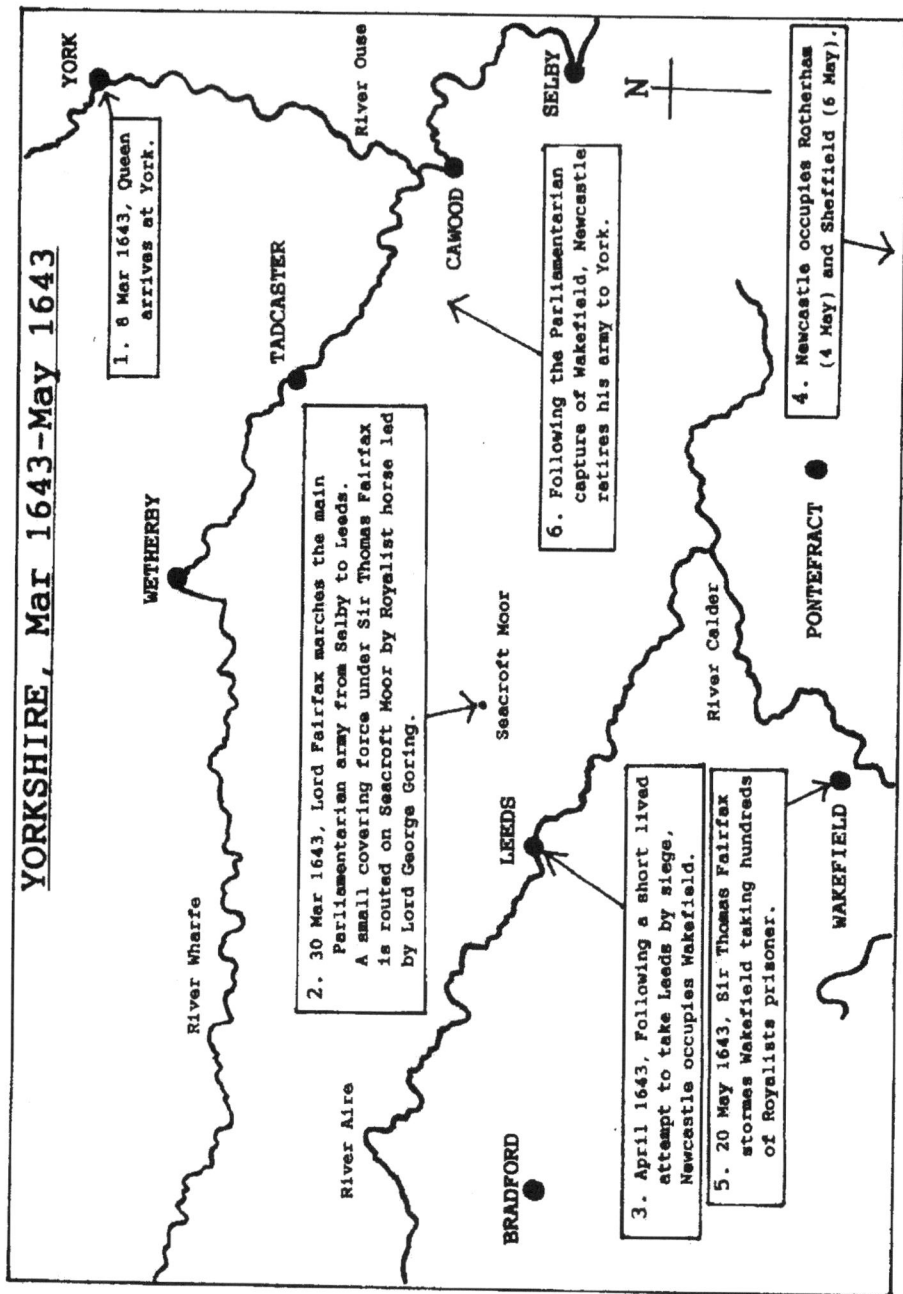

YORKSHIRE, Mar 1643–May 1643

1. 8 Mar 1643, Queen arrives at York.

2. 30 Mar 1643, Lord Fairfax marches the main Parliamentarian army from Selby to Leeds. A small covering force under Sir Thomas Fairfax is routed on Seacroft Moor by Royalist horse led by Lord George Goring.

3. April 1643, Following a short lived attempt to take Leeds by siege, Newcastle occupies Wakefield.

4. Newcastle occupies Rotherham (4 May) and Sheffield (6 May).

5. 20 May 1643, Sir Thomas Fairfax stormes Wakefield taking hundreds of Royalists prisoner.

6. Following the Parliamentarian capture of Wakefield, Newcastle retires his army to York.

YORK

TADCASTER

WETHERBY

River Wharfe

River Aire

River Ouse

CAWOOD

SELBY

Seacroft Moor

LEEDS

BRADFORD

River Calder

PONTEFRACT

WAKEFIELD

N

YORKSHIRE, Mar 1643 – May 1643

Yarm Bridge, King had, however, acquired a reputation for tactical conservatism on the battlefield.[119] Newcastle was nevertheless both delighted and relieved. Immediately arresting his second-in-command the earl of Newport on suspicion of planning to kidnap the Queen, Newcastle appointed King Lieutenant General in Newport's place.[120] Newport's military exploits had in any case inspired little confidence, while the arrival of James King at last provided the experience of battle upon which Newcastle was content to depend. In addition, the appointment of Lord George Goring as General of the Horse placed at Newcastle's disposal a talented and inspirational, if somewhat irresponsible, leader of cavalry.

The steady strengthening of the northern Royalist army was all but completed on 22nd February 1643. Following an unsuccessful intervention by units of the Parliamentarian navy the Queen, accompanied by a large shipment of arms and money, successfully disembarked at Bridlington on the East Yorkshire coast. Newcastle, by virtue of a secret agreement with the Hothams, was permitted to escort the vulnerable convoy to York in return for a commitment not to attack either Beverley or Hull.[121] With the Royalist cause significantly replenished in terms of finance and military hardware, the Queen immediately set about a policy of intrigue designed to win over those Parliamentarian commanders at variance with the Fairfaxes. Following a clandestine audience with Her Majesty, Sir Hugh Cholmley declared Scarborough for the King on 25th March, while Sir John Hotham refused all assistance to Lord Fairfax at Selby.[122] With Scarborough now firmly Royalist and Hull increasingly hostile, Lord Fairfax had little option but to abandon Selby and fall back towards the heartland of his support in the West Riding. On 30th March he made for Leeds while Sir Thomas, with a detachment of horse and foot, was instructed to mask his father's withdrawal by retreating westward from Tadcaster. However, on Seacroft Moor near Leeds, Sir Thomas' foot were caught and badly mauled by a powerful force of Royalist cavalry under the command of Lord George Goring. The Parliamentarians had fatally delayed their departure from Tadcaster, intent on the destruction of the town's fortifications, and so were outstripped in their march by Goring's horse. Although many Parliamentarians were either taken prisoner or wounded, Lord Fairfax's main army arrived in Leeds unmolested. This was, however, an ill-timed and unnecessary reversal, particularly for an army as desperately small as Lord Fairfax's.

Thus reinforced Newcastle left York in early April 1643 with an army of 7000 foot and 3500 horse bound for the West Riding.[123] With the Queen now safely lodged at York, Newcastle, not only concerned to deal with the Fairfaxes as quickly as possible, was once again mindful of the need to secure a safe passage south through Yorkshire in anticipation of the Queen's eventual departure to join the King at Oxford. The earl would have preferred to subdue all opposition in Yorkshire before proceeding with the onerous responsibility of escorting the Queen and her convoy. The swift elimination of the Fairfaxes, combined with a favourable conclusion to the delicate negotiations by which the Hotham's were to be won to the King's cause, would have left Yorkshire safe in Royalist hands, permitting Newcastle to march both his army and his Queen to the King. However, events were to prove otherwise.

Newcastle arrived before Leeds intending to defeat the Fairfaxes by siege. James King, anxious to preserve the strength of the army, cautiously advised against the plan. Newcastle, after a day or two bombarding the town, deferred to his Lieutenant General in order to occupy Wakefield. The South Yorkshire Parliamentary garrisons of Rotherham (4th May) and Sheffield (6th May) were then secured. Sheffield, with important ironworks, was particularly valuable. Though Newcastle had failed to defeat the enemy, his progress south had once again severed West Riding trade routes and had opened up the vital passage to Pontefract Castle.

The Fairfaxes, effectively besieged in their West Riding enclave of Leeds, Bradford and Halifax, were, however, under increasing pressure to obtain the liberty of those Parliamentarian troops captured in the rout at Seacroft Moor. Believing Wakefield to be only lightly held by around 800 Royalists, Sir Thomas Fairfax launched a daring night attack on 20th May. After fierce fighting the town fell, revealing a defending force of over 3000 horse and foot - twice the number of Sir Thomas' small army. Despite the capture of large quantities of supplies and the exchange of Royalist prisoners for those Parliamentarians taken at Seacroft, Fairfax evacuated the town. The Parliamentarian army was not of sufficient strength to garrison effectively beyond its core territory around Leeds and Bradford. Newcastle, suffering not only the ignominy of defeat to a numerically inferior force, had his commander of horse, the able Lord George Goring, taken prisoner.[124] Forced, therefore, to rely increasingly upon the conservative counsel of James King, Newcastle once again retired his army to York. Determined and enterprising, the Fairfaxes had proved to be resilient opponents, to whom the Royalists - for the second time - were forced to concede the issue.

Reinforcements and Strategy

Despite the success of the Wakefield raid - which had compelled Newcastle to at least temporarily abandon his offensive strategy - the Parliamentarian position remained extremely precarious. Forced to retreat into the West Riding, facing an enemy enjoying a significant superiority in numbers, denied access to the strategic garrison of Hull, Lord Fairfax appealed directly to neighbouring counties for assistance. By early June 1643 Cromwell had gathered together an army of perhaps 6000 men at Nottingham, intending to march north into Yorkshire to rescue the Fairfaxes. The plan was foiled by the younger Hotham, also present at Nottingham, who wrote to Lord Fairfax claiming that the threat posed by Newcastle's army no longer justified the reinforcements Fairfax begged for.[125] The Hothams, by now close to declaring themselves for the King, were clearly determined to undermine the Fairfaxes at every opportunity. It was left to the Lancashire Parliamentarians of Manchester, anxious to protect the county from Royalist incursion, to provide their Yorkshire allies with material assistance. Around the middle of June 1643 a small but nevertheless valuable force of around 1600 men was despatched across the border to Halifax.[126] Though remaining desperately short of manpower, the Lancashire reinforcements provided Lord Fairfax with an opportunity to prolong Newcastle's campaign in Yorkshire.

Returning to York, the earl's most pressing concern became the safe despatch of the Queen and her supplies to the King at Oxford. Charles, expecting a siege, was desperate for assistance.[127] Though he had already received, on 13th May, a convoy of arms from Her Majesty, his position remained less than secure.[128] Newcastle, accompanied by the royal entourage, left York on 4th June heading first for the safety of Pontefract Castle. Here a council of war was called to decide strategy. The options were clear. Should Newcastle accede to the King's wishes: deliver the Queen, her supplies, and the whole Northern Royalist army to Oxford? Or should he take the advice of James King: remain in Yorkshire; deal with the Fairfaxes; and despatch only a portion of his force to escort the Queen? Uniting with the King's Oxford army offered the tantalizing possibility of outright military victory. However, leaving an undefeated enemy in the rear of a southward march invited an attack on two fronts. In addition, Royalist troops raised in Yorkshire were understandably reluctant to abandon their homes and property to the marauding and as yet undefeated Fairfaxes. Sir Henry Slingsby, Civil War diarist and Royalist Colonel of the York regiment of foot, described the concluding deliberations:

> Well, this latter was resolved on, of sending some forces only with the Queen, and himself [Newcastle] to stay, and to try the mastery with my Lord Fairfax.[129]

Decisions finally made and agreed upon, Newcastle assembled a royal escort of around 4300 men.[130] The Queen arrived at Newark on 16th June leaving Newcastle free at last to concentrate upon defeating the Fairfaxes. The earl may have reasoned that once the business of Yorkshire had been concluded he could march to the King's aid with a clear sense of 'mission accomplished'. Before his capture at Wakefield in May, George Goring, Newcastle's commander of horse, had written in a letter to his father that the only way to defeat the Fairfaxes was to strike directly into the West Riding.[131] This, after a brief pause to replace lost manpower with a recruiting drive, was precisely what Newcastle did next.

Though not strictly pertinent here, it is perhaps worth making the point that the inevitable lack of reliable information concerning exercises such as recruitment campaigns is one reason why an accurate estimate of the size of the Royalist army at Adwalton Moor is so difficult to arrive at. The problem of calculating the composition and strength of the force Newcastle deployed against Lord Fairfax on 30th June will be discussed in chapter four.

Newcastle's Third Attack: June 1643

Marching north - west from Pontefract towards Bradford and Leeds, Newcastle halted first at the Parliamentary garrison of Howley Hall on 20th June. Though the property of the Royalist Lord Thomas Saville, the house was held for Parliament by his cousin Sir John Saville.[132] Howley was an important outpost strongly defended. It was from the hall, a month earlier, that Sir Thomas Fairfax had launched his successful raid against the 3000 strong Royalist garrison at Wakefield. Newcastle, having first invited Sir John Saville to surrender, laid siege to the house for two days, at which point the building was either stormed, or the defenders - having exhausted their ammunition - surrendered.[133] The capture of Howley by a substantial Royalist force clearly indicated that Newcastle was once again intent upon bringing the Fairfaxes to battle. Having mobilized the entire Royalist field army the earl was heading for the heart of Parliamentarian support in and around the West Riding cloth towns.

Lord Fairfax recognized that the fall of Howley signalled the inevitability of some kind of large scale confrontation. His options, however, were somewhat limited. From the very beginning of Newcastle's Yorkshire campaign the Parliamentarian army had lacked the major reinforcements with which to tackle the enemy in a traditional set-piece battle. It had been the strategy of the Fairfaxes, much to Newcastle's discomfort, to wage a defensive war, attacking when the opportunity presented itself and when the enemy least expected it. Sir Thomas Fairfax's capture of both Leeds and Wakefield had demonstrated how effective relatively small numbers of well led and highly motivated men could be. By avoiding the kind of encounter in which Newcastle could bring his numerical superiority to bear, the Fairfaxes had successfully maintained an army in being. This in turn had compelled Newcastle to remain in Yorkshire when his principal concerns were to deliver both his army and his Queen to the King.

Fairfax's second option, that of defending Bradford against an anticipated siege with all available forces was wholly impracticable - supplies and munitions were only sufficient for a period of 10 or 12 days.[134] Having supported the Parliamentary army for a year the West Riding had been bled dry.[135] The third option, that of withdrawal to the safety of Hull was likewise impossible as Sir John Hotham had already declared his hostility to the Fairfaxes. And the fourth option, that of retreat to another county would only hand Yorkshire over to the Royalists without the prospect of at least stalling Newcastle's formidable forces. Characteristically the Fairfaxes chose to take the initiative. On 29th June, having mustered all the surrounding garrison forces at Bradford - including the newly arrived reinforcements from Lancashire - Lord Fairfax held a council of war. It was a week since Howley had fallen. Fairfax was probably surprised that he had not, in the intervening period, encountered a direct Royalist attack. He realized that he had to act quickly if a pre-emptive strike, such as that which

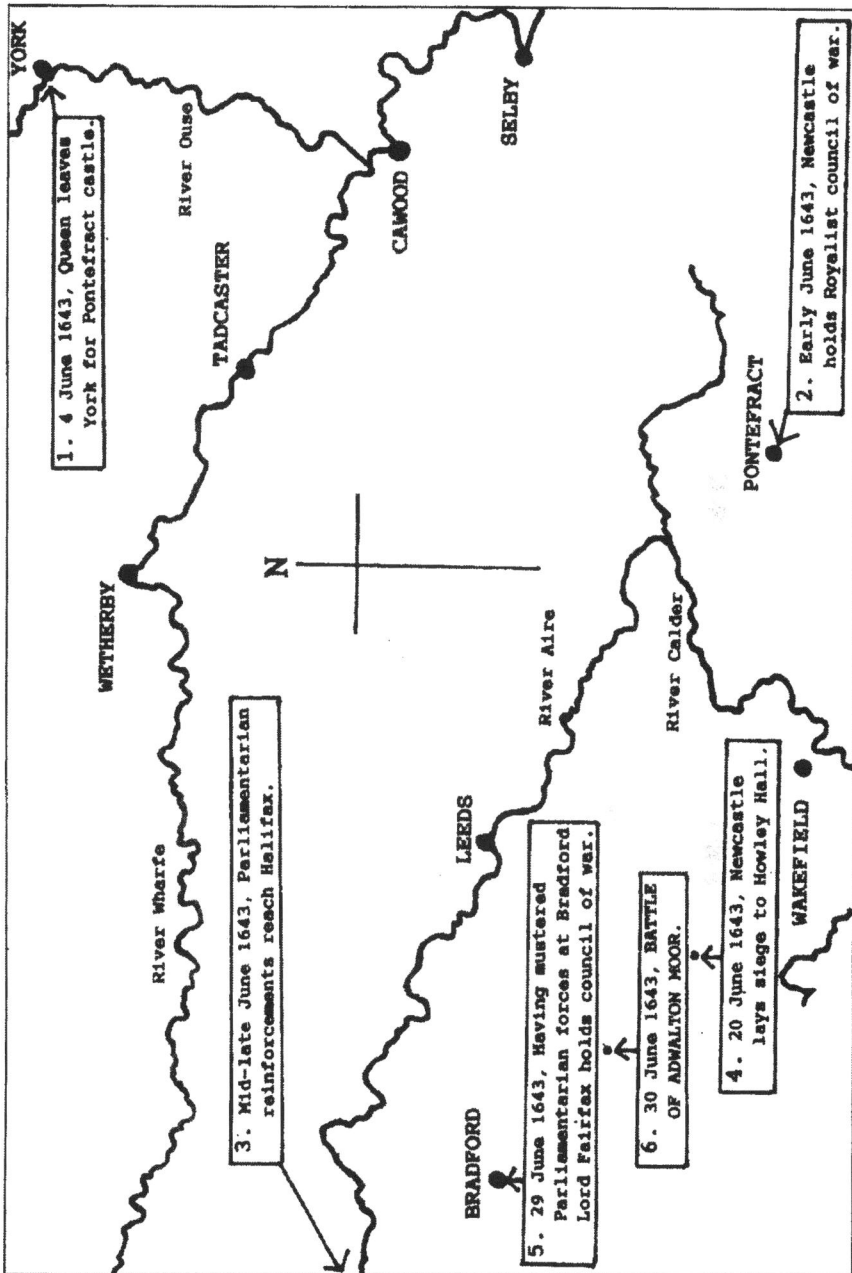

YORKSHIRE, June 1643

1. 4 June 1643, Queen leaves York for Pontefract castle.

2. Early June 1643, Newcastle holds Royalist council of war.

3. Mid-late June 1643, Parliamentarian reinforcements reach Halifax.

4. 20 June 1643, Newcastle lays siege to Howley Hall.

5. 29 June 1643, Having mustered Parliamentarian forces at Bradford Lord Fairfax holds council of war.

6. 30 June 1643, BATTLE OF ADWALTON MOOR.

YORK
SELBY
CAWOOD
TADCASTER
PONTEFRACT
WETHERBY
LEEDS
WAKEFIELD
BRADFORD

River Ouse
River Wharfe
River Aire
River Calder

N

captured Wakefield, was once more to prove successful. Sir Thomas Fairfax described the outcome of their deliberations:

> we resolved, the next morning very early with a party of 3000 men, to attempt his whole Army as they laid in their Quarters, [Howley Hall] 3 miles off: Hoping thereby to put him into some Distraction; which could not (by reason of the unequall number) be done any other way.[136]

Clearly the decision to attack represented a desperate gamble, even allowing for the important advantage of surprise. Newcastle held a potentially decisive superiority in manpower.[137] Yet success offered the possibility of once again sapping Newcastle's strength and determination, forcing another Royalist retreat to York, and buying valuable time to strengthen the Parliamentarian army. If the Fairfaxes were able to inflict sufficient damage without themselves sustaining critical losses they would in all probability derail Newcastle's campaign for a third time.

Despite the intention of the Pontefract council of war to press forward into the West Riding, Newcastle hesitated once Howley Hall had been taken. Margaret Cavendish, his biographer and second wife, claimed that the pause was required to refresh the soldiers and to agree a target to attack next.[138] Sir Henry Slingsby confirmed the indecision, implying that Newcastle may have been waiting for Fairfax to make the next move:

> then he [Newcastle] lay to consider of that which must be the master piece, the taking of Leeds and Bradford, or giving battle if my Lord Fairfax durst venture in the field.[139]

However, the account attributed to Newcastle himself blamed several days of bad weather for the delay.[140] While this may appear at first sight to be a somewhat flimsy excuse it does have an air of credibility. As will be discussed in chapter four, it is claimed that it took the Royalist army no less than two hours to properly draw up and prepare their cannon. Had indeed a prolonged period of inclement weather delayed Newcastle's march, difficult road conditions would certainly have slowed the movement and deployment of heavy field pieces, particularly those intended primarily for the purposes of siege warfare.

Whatever the truth, it is difficult not to sense the inherent caution of the Newcastle/James King partnership, on this occasion, perhaps, tinged with a hint of respect for the Fairfaxes. Finally, in the absence of any move by the Parliamentarians, Newcastle decided to decamp early on the morning of 30th June and strike directly at Bradford.[141] At approximately the same time, Lord Fairfax was marching his army towards Howley Hall. Unknown to either commander, the forces of King and Parliament were set to collide on a ridge of barren West Yorkshire moorland close to the tiny settlement of Adwalton.

As will be demonstrated in chapter four, Adwalton Moor was not to be a traditional set-piece battle such as those that were fought at Edgehill, Marston Moor, and Naseby. In conventional circumstances opposing commanders would carefully select their ground, often arranging their armies in accordance with a predetermined plan of deployment, waiting finally to attack at a pre-arranged signal or to receive their opponents first move. Adwalton Moor, in stark contrast, was a battle fought on the march. Unexpectedly coming to blows approximately half way to their respective destinations, the armies of Newcastle and Fairfax had no alternative but to deploy quickly, making the best possible use of the landscape in which they found themselves compelled to fight. The terrain, not unnaturally given the circumstances, dictated from the outset the way in which the fighting developed and the way in which horse and foot could be utilized. Indeed such was the importance of the battlefield topography that its description runs as a constant thread throughout the principal eyewitness accounts.

In a battle so constrained, as Adwalton Moor was, by the landscape in which it was fought, the reconstruction of that landscape becomes an inescapable prerequisite of any attempt to describe and understand the combat itself. It is to this particular problem that attention is now directed.

CHAPTER 3

ADWALTON MOOR:
The Battlefield Reconstructed

The landscapes in which battles are fought naturally determine the deployment and subsequent use of combatants and their weapons. Military leaders take great care to select the most advantageous ground, to plan, if possible, for fighting to take place in specific locations exhibiting particular topographical features. To properly appreciate the course of any battle the relationship between the soldier and the terrain over which he operates must be understood. Given therefore the importance of battlefield landscape, the reconstruction of terrain becomes an imperative. This not only serves to make sense of the fighting itself but in addition provides evidence for the correct identification of the battlefield site. Anyone familiar with military history will be acutely aware of the various controversies that surround a number of battlefield locations. While military historians will often go to great lengths to research commanders, armies, soldiers, and weapons the overall battle story will always remain incomplete unless the terrain itself is subjected to a similarly comprehensive investigation.

Before considering the specifics of Adwalton Moor battlefield it is perhaps appropriate to say something of the general method by which an historic battlefield landscape is reconstructed. Broadly speaking there are three quite separate but complimentary types or categories of evidence. The first is provided by historic documentation; the second by interpretation of the physical landscape; and the third by archaeological investigation. Each will be considered in turn.

The process of reconstruction begins with and depends fundamentally upon the first type of evidence - historic documentation; in particular the eyewitness and contemporary accounts. Containing vital references to all manner of landscape features, the primary sources provide the raw data upon which the battlefield site is initially identified and located. Historic maps of all kinds, deeds of land ownership and transaction, official and unofficial landscape descriptions of various dates: each of these then provide a specific form of information against which the often precise and particular references of the primary sources can be compared and reconciled.

In some cases, unfortunately, a scarcity of documentation or a lack of pertinent detail can render the evidence of available primary sources inconclusive, confusing or even completely baffling. Of course, to properly understand any battle the site or sites indicated by the written evidence must be subjected to inspection. In difficult instances the careful observation and examination of the terrain can often solve or shed new light upon documentary

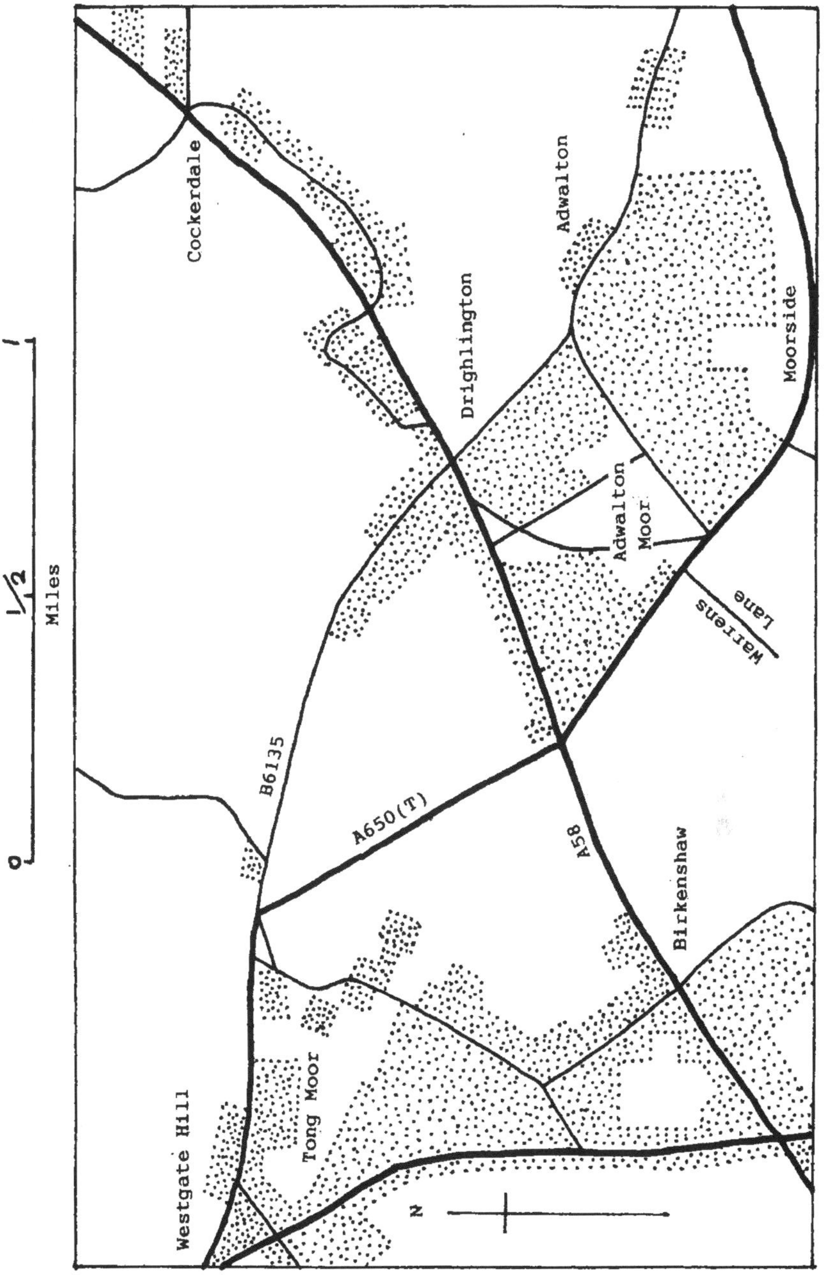
0
1/2
1
Miles
N
Cockerdale
Adwalton
Drighlington
Moorside
Adwalton Moor
Warrens Lane
B6135
A650(T)
A58
Birkenshaw
Westgate Hill
Tong Moor

ADWALTON MOOR BATTLEFIELD 2000

problems as well as serve to confirm the evidence for more straightforward or clear cut battlefield sites. Landscape interpretation - the second category of evidence - has proved to be a significant tool in the work, already referred to, of P.R.Newman, G.Foard, and P.Foss. The landscape is, after all, a primary source of evidence - even if, as in the case of Adwalton Moor, the passage of time has substantially altered its appearance. The technique was adopted in the mid 1990s by English Heritage as the principal means by which its Register of Historic Battlefields was compiled. Intended primarily for purposes of conservation the Register attempted to define the physical extent of each battlefield site by an assessment of the documentary and landscape evidence. It has already been noted that the same process, in perhaps a more rudimentary form, was employed by Norrisson Scatcherd in the early years of the 19th century at Adwalton Moor. Armed with the eyewitness account of Sir Thomas Fairfax, Scatcherd recalled that he had:

> reconnoitred this field of battle, near Adwalton, more times than once, having the foregoing narrative fresh upon my mind; and the impressions then made upon me were committed to writing.[142]

Thus, in the case of Adwalton Moor at least, English Heritage were not the first to examine the battlefield landscape in conjunction with documentary evidence.

The third type of evidence is that provided by archaeological investigation. The careful and systematic recovery and mapping of battlefield artefacts such as, for example, musket balls or arrow heads can dramatically transform an understanding of how and where armies fought. In terms of the English Civil War the painstaking survey work of battlefield archaeologists such as Paul Roberts at Marston Moor has accurately located and identified areas of fighting within the battlefield landscape. Work which in turn serves to illuminate further the documentary testimony of the eyewitness accounts. It has already been noted how a similar project at Naseby has shed new light upon the final stages of that particular battle. This very intensive process is still, however, in its infancy, and has so far been restricted to a small number of sites. Despite the absence of this type of work at battlefields such as Adwalton Moor, some archaeological evidence may nevertheless be available. Isolated and individual archaeological discoveries often find their way into the collections of local museums or onto the pages of the local press, while the published works of numerous 18th and 19th century antiquarians have frequently recorded the discovery of significant military relics. For example, the work of Norrisson Scatcherd has helped to unravel the often very difficult landscape problems at Adwalton Moor.

Adwalton Moor Battlefield

Any battlefield reconstruction must begin with an identification of the general area in which the battle took place. In the case of Adwalton Moor one is immediately presented with two pieces of information. The first, that the battle had some connection with a moor, and the second, that the moor is named Adwalton, raises the distinct possibility that the moorland in question is to be found in the vicinity of a settlement bearing the same name. Confirmation is provided by the First Edition 6" Ordnance Survey map which shows such a moor and village five miles south east of Bradford in West Yorkshire. The map, surveyed in 1847, places the settlement on the main Bradford to Wakefield road adjacent to an area of open land named 'Adwalton Moor'. In addition the site is identified as the location of a battle fought in 1643 between the Royalists and Parliamentarians. These features are described by the first of the accompanying maps. 'Adwalton Moor Battlefield 2000' shows the extent of 20th century urban sprawl and road development in the general battlefield area. The old Bradford to Wakefield road, running north west to south east across the map, is now the B6135, while the remains of the once extensive Adwalton Moor are shown surrounded by 20th century Drighlington and Adwalton villages. Having thus located the general battle site one has then to begin the process by which the topographical references contained within the primary sources are identified and pin pointed. For ease of understanding and to make the reconstruction more intelligible each of the following subsections is accompanied by its own map. Finally these individual maps are combined to produce 'Adwalton Moor Battlefield 1643' - the reconstructed mid 17th century battlefield landscape.

Hills and High Ground

Adwalton Moor sits on a ridge, roughly three-quarters of a mile wide, running north west towards Bradford and south east towards Howley Hall. Hereabouts the ridge, which carries the old Bradford to Wakefield road along its north eastern edge, displays an undulating profile of rising and falling ground. The specific identification of the higher terrain provides the first indication of the extent of the battlefield.

Captain John Hodgson, a Halifax weaver who had enlisted in the Parliamentarian army at Bradford in December 1642 following Sir William Saville's unsuccessful attempt to storm the town, described an important area of high ground in his brief description of the battle of Adwalton Moor:

> All the forces we could spare in Leeds, Halifax, and Bradford, with some Lancashire regiments, were drawn up towards Wiskett hill.[143]

J.Warburton's 'A New and Correct Map of the County of York', engraved in 1720, shows a 'Wisket Hill' lying directly between 'Bradforth' and the village of 'AddWalton or Adderton'. The road along which Lord Fairfax's army would have advanced on its march towards Howley Hall (the Bradford to Wakefield road) is shown running over the summit of the hill. Thomas Jefferys' 1771 map

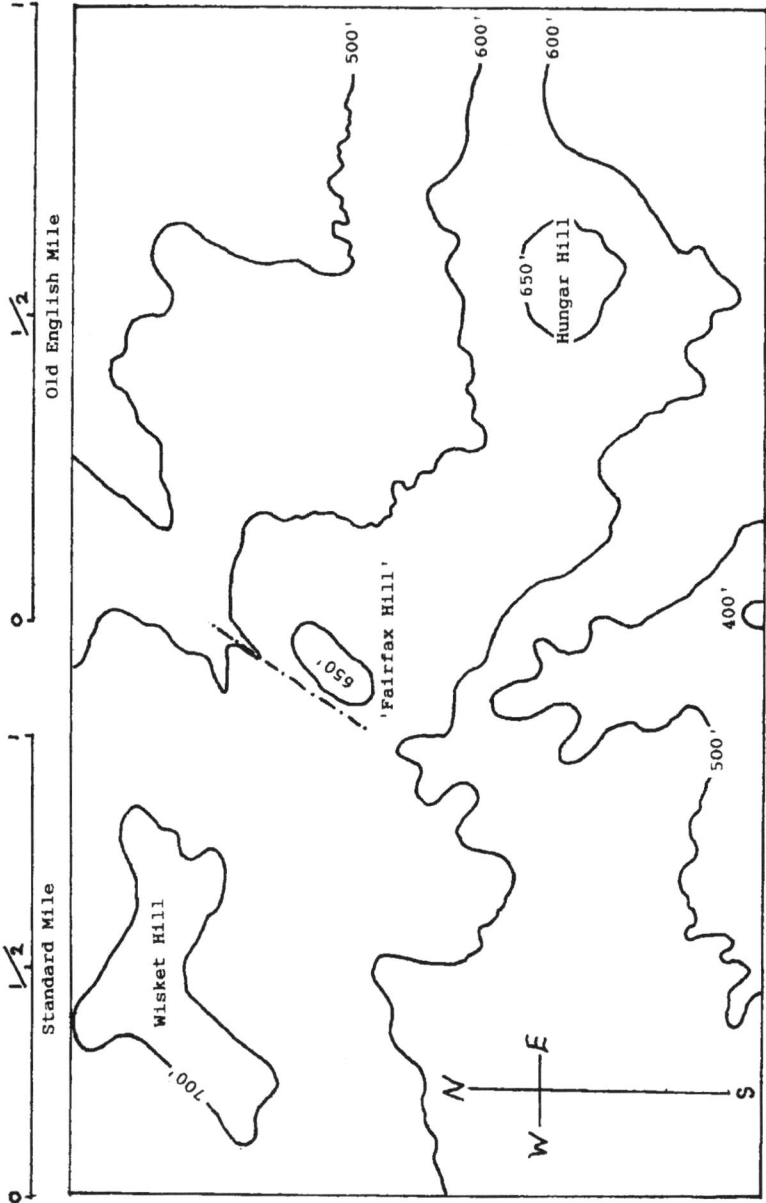

HILLS AND HIGH GROUND

Part of Tong/Drighlington township boundary

Standard Mile

Old English Mile

Wisket Hill

700'

'Fairfax Hill'

650'

Hungar Hill

650'

500'

600'

600'

400'

500'

N
E
W
S

42

View looking south east from the A58 (Whitehall Road) across Adwalton Moor to the site of the final Royalist battle line on the north western slope of Hungar Hill

of 'The County of York' similarly described the Bradford road climbing over 'Wisegate or Wisket Hill'. A comparison with the 'Adwalton Moor Battlefield 2000' map produced here indicates that Hodgson's 'Wiskett Hill' is in fact modern Westgate Hill. Confirmation that the two are one and the same is provided by J.Dickinson's 1725 'Map of the Mannour or Lordship of Tong' which shows Wisket Hill in precisely the same position as modern Westgate Hill.[144]

A second minor Parliamentary source, that of the German military engineer Johan Rosworm, underlined the significance of the hill. Though Rosworm was not present at Adwalton Moor he had fortified Manchester in 1642 and the Pennine passes between Lancashire and Yorkshire in 1643. The Lancashire regiments that fought at Adwalton Moor were raised in Manchester and doubtless provided Rosworm with his information:

The issue was, our men were soundly beaten at Wisked-hill in Yorkshire.[145]

The Lancashire soldiers, possibly unfamiliar with the geography of West Yorkshire in and around the Bradford area, clearly identified the battle with the most prominent local topographical feature. John James, a Bradford historian who twice visited the battlefield in the first half of the 19th century, described archaeological evidence that fighting had taken place on the hill:

> From inquiries made on the spot, I ascertained that it [Wisket Hill] is yet called 'Red-hill'; and that numbers of musket-balls are frequently found burried just beneath its surface.[146]

The evidence of Hodgson and Rosworm raises the interesting possibility that the battle may have been known locally as 'Wisket Hill' for perhaps a short period after 30th June 1643. As will be discussed in chapter four, the battle of Adwalton Moor began as a sharp skirmish for the hill, fought between the advance units of the respective armies. The location of this important landmark is shown in the north west corner of the 'Hills and High Ground' map.

Sir Thomas Fairfax, commander of the Parliamentarian right wing at Adwalton Moor, began his account of the fighting with a further significant reference to an area of high ground:

> We were to goe up a Hill to them, which our fforlorne Hope gained by beating theirs into their maine Body, which was drawne up halfe a mile further, upon a place called Adderton Moore.[147]

In describing what appeared to be the first encounter between the forward troops of the opposing forces ('fforlorne Hope'), Fairfax located the confrontation on a hill half a mile to the north west of Adwalton Moor ('Adderton Moore'). English Heritage have quite reasonably argued that the hill in question is in fact modern Westgate Hill.[148] At the time of the Civil War the old English mile of 2427 yards remained in common use, a measurement considerably larger than the modern mile of only 1760 yards. This has of course to be taken into account when considering 17th century interpretations of distance. Today, half an old English mile south east of Westgate Hill (Wisket Hill) stands a ditch marking the boundary between Tong and Drighlington townships. In traversing the battlefield ridge on a south west to north east axis the ditch also acts as a demarcation between former areas of moorland in Tong and Drighlington. To the immediate south east of the ditch, however, stands an area of rising ground, located as Sir Thomas Fairfax described, half an old English mile from the centre of modern Adwalton Moor. This hill, in fact more of a ridge than a hill, is not named on any historic map, but would appear a plausible alternative to Westgate Hill. Fairfax, familiar with the topography of West Yorkshire, specifically identified the moorland as 'Adderton Moor', but failed to describe the hill as anything other than a hill. One might expect Fairfax, if the hill were in fact Westgate Hill, to identify it as 'Wisket Hill'. This is an important problem, made more difficult by the fluid and ever changing positions of the rival armies. As will be discussed presently, it is also complicated by the precise location and identification of the battlefield's various moorland areas. Nevertheless, the unnamed ridge played a significant part in the fighting of Adwalton Moor. Therefore, in order to avoid confusion with other areas of high ground, it will henceforth be referred to as 'Fairfax Hill'.

A further reference to a hill is contained in a letter written the day after the battle by the Parliamentarian eyewitness Thomas Stockdale. Stockdale, while recounting the deployment of the Royalist army, described the ground upon which Newcastle arrayed his forces as:

> both a great hill and an open moor or common, where our foot could not be able to stand their horse.[149]

Stockdale was almost certainly referring to a third hill - adjacent to the south eastern side of Adwalton Moor - identified as 'Hungar Hill' on Warburton's 1720 map. Norrisson Scatcherd, the 19th century antiquary whose account of the battle was published in his *History of Morley*, described the local tradition that:

> the Earl of Newcastle's troops came out upon the Moor, over that high ridge where there are now collieries of Miss Whiteleg. The soldiers of Fairfax coming from Whisket-Hill, would approach in a direction nearly opposite.[150]

The first 6 inch to the mile Ordnance Survey map of the area, surveyed in 1847 and published in 1852, shows two collieries on the south eastern slope of the hill lying in a direct line between Adwalton Moor and Howley Hall. The deployment of Newcastle's forces from line of march on the Wakefield/Bradford road to battle formation upon Adwalton Moor would have caused large numbers of Royalist soldiers to pass the 19th century site of these collieries on their way over the hill to the moor. In addition the location of the hill adjacent to the Bradford/Wakefield road would, as Scatcherd described, have positioned Newcastle's forces opposite those of the Fairfaxes advancing from modern Westgate Hill. That this hill, identified as 'Penfield' on the 1852 Ordnance Survey map, is in fact the Hungar Hill of Warburton's 1720 map, is confirmed by several field names taken from the 1848 Tithe Award map for Drighlington township.[151] The enclosures named 'Lower Hunger Hill', 'Upper Hunger Hill', 'Hunger Hill', and 'Three Work Hungerhill' are grouped in a position directly commensurate with the position of Warburton's Hungar Hill.

Thus, in terms of relief, the general battlefield area stretches from Westgate Hill in the north west to Hungar Hill in the south east. Westgate Hill rises to a height of just over 725 feet before falling slowly in a south easterly direction to about 625 feet at the ditch marking the Tong/Drighlington township boundary. At just beyond this point the ground rises to over 650 feet along 'Fairfax Hill' before once again falling in stages to 550 feet along the north eastern edge of the battlefield ridge in the vicinity of Adwalton village. Finally, the ground rises to above 650 feet at the highest point of Hungar Hill. Although the battlefield ridge itself is elevated and pronounced the intervals of hills and depressions along its length give an undulating rather than a mountainous appearance.

Roads, Lanes and Villages

The manmade infrastructure of communication routes and settlements are of course an important consideration in the reconstruction of any landscape. Networks of roads and tracks naturally determine the manner in which armies navigate terrain, while the distribution of settlements and strong points such as castles and fortified houses often underpin the planning and fighting of campaigns and battles. Because the armies that fought at Adwalton Moor accidentally ran into one another while in the process of marching towards specific destinations, the roads and tracks that led to, through, and across the battlefield area exercised a significant influence upon the course of the fighting.

The principal means of communication with Adwalton village was and still is the route of the old Bradford to Wakefield road. Running along the north eastern edge of the upland ridge upon which the battle was fought, the road followed a direct line between the Parliamentarian forces advancing from Bradford and the Royalist forces marching from Howley Hall. As English Heritage have argued that the course of the road has changed since the middle of the 17th century it is important to establish its correct line in 1643.

Warburton's map of 1720 is the earliest known cartographic evidence for the road and settlement pattern in the battlefield area before the impact of turnpiking in the middle of the 18th century. Though Warburton mapped the Bradford to Wakefield road running over the summit of Wisket Hill (as it does today) he described the course of the road between the hill and Adwalton village to lie south west of Drighlington village. English Heritage have argued that as Jefferys' map of 1771 shows the same road running *through* Drighlington, the result of improvements carried out by the Wakefield - Tong Lane End Turnpike Trust after 1741, the route of the modern Bradford to Wakefield road must therefore follow a more northerly course than that described by Warburton in 1720.[152] This, however, is unlikely. The first edition Ordnance Survey map of 1852 shows a narrow path named 'Back Lane' and a large house -'Lumb Hall'- to the north east of mid 19th century Drighlington village. This would appear to suggest that the settlement of Drighlington described by the 1852 Ordnance Survey map (south of Warburton's Drighlington village) had developed around the newly improved turnpike road after 1741, while the site of the original Drighlington village - indicated by 'Back Lane' and 'Lumb Hall' - had fallen into a steady and irreversible decline.[153] In addition there are no references to any pre-1741 buildings in Pevsner's description of 'modern' Drighlington village.[154] Thus the evidence strongly suggests that the turnpike company simply improved the existing road without altering its course. That the line of the modern Bradford to Wakefield road follows that of Warburton's 1720 map, south of the original Drighlington village site, becomes significant when considering Royalist cavalry movements towards the end of the battle.

Thomas Stockdale, author of a detailed Parliamentarian first hand

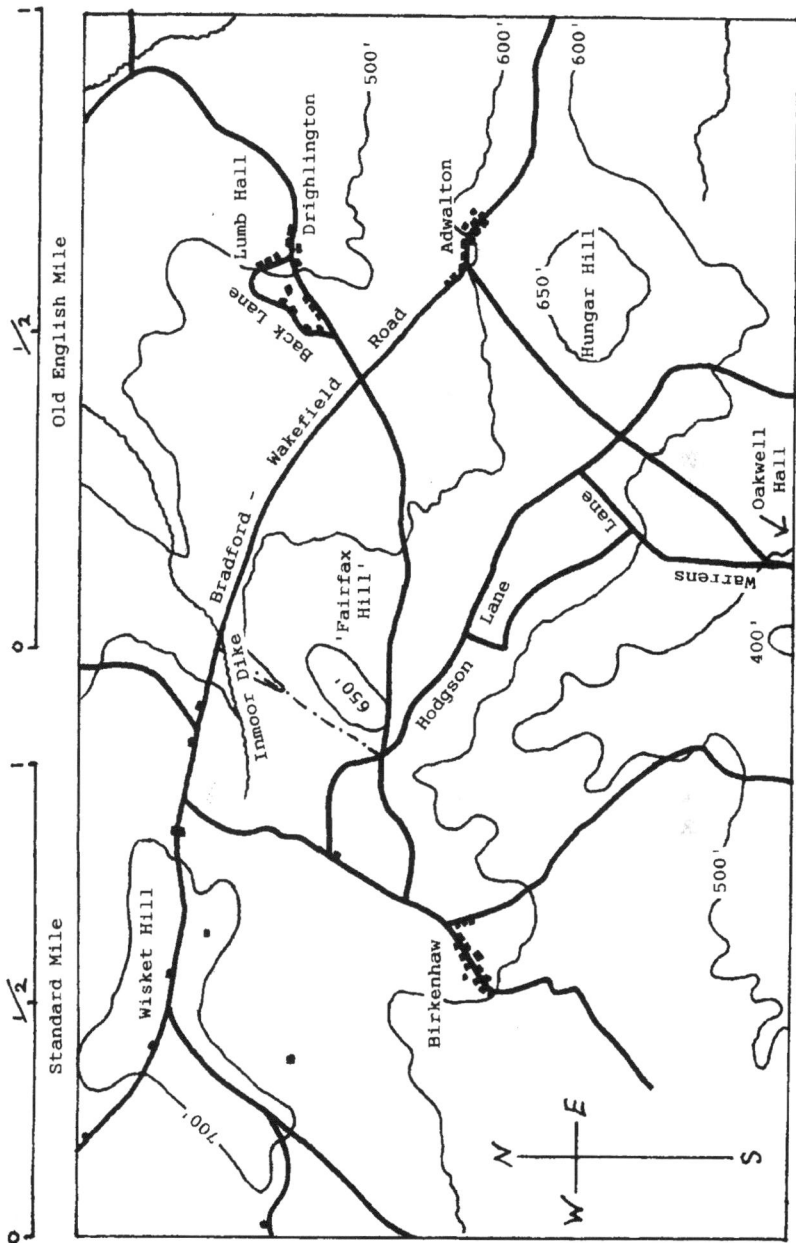

ROADS, LANES AND VILLAGES

View looking north from the disused Bradford to Wakefield railway embankment
showing the stone wall which marks the path of the old track from Adwalton
to Birkenshaw. In the 17th century the land on the near side of the wall
consisted of small hedged enclosures, while the land beyond formed part of
unenclosed Drighlington Common. The ridge line in the distance is that identified
as 'Fairfax Hill'.

account, described the importance of the roads and lanes in the battlefield area:

> [The Royalists] sent out great parties of horse and foot by the lanes and enclosed
> grounds to give us fight.[155]

As will be discussed in chapter four, the battle of Adwalton Moor began as a
skirmish in the immediate vicinity of Westgate Hill. Though small in terms of
the numbers involved, the Royalists were naturally concerned to contain the
initial clash while the vast bulk of the army deployed upon Adwalton Moor. Any
military force is obviously vulnerable in line of march. It therefore became
imperative that once alerted to the situation at Wisket Hill, Newcastle and James
King arrayed their forces in the best and strongest formation as quickly as
possible. Stockdale described how the Royalists despatched forward, from the
army deploying upon Adwalton Moor, significant numbers of horse and foot by
the lanes and enclosures to support those involved in the initial skirmish.

The 1852 first edition Ordnance Survey map indicates that the three most
likely lanes referred to by Stockdale were firstly the Bradford to Wakefield road,
secondly Hodgson Lane - a parallel track to the south west of the Bradford to
Wakefield Road - and thirdly an unnamed lane aligned for the most part on an

east-west axis between Drighlington village and the northern end of Hodgson Lane. These arteries would have enabled William Cavendish to push units of the Royalist army forward with a minimum of delay. English Heritage have argued that as Hodgson Lane appears to follow an old line, not cutting across the local field system, it was probably a feature of the 1643 battlefield landscape.[156] In addition Hodgson Lane is described by Norrisson Scatcherd as the general route by which the Parliamentarian army advanced during the early stages of the fighting.[157] The fact that the track is known as 'Hodgson Lane' may also be significant. Scatcherd raised the possibility that it was named after Captain John Hodgson, whose memoir was referred to earlier, while James Parker related the local tradition that Hodgson stationed soldiers under his command in the lane itself.[158] Though such 'evidence' is not conclusive in itself, the relationship of Hodgson Lane with the adjacent enclosures (yet to be discussed) offers a more substantial proof that the track pre-dated the battle and was therefore an important feature of the battlefield terrain. Similarly the route of the third unnamed track, shown by J.Thorpe's 1822 *Map of the Town of Leeds and the County Circumjacent* (surveyed 1819-1821) as the most direct route between Drighlington and Birkenshaw villages, displayed a significant relationship with the same block of enclosures bounded by Hodgson Lane.

Warburton's map of 1720 shows a major road running south west out of Adwalton village towards Oakwell Hall. Because Warburton's cartography is, by present standards, somewhat primitive, it is easy to confuse this road with the line of the modern A58 connecting Leeds and Halifax via Drighlington on a parallel south west to north east axis. An examination of the 1852 first edition Ordnance Survey map shows that by the middle of the 19th century Warburton's road of 1720 had become little more than a country track, winding its way between the fields from Adwalton village to Oakwell Hall and Great Gomersal. By 1831 the old track had been replaced as a major thoroughfare by the construction of the parallel Whitehall Road (A58). The 1852 Ordnance Survey map clearly shows the path of the new road cutting a straight line across the older field system, indicating that it would not have been present in 1643. Warburton's earlier road of 1720 is important for three reasons. Firstly, as previously mentioned, it was the principal south westerly route out of Adwalton village, secondly its course across Adwalton Moor -broadly indicating the point at which the moorland became Hungar Hill - describes the approximate position to which the Royalist army fell back during the final stages of the battle, and thirdly because it joined with Warrens Lane in the vicinity of Oakwell Hall.

Warrens Lane, running south west from Adwalton Moor towards Oakwell Hall, is conjectured to be the route by which Sir Thomas Fairfax conducted a fighting retreat at the close of the battle. With the Parliamentarian left wing broken and in total disarray, Sir Thomas successfully withdrew the remainder of the army to Halifax. It would appear that Norrisson Scatcherd was the first to record in print the local tradition that it was Warrens Lane which had provided Fairfax and his men with an opportunity to escape:

It is needless, perhaps, to say that this was the way by which Sir Thomas retreated to Halifax, as its very situation indicates as much; besides which, we know that soldiers entered Oakwell Hall on the day of the fight, and of a person having opened a gate for Sir Thomas on his road to Gomersal.[159]

Sir Thomas Fairfax, in his own account, described:

> a lane in the field we were in, which led to Halifax, which, as a happy providence, brought us off without any great loss.[160]

English Heritage have quite correctly made the point that as Sir Thomas did not specifically refer to Warrens Lane by name the possibility remains that the retreat may have followed a different route. In addition, Fairfax stated that the lane in question led from a *field*, whereas Warrens Lane itself leads directly onto *unenclosed* Adwalton Moor. It is possible that either an old track situated to the north of Warrens Lane, or the south easterly continuation of Hodgson Lane, each of which run on to join Warrens Lane at different points, may have been the route to which Fairfax referred. Though a difficult problem to resolve satisfactorily, it is nevertheless important for a clear understanding of the process by which Sir Thomas withdrew from the battle. The question will be returned to in chapter four.

As previously discussed, the battle of Adwalton Moor takes its name from an area of open moorland and an adjacent village. This simple piece of information provides the final evidence for the mid-17th century locations of Adwalton and Drighlington settlements. Thomas Stockdale's statement that:

> we marched from Bradford against the enemy who lay about three miles of us in a village called Adwalton or Atherton and the places thereabouts.[161]

lends weight to the view that Adwalton village was the principal settlement in the immediate area, and that Drighlington - not mentioned by Stockdale or any other eyewitness - was in fact located north east of its present position in 1643. In addition Stockdale's precise wording that the Royalist army deployed *in* and around Adwalton village supports the possibility, explored in chapter four, that Newcastle's forces occupied a far larger area than traditional accounts have hitherto allowed. The outcome being that the 'battlefield' - defined to include the deployment of the rival armies as well as the fighting itself - is more extensive than the area designated by English Heritage in its register of battlefield sites.

Therefore, the probable relationship of tracks and settlements at the time of the battle, based primarily upon the evidence of Warburton's 1720 cartography, is described by the accompanying 'Roads, Lanes and Villages' map.

Moors and Enclosures

In 1643 the area of land that was to become Adwalton Moor battlefield consisted of two quite distinct types of terrain: open moorland and hedged enclosures. Because the eyewitness descriptions of the fighting specifically differentiate between the two, it is clearly important to establish the precise location and extent of both moorland and enclosures.

The importance of hedged fields and hedgerows, clearly significant for the protection they afforded defending forces as well as for the difficulties they presented to attacking forces, not unnaturally prompted several primary source references to the way in which they were utilized at Adwalton Moor battlefield. Thomas Stockdale, Parliamentarian eyewitness and adviser to General Lord Fairfax, thus described the initial deployment of the Royalist army:

> Upon Atherton moor they planted their ordnance and ordered their battalia, but they manned divers houses standing in the enclosed grounds betwixt Bradford and Atherton moor with musketeers.[162]

Sir Thomas Fairfax, commander of the Parliamentarian right wing, confirmed Stockdale's description of enclosed land between the Parliamentarian forces and the Royalist army on Adwalton Moor:

> We advanced through the enclosed Grounds till we came to the moor.[163]

Margaret Cavendish, second wife and biographer of the earl of Newcastle, described how the Parliamentarian army had:

> drawn up in a place full of hedges, called Atherton Moor.[164]

Similarly the first hand account attributed to Newcastle himself, *An Express Relation of the Passages and Proceedings of his Majesty's Army, under the Command of his Excellence the Earl of Newcastle*, described how the Parliamentarian army had:

> possessed a place called Adderton Moor, and taken the most advantageous places thereof, and lined several hedges with musketeers.[165]

It has already been noted that the battlefield ran from Wisket Hill in the north west to Hungar Hill in the south east. Broadly speaking the land so described is conveniently divided around its midpoint by a section of the Tong/Drighlington township boundary. Conveniently divided because the documentary evidence

— — — Line of modern A58

— · · — · · — Part of Tong/Drighlington township boundary

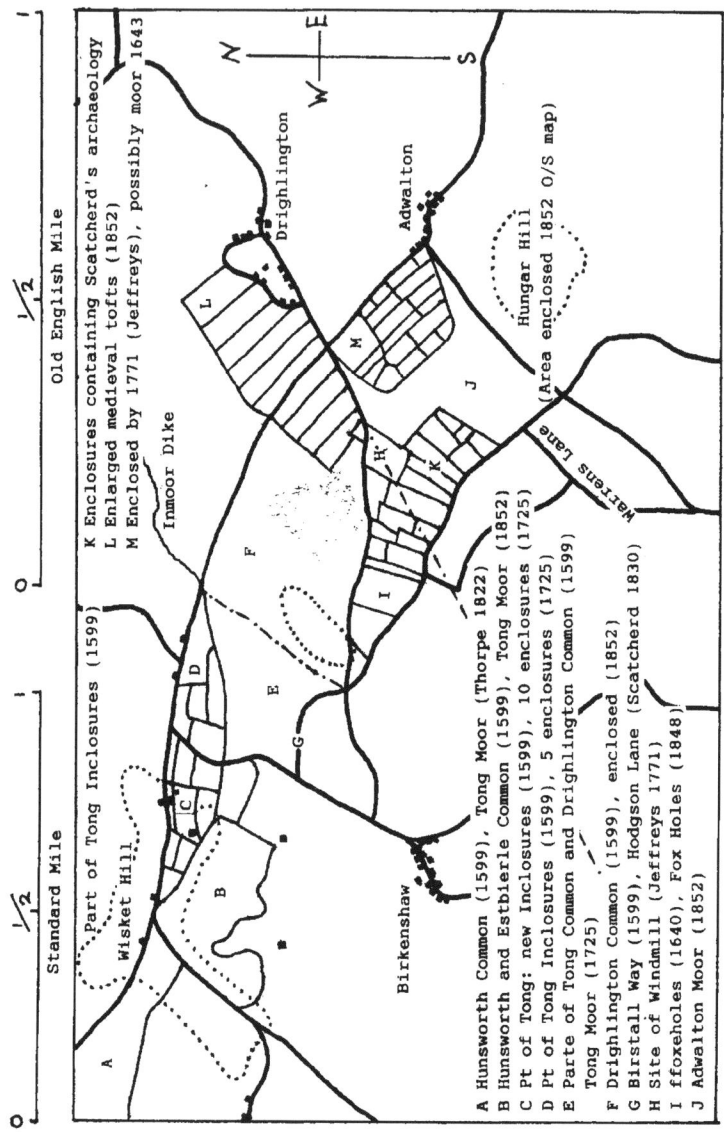

Standard Mile

Old English Mile

Part of Tong Inclosures (1599)

Wisket Hill

Inmoor Dike

Drighlington

Adwalton

Hunger Hill

(Area enclosed 1852 O/S map)

Warrens Lane

Birkenshaw

N
W — E
S

K Enclosures containing Scatcherd's archaeology
L Enlarged medieval tofts (1852)
M Enclosed by 1771 (Jeffreys), possibly moor 1643

A Hunsworth Common (1599), Tong Moor (Thorpe 1822)
B Hunsworth and Estbierle Common (1599), Tong Moor (1852)
C Pt of Tong: new Inclosures (1599), 10 enclosures (1725)
D Pt of Tong Inclosures (1599), 5 enclosures (1725)
E Parte of Tong Common and Drighlington Common (1599)
  Tong Moor (1725)
F Drighlington Common (1599), enclosed (1852)
G Birstall Way (1599), Hodgson Lane (Scatcherd 1830)
H Site of Windmill (Jeffreys 1771)
I ffoxeholes (1640), Fox Holes (1848)
J Adwalton Moor (1852)

MOORS AND ENCLOSURES

View looking north west from the Royalist line on Hungar Hill across Adwalton Moor towards the hedged enclosures. The long thick grass in the foreground probably covered the entire moor in 1643.

concerning the moors and enclosures in each of the townships is location specific, and therefore best considered separately. Particularly as the absence of any homogeneous data, such as that which would have been provided by Parliamentary Enclosure Awards, precludes a unified approach.

To take Tong township first. It is fortunate that the survival of key cartographic evidence provides a detailed record, both before and after the battle, of the distribution of enclosures and moorland from Wisket Hill to the Tong/Drighlington township boundary. Christopher Saxton's 1599 survey of Hunsworth and East Bierley Common[166] together with Dickinson's 1725 estate map of the Manor of Tong[167] describe the topography of Tong township 44 years before Adwalton Moor and 82 years after. A comparison of the two is therefore likely to indicate the nature of the terrain in 1643.

Saxton's 1599 map shows Wisket Hill in the centre of 'the way from Bradforde to Wakefelde' (Bradford to Wakefield road). To the west of Wisket Hill, in the direction of Bradford and encompassing the road, Saxton describes an area of unenclosed land named Hunsworth Common. The Bradford to Wakefield road is undefined as it crosses the common on its approach to Wisket Hill, possibly indicating that the Parliamentarian army would not have been

Christopher Saxton's 1599 map of East Bierley

constrained at the beginning of the battle by a narrow thoroughfare as it attacked the Royalist forlorn hope defending the hill.

To the east of Wisket Hill and immediately south of the Bradford to Wakefield road Saxton shows three separate areas of enclosed land. The first, beginning on the eastern slope of the hill itself, is labelled 'Hunsworth and Estbierle Common Inclosed and Sowen'. The second, divided from the first by a lane running in a south easterly direction away from the Bradford to Wakefield road, is named 'pt of Tong: new Inclosures'; while the third, separated from the second by a lane running in a southerly direction, is labelled 'Pt of Tong Inclosures'. To the south and east of these enclosures, extending to the Tong/Drighlington township boundary, Saxton described a large area of open land as 'Parte of Tong common and Drighlington Common'. This, significantly, implies that the remainder of Tong and Drighlinton Common is located off the map in Drighlington township, an important consideration when attempting to identify the extent of land occupied by hedged enclosures adjacent to Adwalton Moor.

In addition Saxton shows a broken line labelled 'Birstall Way' running on an east-west axis to the south of the Tong and Drighlington Common. The broken line follows the path of present day Hodgson Lane, and may therefore indicate that it was indeed after the battle that the track to Birstall became known as 'Hodgson Lane' in honour of the local Parliamentarian soldier referred to earlier. This, if correct, would in turn bestow the status of eyewitness testimony upon Hodgson's brief but consequently important account of the battle. Alternatively it is entirely possible that the track was known as Hodgson Lane before the battle and that Saxton's description was purely functional, simply indicating that it was in fact the way to Birstall village.

Finally Saxton described a number of houses, mostly aligned along the northern edge of the Bradford/Wakefield road, but with one or two others positioned in or adjacent to the blocks of enclosures. Interestingly Saxton adds the surnames of the owners and/or tenants. Thomas Stockdale's account, noted above, describing the Royalist occupation of several houses standing in the enclosed grounds, may refer to those buildings indicated by Saxton's map, but may equally describe similar dwellings located to the east in Drighlington township. Hugh Kendall's explanation that:

> A State paper of 1638 tells us that the clothiers had spread themselves all over the country, as well in closes and parcels of waste land as in towns[168]

is supported by West Yorkshire Archaeology Service research documenting the 16th century enclosure of land at Wisket Hill and Tong Moor, and the conveyancing of land to a number of clothiers.[169] While it is plausible that Stockdale's houses are those described by the documentary evidence to be occupied by clothiers, it is also a possibility that the houses named and drawn by

Saxton are of a higher status, and that the more rudimentary clothiers' cottages are not indicated.

Saxton's survey provided a clear and readily understood record of the battlefield terrain in Tong township at the close of the 16th century. His depiction of enclosures and moorland to the east of Wisket Hill accords with the eyewitness accounts and is confirmed by documentary land transaction evidence. The map was created 44 years before Adwalton Moor was fought, sufficient time for major changes to have occurred in the landscape. A comparison with Dickinson's 1725 map will thus determine which areas remained unchanged - and were therefore part of the 1643 terrain - and which areas appear to have altered, and are hence problematic.

Dickinson's 1725 map of the Lordship and Manor of Tong is a large and impressive example of eighteenth century cartography. However, it is only the southern portion of the map, where the land rises to form the ridge running south east from Wisket Hill, that coincides with the area depicted by Saxton in 1599. Despite the 126 year interval between the creation of the two documents a marked similarity is evident; indicating that Saxton's 1599 map would have remained in 1643 an accurate representation of the terrain over which the Tong portion of the battle was fought.

Because Dickinson's map is concerned solely with Tong township, only a small portion of Saxton's Hunsworth Common, situated to the west of Wisket Hill, is shown immediately south of the Bradford to Wakefield road. Dickinson renamed the common 'Tong Moor' indicating that the area had remained open and unenclosed throughout the 17th century.

For the same reason Dickinson does not show the area to the immediate south east of Wisket Hill described by Saxton as 'Hunsworth and Estbierle Common Inclosed and Sowen'. However Thorpe's 1822 map (surveyed 1819-1821) shows virtually the same area as 'Common'; and those parts of it still recorded as common by the Ordnance Survey map of 1852 were once again renamed 'Tong Moor'. It would appear that the large common described as 'Inclosed and Sowen' by Saxton in 1599 was possibly part of the field system belonging to East Bierley village. Though enclosed at its perimeter and under cultivation in 1599 it was not subdivided by further enclosure. This may indicate that the former pastureland of the common had been turned over to cultivation in order to yield crops of some description. This may in turn reflect a rise in the local population, thereby creating an increased demand for food. By the 19th century Thorpe's map shows that the bulk of the land described as 'Inclosed and Sowen' by Saxton had returned to wasteland, becoming part of 'Tong Moor'. This would appear to indicate that although enclosed as a single large field the land had remained essentially open during the period of the Civil War.

To follow Saxton's map eastwards; Dickinson depicts as a block of ten individual enclosures *precisely* and *exactly* the area described by Saxton as 'pt of Tong: new Inclosures'. As Saxton labelled the land *'new inclosures'* (ie plural), and as Dickinson represented individually each of the ten enclosures within the same piece of land, it is not unreasonable to suppose that the arrangement given in 1725 by Dickinson is in fact that confronted by the Royalist and Parliamentarian armies in 1643. Similarly, the most easterly block of Saxton's 1599 enclosures, labelled 'Pt of Tong Inclosures', occupied *precisely* the same area of land in 1725. Again, while Dickinson had subdivided the block further, this time into five smaller enclosures, the total extent of the land was *exactly* that given by Saxton 126 years earlier. The only difference being that Dickinson showed the southern boundary of the enclosures to be the Inmoor Dike, a ditch running on a south west to north east axis, thereby drawing attention to the logical use of a physical rather than an arbitrary perimeter.

Further confirmation that the extent of enclosed land in this part of Tong township had not increased between 1599 and 1725 is provided by Dickinson's depiction of Tong Moor. This is shown to cover an area identical to that described by Saxton as 'Parte of Tong common and Drighlington Common'. In addition both are bounded to the south by the line of modern Hodgson Lane. Similarly the land north of the Bradford to Wakefield road, and therefore north of the ridge upon which the battle was fought, is described by Saxton as 'Part of Tong Inclosures', while Dickinson shows the same land to be completely enclosed in 1725. As Dickinson's map of the Tong estate confirms in almost every detail the earlier survey of 1599, it is clear that Saxton's work is an accurate representation of the 1643 battlefield terrain.

By contrast, the extent of enclosure and moorland in Drighlington township is more difficult to ascertain. While cartographic evidence for Tong township described the landscape both before and after the battle, the absence of similarly early documentation for Drighlington township requires the evaluation of alternative forms of evidence. However, it is appropriate to begin with the cartographic evidence, such as it is.

Thomas Jefferys' 1771 map of The County of York (surveyed 1767-1770) is the earliest known drawing to show any useful detail for Drighlington township. Based on a scale of one inch to a mile, the 1771 map describes an unnamed area of land south west of Drighlington and Adwalton villages that broadly corresponds with the area designated 'Adwalton Moor' on the first edition Ordnance Survey map of 1852. As the extent of Adwalton Moor described by the Ordnance Survey in 1852 is not dissimilar to that which exists today, it may be deduced that the area occupied by the moor in 1771 has remained largely unaltered to the present day. What is important is that Jefferys shows in 1771 an area of land bounded to the north west by the route of the modern A58, to the south east by Hungar Hill, to the south west by the line of Hodgson Lane, and to the north east by the Bradford to Wakefield road. As Jeffreys' map was created over a century after the battle, it must consequently be assumed that the 1771 depiction of Adwalton Moor represents a conservative estimate of the likely extent of the moor in 1643. This is inferred firstly by the Ordnance Survey map of 1852 which shows areas of Tong Moor known to have been unenclosed in 1725 as hedged fields, and secondly by Norrisson

Scatcherd's observation of 1830 that a creeping erosion of the land once occupied by Adwalton Moor had taken place since the days of Sir Thomas Fairfax:

> some inclosures, however, and many alterations have been made in and near this field [ie Adwalton Moor] since his days, and the lanes are fast disappearing.[170]

As the 1852 Ordnance Survey map shows a block of enclosed fields standing to the immediate north west of the Tong/Drighlington township boundary, occupying an area known to have formed part of *unenclosed* Tong Moor in 1725, it is reasonable to suppose the similar enclosure of moorland in adjacent Drighlington township during the same period. The 1852 Ordnance Survey map shows the land extending south east from the Tong/Drighlington township boundary to the line of the modern A58 to be completely enclosed. To the immediate south east of the A58 the same map describes unenclosed Adwalton Moor stretching further south east to the enclosed heights of Hungar Hill. As it has been noted that Thomas Stockdale's account described enclosed grounds *between* Bradford and Adwalton Moor, and that Sir Thomas Fairfax recalled the advance of Parliamentarian soldiers through enclosures to the edge of the moor, it would appear that an area of land somewhere between the Tong/Drighlington boundary and the north western edge of Adwalton Moor was enclosed in 1643. As Sir Thomas Fairfax went on to describe in detail the heavy and protracted fighting that occurred in and around the hedgerows dividing the enclosures from the moor, one would expect that the recovery of substantial archaeological evidence would clearly indicate the area in question. Significantly Norrisson Scatcherd's 1830 account of the terrain over which the battle was fought described the widespread discovery of such archaeology to the immediate west and north west of modern Adwalton Moor:

> In the inclosures on the right of Warren's-Lane, as you enter it from the Moor, many cannon balls of iron and lead - horse shoes of singular forms - grape or cannister shot - bridlebits with chains - bullets of different sizes - have been repeatedly turned up even of late years; and the same thing may be said as to all the inclosures, till you get a field or two North East of the windmill, when they cease to appear. In the fields North West of the windmill the quantity of bullets discovered, has been so great, that a dozen have been found on one day, and in a little garden, on the West skirts of the Moor, a woman told me her husband had found scores of them, which had been given to their children for 'taws'.[171]

Scatcherd's archaeology, plotted on the 'Moors and Enclosures' map, very neatly coincides with a series of small rectangular enclosures readily identified by the 1852 Ordnance Survey map. They are bounded to the south west by the line of Hodgson Lane and to the north by the gently meandering path of the track connecting Adwalton and Birkenshaw villages. These enclosures differ markedly, both in shape and size, from those shown by the same map to extend north west to the Tong/Drighlington township boundary. This strongly suggests that the latter enclosures, bounded to the north west by the Tong/Drighlington boundary and to the south east by the smaller enclosures containing the battlefield archaeology, were unenclosed moorland in 1643. A continuation, in fact, of unenclosed Tong Moor across the township boundary into Drighlington township - as Saxton's 1599 survey suggested - and indeed described by Saxton as 'Tong *and* Drighlington Common'. The position of the windmill described by Scatcherd is indicated by Jeffreys' 1771 map and confirmed by the location of two named fields ('Windmill Close' and 'Low Windmill Close') taken from the 1848 Drighlington Tithe Award Map.[172]

Thus it would appear that in 1643 the upland ridge stretching south east from Wisket Hill to Hungar Hill contained, by name, three distinct areas of moorland. Tong Moor ran from an area south of Wisket Hill to the township boundary, Drighlington 'Common' continued in a south easterly direction from the boundary to the enclosures, and finally Adwalton Moor extended further to the south east, probably encompassing the heights of Hungar Hill as it did so. Thomas Stockdale's reference to the retreat of Royalist units across Adwalton Moor to higher ground may indicate that the moorland encompassed a large proportion of Hungar Hill in 1643:

> and after some dispute beat the enemy both out of the houses they had manned and from the skirts of the moor to the height[173]

Stockdale's description of a Royalist withdrawal to the highest point of the moor would appear to indicate that Hungar Hill was unenclosed in 1643. As the hill stands to the south east of Adwalton Moor, the direction in which the Royalist army would have retreated, the summit and areas roundabout would have appeared as 'the height' to the Parliamentarian forces away to the north west. In addition Stockdale's reference to houses may have included an old cottage which once stood on the western side of Adwalton Moor, possibly in Hodgson Lane, the roof of which, according to local tradition, provided a vantage point from which a small boy witnessed the battle. Norrisson Scatcherd's description of the cottage, and the ancient method by which it was constructed, lends support to the view that Hodgson Lane may well have been the location of several such dwellings in the mid 17th century.[174]

As the landscape reconstruction proposed above describes separate and distinct blocks of enclosures in both Tong and Drighlington townships, it is consequently plausible to suggest the existence of alternative battlefield sites. However, Norrisson Scatcherd's substantial archaeological evidence for Drighlington township, set against a lack of similar evidence for Tong enclosures - save for John James' 1841 references to discoveries at Wisket Hill - strongly supports the view that the heaviest fighting occurred in the vicinity of the proposed enclosures adjacent to Adwalton Moor. Indeed, documentary evidence demonstrates that part of the moor in Drighlington township, situated between Hodgson Lane and the track running from Adwalton village to Birkenshaw, had in fact been enclosed by 1640. The location of the enclosure, referred to as the 'ffoxeholes' in 1640, is given as a named field - 'Fox Holes' - by the 1848 Tithe Award Map for Drighlington township.[175]

The 1848 Tithe Award Map for Drighlington township also shows two further blocks of enclosures which, by virtue of their shape and size, may also have formed part of the battlefield topography of 1643. The first block, situated to the west and north west of old Drighlington village, consists of a series of long and relatively narrow fields. Each of these enclosures may have been formed by the amalgamation of perhaps two or three even narrower medieval tofts. It is possible that the left wing of the Parliamentarian army may have advanced through those to the west of Drighlington village in order to reach Adwalton Moor. The second block of possible 1643 enclosures is situated to the west of Adwalton village encroaching upon the eastern side of Adwalton Moor. These fields, if they were present at the time of the battle, would have seriously impeded the initial deployment of the Royalist army. As will be discussed below, Newcastle's principal concerns appear to have been disused coal pits, a large ditch, and a high bank rather than a cluster of enclosed fields. The free movement of forces back and forth across Adwalton Moor suggests that the moor hereabouts was largely unenclosed, with perhaps a small paddock or two adjacent to the Bradford to Wakefield road.

Ditches, Banks and Coal Pits

In describing the difficulty with which the Royalist army deployed for battle Margaret Cavendish drew attention to several important topographical features:

> no place was left to draw up my Lord's horse, but amongst old coal-pits. Neither could they charge the enemy, by reason of a great ditch and high bank betwixt my Lord's and the enemys troops, but by two on a breast, and that within musket shot; the enemy being drawn up in hedges[176]

To take the reference to coal pits first. The seams of the Yorkshire Coalfield, extending south from Leeds and Bradford, lay just beneath the surface of the battlefield and surrounding area. As a consequence the West Riding was an early producer of coal:

> there can still be traced the ancient open-cast workings and bell pits which marked the commencement of the coal and iron industry of Yorkshire.[177]

The 1852 Ordnance Survey map plots the individual positions of numerous old workings, but shows only two clusters of pits on the battlefield itself. The first, located in an enclosed field named 'Pit Hole Plantation', is

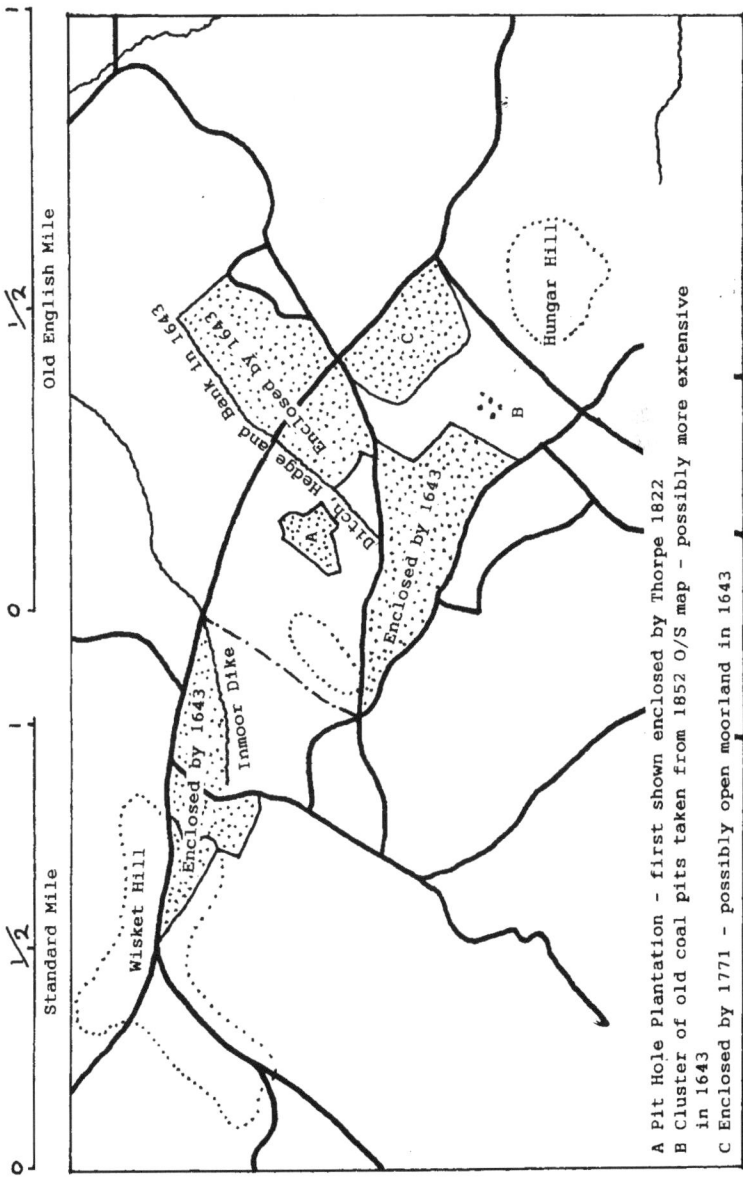

Part of Tong/Drighlington township boundary

Standard Mile

Old English Mile

DITCHES, BANKS AND COAL PITS

A Pit Hole Plantation - first shown enclosed by Thorpe 1822
B Cluster of old coal pits taken from 1852 O/S map - possibly more extensive in 1643
C Enclosed by 1771 - possibly open moorland in 1643

Wisket Hill

Hungar Hill

Enclosed by 1643

Inmoor Dike

Ditch, Hedge and Bank in 1643

Enclosed by 1643

61

situated to the west of Drighlington village. However, these pits stand too far to the north west of Adwalton Moor to have disrupted the deployment of Newcastle's cavalry. A much more likely candidate is the small grouping shown by the 1852 map to have stood in the centre of the moor. These old pits would have occupied precisely the ground upon which the left wing of Royalist horse made an initial and probably hurried deployment. As will be discussed presently, the mounted arm formed so disproportionately large a part of Newcastle's army that any restriction placed upon it would have been of the utmost concern. Given the apparent ease with which the coal could be exposed, it is likely that the concentration of old workings in which the cavalry formed up would have been more extensive in 1643 than indicated by the map of 1852. This is certainly the impression conveyed both by the duchess and the account attributed to her husband.[178] In addition the moor of 1643 would in all probability have been covered by the long coarse tussocky grass that can today still be found at its south eastern edge. This thick covering may have obscured some of the old coal pits, thereby hindering further the deployment and mobility of the left flank of Royalist horse.

Margaret Cavendish also complained about a great ditch and high bank that stood between the rival armies and which apparently prevented a mass Royalist attack. The 1852 Ordnance Survey map shows a ditch running on a south west to north east alignment, at which 17th Century Drighlington Common gave way to the enclosed ground north west of Adwalton Moor. In 1643 this ditch would indeed have stood between the Royalists on Adwalton Moor and the Parliamentarians advancing from Wisket Hill. The ditch today is shallow, narrow, and insignificant; hardly an obstacle to military operations. However, in the middle of the 17th century it may well have been a well maintained and defensible barrier, particularly as its principal purpose would have been the protection of cultivated land or the control of livestock. To this end the ditch would have had associated with it a substantial stockproof hedge planted upon a supporting bank. There is today no evidence of such a bank or earthwork, but this does not mean that one did not exist in 1643. The changing demands of agriculture are likely to produce dramatic alterations in any landscape, and it is not unknown, in the pursuit of agricultural improvement, for such banks to be removed and levelled. The duchess' final remark concerning the proximity of hedges is a clear reference to the enclosures bordering the north western edge of Adwalton Moor.

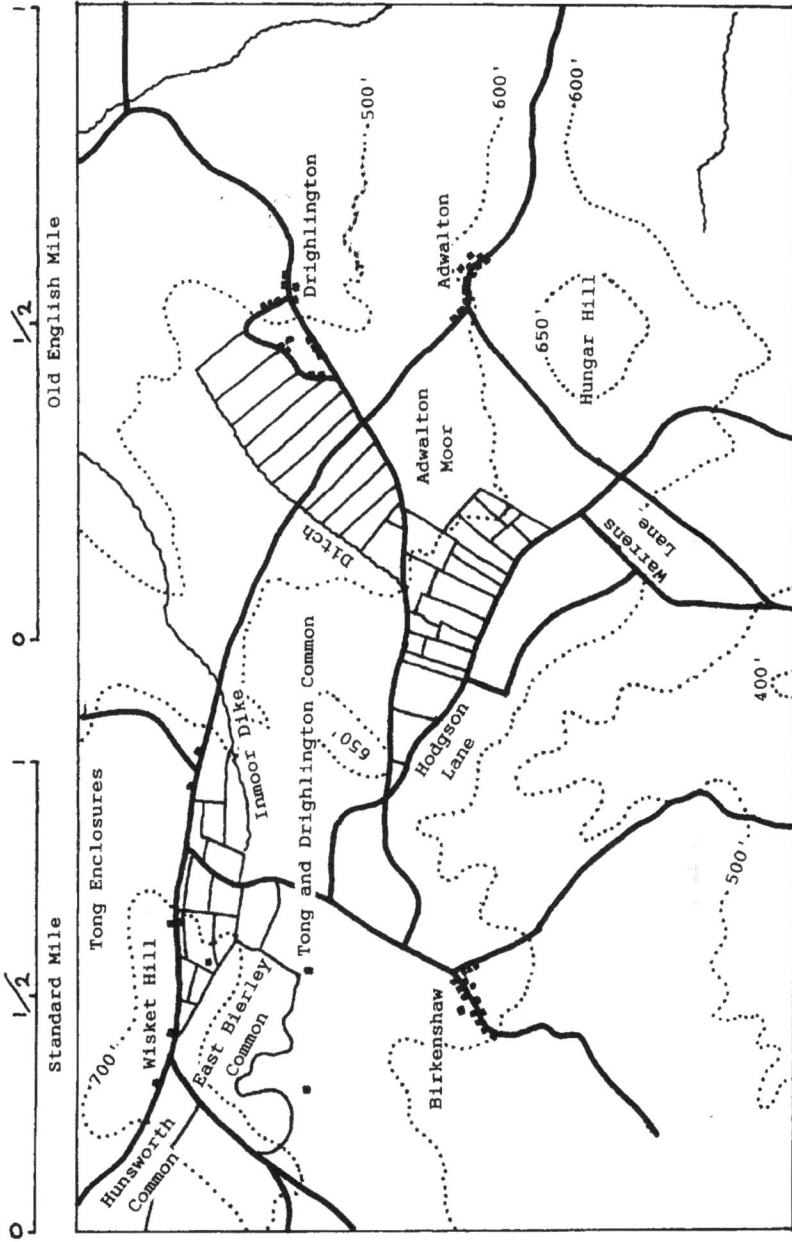

ADWALTON MOOR BATTLEFIELD 1643

CHAPTER 4

THE BATTLE OF ADWALTON MOOR

The Royalist campaign to defeat the Fairfaxes - outlined in chapter two - had endured several unexpected and frustrating setbacks since Newcastle first marched into Yorkshire at the beginning of December 1642. However, despite seven months of unrelenting Parliamentarian resistance, the earl was at last free to concentrate upon the destruction of the Yorkshire rebels. The Queen, for whom Newcastle had assumed responsibility following her landing at Bridlington in February 1643, had at last departed for Newark en route to the King at Oxford. Though Newcastle's campaign had been delayed by several days of bad weather, the Royalist army finally vacated its temporary base at Howley Hall early on the morning of Friday 30th June 1643. Unaware that Newcastle was marching for Bradford, Lord Ferdinando Fairfax and his son Sir Thomas had coincidentally mobilized the same morning, intent upon a surprise attack against an unsuspecting enemy. The battle of Adwalton Moor - the result of two armies unwittingly marching towards each other - took place by chance rather than design. Neither Newcastle or the Fairfaxes envisaged the kind of confrontation that was to take place, nor one might suspect, the dramatic twist of fortune that was to precipitate a decisive conclusion to the day's fighting.

Before detailing the events of 30th June 1643 it is appropriate to consider the composition and strength of the rival armies. To accomplish this satisfactorily it is necessary first to examine the Parliamentarian force. As will become apparent, the regrettably slight evidence for the Royalist army becomes more intelligible when set against the established size of the rebel force. Fortunately the corpus of extant documentation includes a particularly detailed eyewitness description of the Parliamentarian order of battle.

The Parliamentarian Army

Thomas Stockdale's account of Adwalton Moor, written the day after the battle, includes an itemized breakdown of the force Lord Fairfax had assembled at Bradford by the morning of 30th June 1643. Stockdale described it as:

> consisting of 1200 commanded men of the garrison of Leeds, seven companies of Bradford, 500 men of Halifax, Pomfret [Pontefract], Paddleworth [probably 'Saddleworth'], Almonberry, and the county thereabouts, twelve companies of foot brought out of Lancashire, and of horse we had ten troops of our own and three from Lancashire, but the troops for the most part weak; we had four pieces

of brass ordnance with us and a great part of our powder and match, and many club-men followed us, who are fit to do execution upon a flying enemy, but unfit for other service, for I am sure they did us none; and with this strength, being not full 4000 men horse and foot armed,[179]

In reporting the strength of the Parliamentarian army to be less than 4000 armed men, Stockdale accounted for 1700 as infantry drawn predominantly from Leeds and Halifax. The remainder, approximately 2300, were described as twelve companies of Lancashire foot, seven companies of Bradford foot, ten troops of Yorkshire horse and three troops of Lancashire horse. As a consequence it is difficult to establish a precise numerical value for each of these particular units. Helpfully, perhaps, the Parliamentarian newsbook *Certaine Informations*, 26th June to 3rd July 1643, claimed that the contingent of Lancashire foot consisted in total of 1500 men.[180] This, if true, would mean that the combined strength of the seven companies of Bradford foot *and* the thirteen troops of Lancashire and Yorkshire horse could amount to no more than 800 men. Stockdale's testimony that the Lancashire foot were drawn up into twelve companies must have meant that these units, if indeed their number amounted to 1500, were pretty much at full strength. While such a situation is unusual for an army on campaign, the fact that these particular soldiers had only recently marched into West Yorkshire from Manchester may indicate that their individual companies had been brought up to full compliment before setting out. Stockdale's further observation that the troops of horse were for the most part weak presents a clue with which to estimate their strength. A drill manual troop of cavalry could amount to as many as eighty mounted men. However, a weakened unit would obviously consist of far fewer - perhaps half strength of forty horse per troop might be a reasonable estimate. Given this scenario the thirteen troops of Parliamentarian cavalry at Adwalton Moor would have amounted to around 500 horse in total; thereby leaving no more than 300 foot for the seven Bradford infantry companies.

Therefore, based upon the data provided by Thomas Stockdale and the Parliamentarian propaganda newsbook *Certaine Informations*, combined with the conjectures outlined above, the composition and strength of Lord Fairfax's army on 30th June 1643 was probably as follows:

FOOT

Leeds Garrison		1200
Bradford Garrison (7 companies)	approx	300
Halifax Garrison & Locality		500
Lancashire Foot (12 companies)		1500

TOTAL FOOT **3500**

<u>HORSE</u>

Yorkshire & Lancashire Horse (13 troops)   approx 500

TOTAL HORSE **500**

TOTAL (Horse & Foot) approx **4000**

Though Stockdale claimed that the Parliamentarian army numbered slightly less than 4000 armed men all told, the estimate provided here of around 3500 foot and about 500 horse would appear a reasonable working assumption. Sir Thomas Fairfax, writing more than twenty years after Adwalton Moor, stated that his father's army had consisted of only 3000 men.[181] However, given that Stockdale's account was both contemporary and detailed, the weight of evidence strongly suggests that a Parliamentarian force of approximately 4000 was the more likely estimate of the two.

In addition to four pieces of artillery Stockdale also made reference to a large, but unspecified, number of Clubmen that had followed Lord Fairfax and his army to the field of battle. The term Clubmen is generally applied to those who took up arms against both King and Parliament, as the situation demanded, in order to drive the Civil War and its armies from a particular locality. However, the earliest use of the term may well refer to the West Riding Clubmen that regularly attached themselves to Lord Fairfax's army during 1642 and 1643. J. Jones has argued that these men were zealous Parliamentarians who, receiving no pay, were engaged on a short term basis as and when required. Drawn from the poorer classes of the clothing districts, their prime function was to inflate the desperately small size of the Yorkshire Parliamentarian army.[182] As one might expect, Clubmen were armed with all manner of weapons, primarily of an agricultural nature, from which their name is believed to derive. Interestingly, the point has recently been made that the term referred not to the type of weapon carried but to the fact that these men belonged to local associations or *clubs*.[183] Stockdale's survey of the Parliamentarian army is assumed here to imply roughly 4000 armed men *plus* an unquantifiable number of Clubmen. However, an alternative reading of Stockdale might imply 4000 horse and foot *including* Clubmen. In the latter case it would be difficult to conceive that the Clubmen totalled more than 500, particularly when one considers Stockdale's figures for the Leeds and Halifax garrisons plus the likely size of the Lancashire contingent. Finally, Stockdale's somewhat caustic comment that the Clubmen performed no useful service may provide a clue to the sudden collapse of the Parliamentarian left at what turned out to be the critical moment of the battle. This will be returned to below.

The Royalist Army

One of the principal difficulties confronting any attempt to write about the battle of Adwalton Moor is the problem of reconstructing the Royalist order of battle. So much so that Stuart Reid has commented:

> The composition of the Royalist army is impossible to establish. Indeed it is difficult enough to ascertain just how strong it was.[184]

Though the Parliamentarian sources offer estimates of Royalist numbers the real problem arises from a total absence of any such detail in the Royalist accounts themselves. J. Jones has attributed this apparent reluctance to divulge the true size of Newcastle's army to embarrassment over the success of the smaller Parliamentarian army during the first half of the battle.[185] However, by careful examination of the claims made by Thomas Stockdale and Sir Thomas Fairfax, plus a *between the lines* reading of the Royalist sources, it is possible to arrive at a tentative conclusion for both the strength and composition of Newcastle's army. To take the rebel accounts first.

In his report to the House of Commons the Parliamentarian eyewitness Thomas Stockdale provided several useful pieces of information:

> Their army consisted of 8000 of their old foot, and about 7000 new men raised by the Commission of Array, and, as most men say, 4000 horse, which I could not conceive by view, though the truth is they had 80 cornets, and so might have had more, if their companies had been full and well armed, but indeed there are many both of their horse and foot very slenderly armed.[186]

In describing the composition of the Royalist foot one can plausibly assume that Stockdale was making a distinction between what he believed to be the number of troops raised in County Durham and Northumberland during the second half of 1642 (8000) and those recruited at the same time and later by the Commission of Array for Yorkshire (7000). However, the combined total of 15000 infantry would appear somewhat excessive, particularly when one considers the evidence for Newcastle's army in the months immediately preceding Adwalton Moor. In addition, Stockdale's admission that his personal vantage point did not permit a complete appreciation of the entire Royalist army is pertinent not only here, but also in terms of the extent to which Newcastle's deployment, discussed below, extended beyond the visible horizons of Adwalton Moor.

Stockdale's claim of 19000 Royalist horse and foot is best examined in the light of two further, but quite independent, pieces of evidence. The first was provided by none other than the Queen herself. Her Majesty had observed that in April 1643 the earl of Newcastle had commanded into the West Riding against the Fairfaxes a field army of 7000 foot and 3500 horse - a considerably smaller army than that described by Stockdale.[187] This total would not, however, have included those forces that remained in York to garrison the town and protect the Queen. Conveniently the second piece of evidence provides a numerical clue to the possible size of the bodyguard that Newcastle may have felt compelled to leave at York. In a letter written shortly before Adwalton Moor, Oliver Cromwell estimated the strength of the Queen's escort from Pontefract to Newark, despatched by Newcastle in June 1643, to consist of 1200 horse and 3000 foot.[188] Though by no means a precise or scientific total of Royalist numbers, a combining of these two armies would produce a force of almost 15000 men. This is perhaps a more realistic estimate of the size of the army Stockdale *believed* Newcastle to have at his disposal in the period immediately preceding Adwalton Moor.

Though it is unquestionably significant that Stockdale qualified his report with the admission that his statistics were not wholly based on personal observation, Stockdale's figure of 80 cornets (troops) of Royalist horse would in all probability have resulted in a total of at least 4000 mounted men.[189] It may be conjectured that Stockdale's estimate of the Royalist horse was possibly more reliable than his estimate of Newcastle's foot. As a means of battlefield identification each troop (or Cornet) of horse carried at its head a colour (flag). Stockdale's account would appear to suggest that the number of Royalist horse had been based upon the number of colours present. Stockdale, while admitting that his view of the Royalist army was incomplete, would appear to have received information concerning the quantity of Royalist cornets. Stockdale's account of Newcastle's army placed particular emphasis upon the potential vulnerability of Lord Fairfax's foot to massed ranks of Royalist horse. It may well be the case that Stockdale's principal concern was defence against cavalry attack, particularly as this unexpected engagement was to take place in a partly open moorland landscape. This emphasis and concern makes even more sense when Royalist accounts of Newcastle's army are examined. Thus while Stockdale's overall report of Royalist strength might appear suspect, his reference to cavalry numbers is perhaps more credible. In terms of Royalist infantry, it would appear plausible that Stockdale had simply not taken into account the loss to Newcastle's army of the considerable force of foot described by Cromwell to have formed part of the Queen's escort.

Research conducted by P.R.Newman has revealed that the King's various Civil War armies were fatally imbalanced in favour of cavalry. Newman stated that a properly constituted army would exhibit a ratio of horse to foot of 1:3. Newman claimed this was never achieved; and that the resulting imbalance in favour of the mounted arm represented a significant factor in the King's ultimate defeat. Newman stated that Newcastle's northern army was beset by the same problem.[190] Therefore, if Newman is correct, Newcastle's army may have consisted of only one third horse to two thirds foot. This would produce - given Stockdale's estimate of 4000 cavalry - a total of around 8000 Royalist infantry at Adwalton Moor. It may be significant that the strength of Newcastle's field army described by the Queen in April 1643 - 3500 horse and 7000 foot - exhibited precisely this ratio of 1:2. Sir Thomas Fairfax believed the Royalist army at Adwalton Moor to have consisted of 10 or 12000 men.[191] This again would accord with Stockdale's figure of 4000 horse plus a projected addition of 8000 foot based on a 1:2 ratio.

Given the evidence of the Parliamentarian accounts - Stockdale and Fairfax - it would appear fairly certain that the Royalist army consisted of at least 10000 men. A total of 4000 horse is a strong possibility, while the number of foot is more debatable. However, these to some extent conjectural statistics of 4000 Parliamentarians and 10000 or more Royalists provide an important benchmark against which the claims of the Royalist accounts can be evaluated.

As previously noted, the Royalist sources declined to provide either a detailed breakdown of Newcastle's army or even a rough estimate of its total strength. However, it is possible to draw one or two tentative conclusions from a cryptic reference made by the duchess of Newcastle. Describing the Parliamentarian army, Margaret Cavendish claimed that:

> in their army there were near 5000 musketeers, and eighteen troops of horse......ready to encounter my Lord's forces, which then contained not above half so many musketeers as the enemy had : their chiefest strength consisting in horse.[192]

By exaggerating the number of musket armed Parliamentarian foot the duchess implied that the Royalist army consisted of no more than 2500 musketeers. At first glance this might appear a preposterous assertion for an army of perhaps 12000 men, particularly one that may have included as many as 8000 foot. However, despite the fact that the proper ratio of Civil War infantry was considered to be two muskets to each pike, both the Royalists and Parliamentarians struggled to acquire sufficient quantities of firearms during 1642 and in to 1643. The result was a widespread parity in the numbers of pike and shot.[193] Margaret's claim of around 2500 musketeers therefore becomes more plausible in this context, and is in fact supported by the evidence of the fighting once the battle begins. The first half of Adwalton Moor consisted essentially of an escalating fire-fight, first of all for Wisket Hill and then for the enclosures that led to Adwalton Moor itself. This fire-fight was characterized by the steady and unflinching progress of the Parliamentarian musketeers, despite the opposition of Newcastle's full compliment of musket armed foot. Considering the territory that the Royalists were attempting to defend - high ground, houses, and hedged enclosures - Parliamentarian success would only appear likely given superiority, or at the very least equality, in musketeers. It has already been demonstrated that Lord Fairfax commanded between 3000 and 3500 foot - depending upon how Stockdale is to be interpreted - and while this number must have included a proportion of pike, it is entirely possible that Fairfax's musketeers outnumbered Newcastle's, particularly if the earl in fact deployed *less* than 2500. Although contentious, the evidence, such as it is, would appear to allow such a conclusion. Parliamentarian progress at Adwalton Moor finally foundered upon the determination of the Royalist pike blocks. For this to have occurred it has to be assumed that Newcastle was adequately provisioned in that department. Parity with the musketeers would give around 2500 pikemen, or perhaps 3000 if Newcastle deployed as few as 2000 muskets. However surprising, it may well be the case that the Royalist army at Adwalton Moor fielded in total no more than 5000 foot.

The duchess claimed that the chief strength of her husband's army lay in its cavalry. It has been established that Newcastle probably had at his disposal somewhere in the region of 4000 horse. However, Stockdale believed that the figure could have been higher, while Margaret's assertion that the mounted arm formed the principal component of the Royalist force introduces the possibility that Newcastle deployed a greater number of horse than foot. An army of around 5000 foot and perhaps 5000 horse would be entirely consistent with the way in which the battle was fought and the manner in which both Parliamentarian and Royalist accounts expressed particular concerns over the battlefield terrain and its utilization. As will become apparent, it was a source of frustration, and perhaps even exasperation, that Newcastle was unable to deploy the horse to advantage until Parliamentarian momentum had been broken by the Royalist pike and cannon.

The account attributed by Firth to the earl of Newcastle stated that the Parliamentarian army had consisted of:

> a greater number of foot than we, and almost all musketeers, and some twenty troops of horse.[194]

It has been demonstrated that the Fairfaxes commanded no more than 13 troops of horse; Newcastle's figure of 20 was in all probability a further attempt to disguise the small size of the Parliamentarian army. A similar motive might explain the earl's claim to have been outnumbered by Ferdinando Fairfax's infantry. Alternatively, due to the potentially large number of Clubmen that accompanied Lord Fairfax's army, it is possible that Newcastle may have unwittingly overestimated the number of regular Parliamentarian foot. It is feasible that the combined strength of Fairfax's infantry and West Riding Clubmen could have outnumbered or equalled Newcastle's foot. However, the earl's assertion that most were musketeers would appear difficult to sustain given the type of arms carried by the Clubmen. As a consequence of the paucity of detail concerning the true size of the Royalist army the conjectures outlined above represent possibilities, though occasionally the term probability might credibly be used. Yet despite this important caveat, it would appear reasonable to suggest that Newcastle's forces at Adwalton Moor consisted of perhaps as many as 5000 horse and as few as 5000 foot. The critical point being that the potency of the army was compromised by what would appear to be a severe shortage of musketeers. However, setting aside the difficult question of composition, this total would broadly accord with the estimate provided by Sir Thomas Fairfax of between 10000 and 12000 men.

The original intention of the Royalist army was to lay siege to the town of Bradford - an undertaking that would require an adequate train of artillery. Though precise details of the number and type of cannon deployed by the earl of Newcastle are unknown, it has to be assumed that the Royalists possessed the means by which an effective bombardment of the town could be undertaken. It is almost certain that the Royalists mobilized two Demi-Culverins, known alternatively as 'the Queen's Pocket Pistols' or 'Gog and Magog'.[195] A Demi-Culverin was the largest type of cannon normally found on an English Civil War battlefield. Usually deployed for siege warfare, the weapon could propel a 9lb iron canon ball 2400 yards. However, the Demi-Culverin's mobility, dependent upon a team of 36 horses, was restricted by its excessive weight (3600 lbs).[196] As will be shown presently, the Royalist cannon at Adwalton Moor - once properly deployed - played an unusually prominent role towards the end of the battle. This despite the duchess of Newcastle's assertion that her husband had significantly weakened his army by the despatch of a good number of cannon with the Queen's escort.[197]

Muster and March

The historian Charles Carlton has argued that:

Those who went into a civil war battle rarely did so with a clearly defined set of objectives.[198]

Yet, as has been demonstrated in chapter two, both the earl of Newcastle and the Fairfaxes had prepared for action having first devised specific plans by which particular objectives were to be achieved. The Royalist campaign in Yorkshire was about to enter its eighth month, the anticipated siege of Bradford at last presented Newcastle with the kind of opportunity he had been seeking to finally crush the obstinate resistance of Lord Fairfax and his son. Once victory had been secured the northern Royalists would then be free to directly support the King's operations against the earl of Essex on the central front. The Fairfaxes, in order to prevent the inevitability of defeat by siege, had resolved to launch a surprise attack against the Royalist camp at Howley Hall. Such an enterprise had succeeded in May 1643 when Sir Thomas Fairfax captured Wakefield. An attack against Howley however represented a huge gamble, yet the desperate situation with which the Fairfaxes were confronted required an equally desperate response. Thus both the Royalists and Parliamentarians had not only defined their objectives with some clarity, but had also prepared plans of attack by which they might be realized. The intentions of the Fairfaxes, for example, were confirmed in a letter to Westminster, despatched shortly after the Parliamentarian march had begun, declaring that Lord Fairfax had gathered his

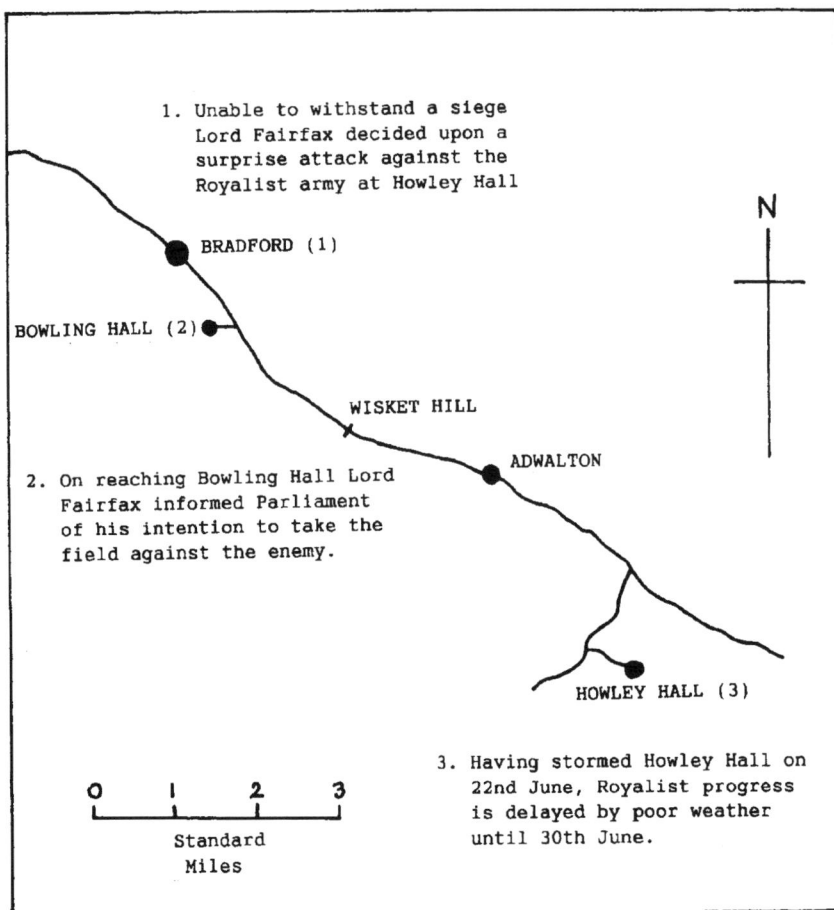

1. Unable to withstand a siege Lord Fairfax decided upon a surprise attack against the Royalist army at Howley Hall

BRADFORD (1)

BOWLING HALL (2)

WISKET HILL

ADWALTON

N

2. On reaching Bowling Hall Lord Fairfax informed Parliament of his intention to take the field against the enemy.

HOWLEY HALL (3)

0   1   2   3

Standard Miles

3. Having stormed Howley Hall on 22nd June, Royalist progress is delayed by poor weather until 30th June.

MUSTER AND MARCH: 30th JUNE 1643

forces and was that day intent upon enforcing a Royalist retreat.[199]

At this point in the narrative it is necessary to clarify two particular issues concerning the mobilization and march of the respective armies. The first issue concerns the exact date upon which the Royalist army arrived at Adwalton village and the adjacent moorland. Clements Markham, in his biography of Sir Thomas Fairfax, stated that after the capture of Howley Hall:

> The Royalists then advanced towards Bradford, and came out upon Adwalton Moor, four miles south-east of the town, in the evening of June 29.[200]

Markham's chronology of events perhaps implies support for the belief shared by Stockdale and Sir Thomas Fairfax that the Royalists had acquired intelligence of Parliamentarian intentions and had taken up a position to frustrate the planned attack upon Howley Hall. However, the account attributed to the earl of

Newcastle stated quite clearly that the Royalist army set out from Howley Hall early on the *morning of 30th June*. Newcastle's testimony, though confirming that march and battle took place upon the same day, does not itself preclude prior Royalist knowledge of Parliamentarian intentions, this being the crux of the second contentious issue: did the Royalists know in advance that which Lord Fairfax and his council of war had planned?

As has been established, Newcastle's army, rested after a week of inactivity, vacated Howley for Bradford on the morning of Friday 30th June. Meanwhile, according to Sir Thomas Fairfax, Parliamentarian preparations had already fallen behind schedule:

> my Father appointed 4 of the clock the next morning, to begin to march; but Major Gen: Gyffard, Who had the ordering of the businesse, so delayed the execution of it, that it was 7 or 8 before we began to move; & not without much suspition of trechery in it; For when we were neare the place we Intended, the enemys whole Army was drawne up in Battalia.[201]

As will become clear, Sir Thomas Fairfax was convinced that defeat at Adwalton Moor was almost entirely due to the conduct of Major General Gifford. From Bradford the Parliamentarian army would have had to march a distance of approximately eight (standard) miles to reach Howley Hall. Given the planned four o'clock start time referred to by Fairfax, plus a marching speed of perhaps two or three miles per hour, the Parliamentarian army could have arrived at its destination by seven o'clock. As will be demonstrated, this would possibly have been just early enough to launch the intended surprise attack against the Royalist camp. In these circumstances it is perhaps understandable that the failure of a design so heavily dependent upon timing and secrecy should arouse suspicions of treachery. Thomas Stockdale - without making accusations - clearly believed that the Royalists had somehow acquired knowledge of the Parliamentarian plan of attack:

> we marched from Bradford against the enemy who lay about three miles of us in a village called Aldwalton or Atherton and the places thereabouts. They hearing of our preparations had left their quarters about Howley and chosen that place of advantage being both a great hill and an open moor or common, where our foot could not be able to stand their horse.[202]

However the account of the Royalist infantry colonel Sir Henry Slingsby - compiled sometime after the battle - revealed that Newcastle had in fact no such intelligence of a surprise Parliamentarian attack:

> It is resolved on both sides to give battle and yet neither knew of the others intention.[203]

It therefore seems likely that Fairfax's suspicions of treachery - and perhaps Stockdale's as well - were in reality a despairing and frustrated reaction to a crushing military defeat sustained in a critical situation. Particularly when one takes into account the delicate balance of the battle and the tantalizing closeness with which the Parliamentarians came to success. The conduct of the Stockdale/Fairfax post-mortem will be fully examined in due course.

Once Major General Gifford had completed the assembly and ordering of the Parliamentarian army, Lord Fairfax and his men finally began the march from Bradford to Howley Hall. Thomas Stockdale provided an important account of the composition of the army as it deployed in line of march along the Bradford/Wakefield road.[204] The great value of Stockdale's description lies in the extrapolation from it of the subsequent deployment of the Parliamentarian army into battle formation. This vital piece of evidence then becomes instrumental in making sense of the way in which Lord Fairfax's forces fragmented during the later stages of the fighting. Stockdale stated that the march was led by a detachment of skirmishing troops known as a 'forlorn hope'. Consisting of horse, foot, and dragoons (mounted infantry) - totalling perhaps 300 men[205] - the forlorn hope comprised six troops or companies under the command of Captain Mildmay. The 'van', or more properly the 'vanguard', formed the first of three separate contingents into which the army proper was then divided. Commanded by Major General Gifford, the van consisted of the 1200 strong garrison force despatched from Leeds. Next, the 'main battle', led by General Lord Ferdinando Fairfax, no doubt with Thomas Stockdale at his side, comprised the 1500 Lancashire foot (and possibly the three troops of Lancashire horse), plus the 500 foot from Halifax and the surrounding moors. The Lancashire forces - according to the Parliamentarian newsbook referred to earlier - were commanded by Colonel Shuttleworth, Colonel Ashton, and Colonel Holland.[180] As Stuart Reid has identified the latter two commanders as colonels of foot, it would appear likely that the 1500 infantry were divided into two battalions of six companies each, and that the three troops of Lancashire horse were led by Colonel Shuttleworth.[206] Finally, the 'rear' consisted of the seven companies of foot taken from the Bradford garrison under Lieutenant Colonel Forbes. In addition Sir Thomas Fairfax led the horse - although his position in the formation is not mentioned by Stockdale. However, a clue to the possible deployment of the horse amongst the marching infantry is provided by a description of the small English army that fought at Rathconnel in Ireland in 1642.[207] The cavalry were divided into three bodies. The first was positioned at the head of the march, forward of a musket detachment forming the English forlorn hope. The second was placed in the centre, amid the main battle, while the third brought up the rear of the army, forming the final component of the rearguard. The possible similarities to the Parliamentarian line of march are marked. Stockdale confirmed that Lord Fairfax's forlorn hope consisted of horse and foot, while it is not inconceivable that the Lancashire horse rode with the Lancashire foot in the main battle. Finally the rear of the Parliamentarian army could well have comprised in part the remaining troops of the Yorkshire horse. This arrangement would in fact make sense given the need to deploy cavalry to either flank once the move from line of march to battle formation had commenced. In addition, the position of the Lancashire horse would facilitate its deployment to the rear of the centre as part of the reserve.

Wisket Hill Skirmish

What is absolutely certain is that the battle of Adwalton Moor began as a skirmish fought between the Parliamentarian and Royalist forlorn hopes on or in the immediate vicinity of the Bradford/Wakefield road. Though the action was small in scale, consisting perhaps of no more than 1000 men, the skirmish was nevertheless critical in shaping much of what followed. What is at first glance less certain is the precise location and subsequent development of this preliminary engagement. Despite eyewitness and contemporary evidence of an apparently contradictory nature, a careful reading nevertheless reveals a logical and perfectly coherent account of the fighting.

It was noted above how the Bradford historian John James had reported that well into the 19th century musket balls were frequently discovered beneath the surface of Wisket Hill. In addition the minor accounts of the German engineer Rosworm and the local Parliamentarian Captain John Hodgson had described a strong association between Wisket Hill and the battle of Adwalton Moor. Intriguingly, and less specifically, Sir Thomas Fairfax described the initial clash to have taken place upon an unnamed area of high ground:

> We were to go up a Hill to them, which our fflorne Hope gained by beating theirs into their maine Body, which was drawne up halfe a mile furthur, upon a place called Adderton Moor.[208]

The distance between Wisket Hill and Adwalton Moor is fully one old English mile. Unless Fairfax's estimate of distance was completely inaccurate, Sir Thomas must have been describing an entirely different hill. As discussed in chapter three, Fairfax appeared to be referring to the unnamed ridge of rising ground standing just to the east of the Drighlington township boundary, *half* an old English mile from 'Adderton' Moor. But how then does one account for the archaeological discoveries recorded at Wisket Hill? One possibility is that these finds indicate the route by which the retreating left flank of the Parliamentarian army attempted to make an escape during the final stage of the battle. However, a more credible explanation is provided by Sir Henry Slingsby. Though not present at the battle, Sir Henry's account makes sense of both the archaeology and Sir Thomas Fairfax's estimation of distance. Slingsby is occasionally difficult to read and properly understand. However, careful study is handsomely rewarded. Sir Henry recorded that:

Standard Mile

Old English Mile

1 Advancing along the Bradford to Wakefield Road the Parliamentarian forlorn hope launch an attack against the Royalist forces occupying Wisket Hill.

2 The Royalist forlorn hope stage a fighting retreat through the enclosures to 'Fairfax' Hill.

3 The earl of Newcastle rallies his men upon 'Fairfax' Hill. The Parliamentarian advance is temporarily halted.

4 Determined Parliamentarian attacks force the Royalist forlorn Hope to retreat to Adwalton Moor. Here the Royalist army is deploying across the ridge having marched over Hungar Hill.

5 Many Royalist troops are still advancing in line of march towards Adwalton village. It will take two hours to deploy the entire army.

Hunsworth Common

700'

Wisket Hill

East Biereley Common

Birkenshaw

'Fairfax' Hill

650'

Ditch

Hodgson Lane

Drighlington

500'

Adwalton

Adwalton Moor

600'

Hungar Hill

650'

600'

Enclosures

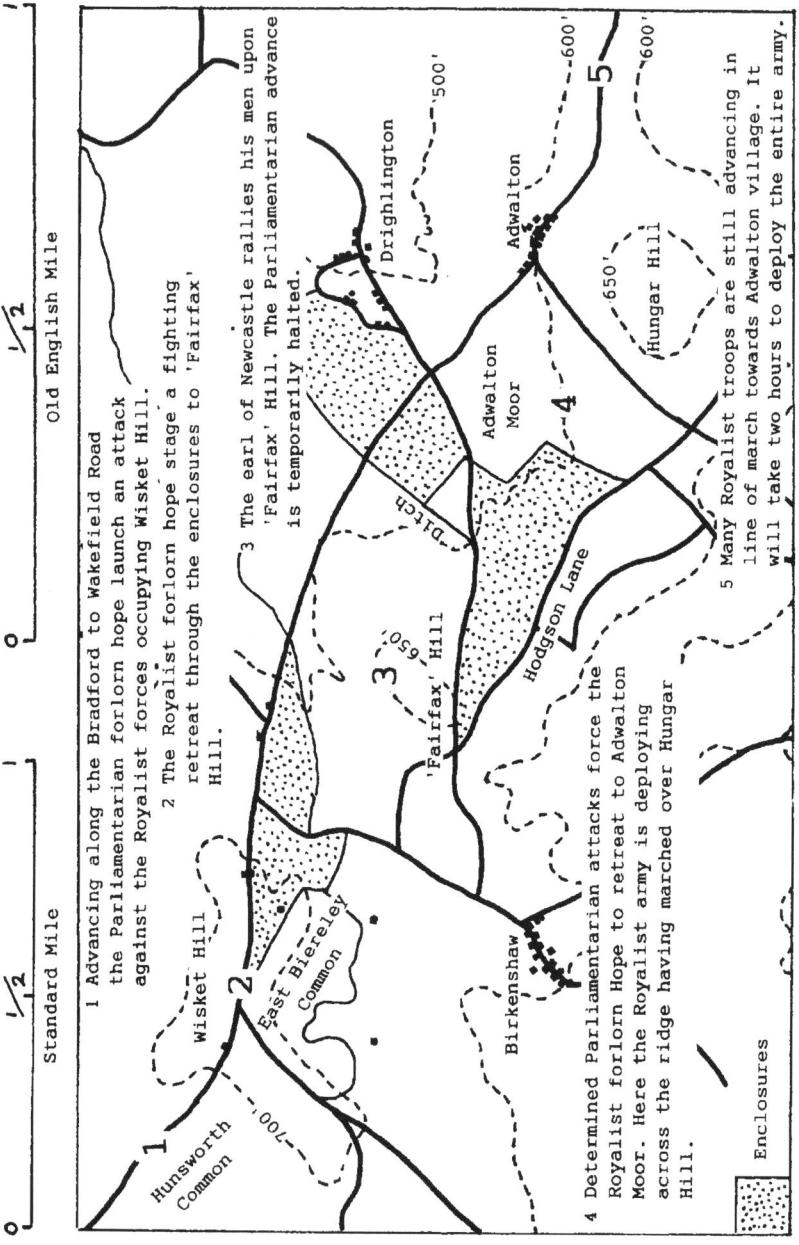

WISKET HILL SKIRMISH

> The forlorn hope of his excellenc's [Newcastle's] army met unexpectedly with the van of the enemy. They skirmish and [Royalists] are put to retreat. He [Newcastle] encourageth his men and puts the enemy [Parliamentarians] to a stand. They [Parliamentarians] come on fiercer, and beats enemy [Royalists] from one hedge, from one house to another; at last they [Royalists] are driven to retreat and we recover the moor [Adwalton Moor].[209]

Though Slingsby telescoped the preliminary skirmish into the battle proper, the correct sequence of events is nevertheless thrown into focus. As the archaeology suggests, the skirmish began as a sharp fire fight for Wisket Hill. Slingsby then described the intervention of the earl of Newcastle who, receiving word or hearing the engagement for himself, raced forward in time to rally his retreating forlorn hope. The logical location for such a stand would have been the rising ground here identified as 'Fairfax Hill'. The Parliamentarians then renewed their attack with even greater vigour and once again forced the Royalists to retreat - this time through the houses and enclosures to Adwalton Moor. The second retreat, as revealed below, was in fact the initial phase of the battle proper, occurring when both sides were in a position to commit greater numbers to the fighting. The significance of its inclusion here is to indicate the position at which Newcastle inspired his troops to rally and stand. The enclosures described by Slingsby are those to the north west of Adwalton Moor and the houses are those that fronted onto Hodgson Lane. The next defensible point north west of these enclosures and houses was 'Fairfax Hill'. When beaten from this hill the Royalist forlorn hope regrouped, as Slingsby described, amongst the enclosures, supported by musketeers and horse despatched forward from Adwalton Moor. The Parliamentarians then deployed across 'Fairfax Hill' before launching a fresh attack that was to drive Newcastle's men back to the moor. What all this means is that the hill from which the Royalist forlorn hope was finally forced to withdraw stood, as Sir Thomas Fairfax described, *half* an old English mile from Adwalton Moor. Thus the skirmish of the forlorn hopes began upon Wisket Hill and came to a close upon 'Fairfax Hill': the evidence provided by the archaeology and the testimony provided by Sir Thomas Fairfax are thereby reconciled and satisfied.

Having established that the fighting of Adwalton Moor commenced upon Wisket Hill it is now possible to return to the question of Lord Fairfax's intended attack upon the Royalist camp at Howley Hall. Wisket Hill lies three standard miles from Bradford and about five standard miles by road from Howley. If the Parliamentarian army had set off as intended at 4 o'clock Lord Fairfax, given an average marching speed of two to three miles per hour, could have reached the hall by 7 o'clock. This is probably the time at which Newcastle began his march towards Bradford. Assuming a similar marching speed of between two and three miles per hour, the Royalist forlorn hope would have travelled the five standard miles to Wisket Hill in about two hours, arriving at around 9 o'clock. If, as seems likely, Lord Fairfax had set off at around 8 o'clock, his forlorn hope would have approached the hill just as the Royalists were reaching the summit. Thus it is entirely possible that the delayed departure from Bradford, for whatever reason, may have cost the Fairfaxes a famous victory. It is conjectured below that the Parliamentarian march may have been intended to bypass the Bradford/Wakefield road so as to advance from Wisket Hill to Howley Hall via Hodgson Lane. Though a more direct route the potentially difficult nature of the terrain over the final approach to Howley would probably have failed to save any additional time. The attraction of the Hodgson Lane advance lay in the concealment it would have provided for the Parliamentarian army.

Thomas Stockdale's report that the Parliamentarian forlorn hope - led by Captain Mildmay with Captain Askwith, Captain Morgan, Captain Farrar, Captain Salmon and Captain Mudd - consisted of horse, foot and dragoons has already been noted. The Royalist forlorn hope was commanded by Sir Robert Clavering, a young Northumberland gentleman who had been knighted by the earl of Newcastle in 1642. As the Royalist cavalry colonel Sir Marmaduke Langdale was later to recall, Clavering had been an active and committed figure from the very outset of the Civil War:

> in the beginning of the said troubles, at his own charge, he raised a regiment of horse and another of foot, with some Troops of Dragoons: with these he often eminently served his late Majesty, as appeared by their many engagements, more particularly at Anderton Moor fight when he (commanding the forlorn hope) was very instrumental in gaining that great victory which then made us masters of the north.[210]

Given that the Parliamentarian forlorn hope consisted of horse, foot and dragoons, it is reasonable to assume that the Royalist forlorn hope exhibited a similar balance of forces, particularly when one considers that Clavering, the forlorn hope commander, had himself raised units of all three. It is certainly possible that the Royalist forlorn hope at Adwalton Moor was made up of those forces that Clavering had personally recruited in 1642.

On the morning of Friday 30th June 1643 however, having led his contingent along the Bradford road to the brow of Wisket Hill, Clavering was suddenly and unexpectedly confronted by the leading units of Lord Fairfax's army. In addition, receding into the distance towards Bradford, Clavering would have been able to make out the bulk of the Parliamentarian force. Comprehending at once the gravity of the situation, Clavering would have hastily despatched a rider to Newcastle, or another of the earl's senior commanders, while drawing up the forces at hand to defend the hill. Sir Robert had one simple objective: to delay the enemy advance until the Royalist army had safely deployed into battle formation. A potential catastrophe, that of being attacked in line of march, had at all costs to be averted.

Taking the initiative however, Captain Mildmay led a determined Parliamentarian attack against the Royalists on the hill. Thomas Stockdale recalled that:

> Our forlorn hope beat back the enemies out of the lanes and enclosed grounds, killing many and taking some prisoners.[211]

Stockdale made no reference to Mildmay's assault upon Wisket Hill, but described instead the fighting that took place in the enclosures to the immediate south of the Bradford/Wakefield road between Wisket Hill and 'Fairfax Hill'. This was, in all probability, because Stockdale rode with the Lord General in the centre of the Parliamentarian army. By the time Stockdale reached Wisket Hill Captain Mildmay had forced Clavering from the summit and was in the process of ejecting the Royalists from the lanes and enclosures that lay beyond. It will be recalled that in describing the same action Sir Thomas Fairfax had stated that, '*We* were to go up a hill to them'. Sir Thomas clearly recalled *a hill*, most probably because he participated in Mildmay's attack against it. If Fairfax had placed himself in command of that portion of the Parliamentarian horse positioned towards the front of the march, he would have been able to lend swift support to Mildmay's subsequent action against 'Fairfax Hill'. This, of course, would be entirely consistent with everything that is known of Sir Thomas. It is possible that the extra numbers provided by Fairfax's cavalry persuaded Clavering to conduct a fighting withdrawal rather than the defence of a single static position.

It has already been noted that the Wisket Hill fight had been evidenced by the discovery of archaeology in the 19th century. In recent years, prompted by the threat of development, attempts have been made to recover battlefield relics from the area between Wisket Hill and 'Fairfax Hill'. Though unsuccessful the exercise was in fact somewhat limited in scale, examining only a small number of isolated points within the battlefield landscape. As the fighting involved a relatively small number of men, a high proportion of which were mounted, the recovery of archaeology in this rather restricted manner was always likely to be a matter of good fortune rather than good judgement. Evidence of the skirmish will continue to remain elusive until the kind of comprehensive survey conducted by Paul Roberts at Marston Moor is repeated here.

By the time Newcastle arrived the fighting had become centred upon the struggle for possession of 'Fairfax Hill'. According to Sir Henry Slingsby it was here that the earl rallied his men and successfully brought the Parliamentarian advance to a temporary halt. From the brow of 'Fairfax Hill' Newcastle would have witnessed, with some alarm perhaps, the appearance of an increasing number of enemy troops; while to his rear the earl would have commanded an excellent view of the Royalist army deploying across Adwalton Moor. Given Newcastle's central location the decision to defend 'Fairfax Hill' must indicate that the majority of Royalists troops had yet to complete their dispositions, and that they remained, for the time being, in a dangerously vulnerable posture. Though, as Slingsby reported, the vigour with which the Parliamentarians renewed their attack was ultimately to sweep Clavering's men from 'Fairfax Hill', Sir Robert's fighting retreat was nevertheless to buy Newcastle the time he desperately required. Sir Thomas Fairfax, on gaining the top of the hill, was immediately confronted by the panorama of Newcastle's army strung out across Adwalton Moor. He was also confronted, as will be discussed presently, by units of Royalist horse and musket freshly drawn up in the enclosures before him and along the line of the ditch. It would have been immediately apparent that the Parliamentarian pursuit could not continue until the whole of Lord Fairfax's force had been deployed. However, the account attributed to the earl of Newcastle made it clear that fully two hours was to elapse before the Royalist foot and artillery were properly positioned.[213] Therefore Clavering's rearguard action, perhaps lasting an hour at the very most, drew to an end well before the Royalist army was able to respond effectively. Clavering delayed the Fairfaxes long enough for supporting Royalist forces to arrive, thus compelling the Parliamentarians to call a halt to their advance and to deploy in battle formation upon 'Fairfax Hill'. Though, in the face of renewed attacks, the Royalist position could not be held, Sir Robert's men had nevertheless played a critical part. A point, previously noted, that was fully appreciated by Sir Marmaduke Langdale. It was, therefore, Clavering's achievement that he had enabled the earl of Newcastle to secure a defensible position upon Adwalton Moor. It was to be some time, however, before that same position would become one from which an effective counterattack could be launched.

Battle Lines and Battalia

Having occupied the crest of 'Fairfax Hill' the Parliamentarian forlorn hope, probably supported by elements of Sir Thomas Fairfax's horse, held its position until joined by the remainder of Lord Fairfax's forces. It was at this point, with the respective battle lines in the process of being drawn up, that the terrain over which the fighting was to take place, and which would initially divide the two armies, was revealed. Though the battle had begun with an impromptu skirmish for Wisket Hill, it was only upon the Parliamentarian capture of 'Fairfax Hill' that Lord Fairfax and the earl of Newcastle were able to fully assess their own deployments as well as those of the enemy. Separated by roughly half an old English mile of open moorland and hedged enclosures, the battle which Newcastle had waited seven months to fight was finally to take place.

Though the Parliamentarian army had advanced as far as Wisket Hill by means of the Bradford/Wakefield road the circumstantial evidence suggests that once to the east of the hill the march was planned to continue via Hodgson Lane. J.Thorpe's map of 1822 shows that the most direct route from Wisket Hill to Howley Hall followed Hodgson Lane along the southern edge of the battlefield

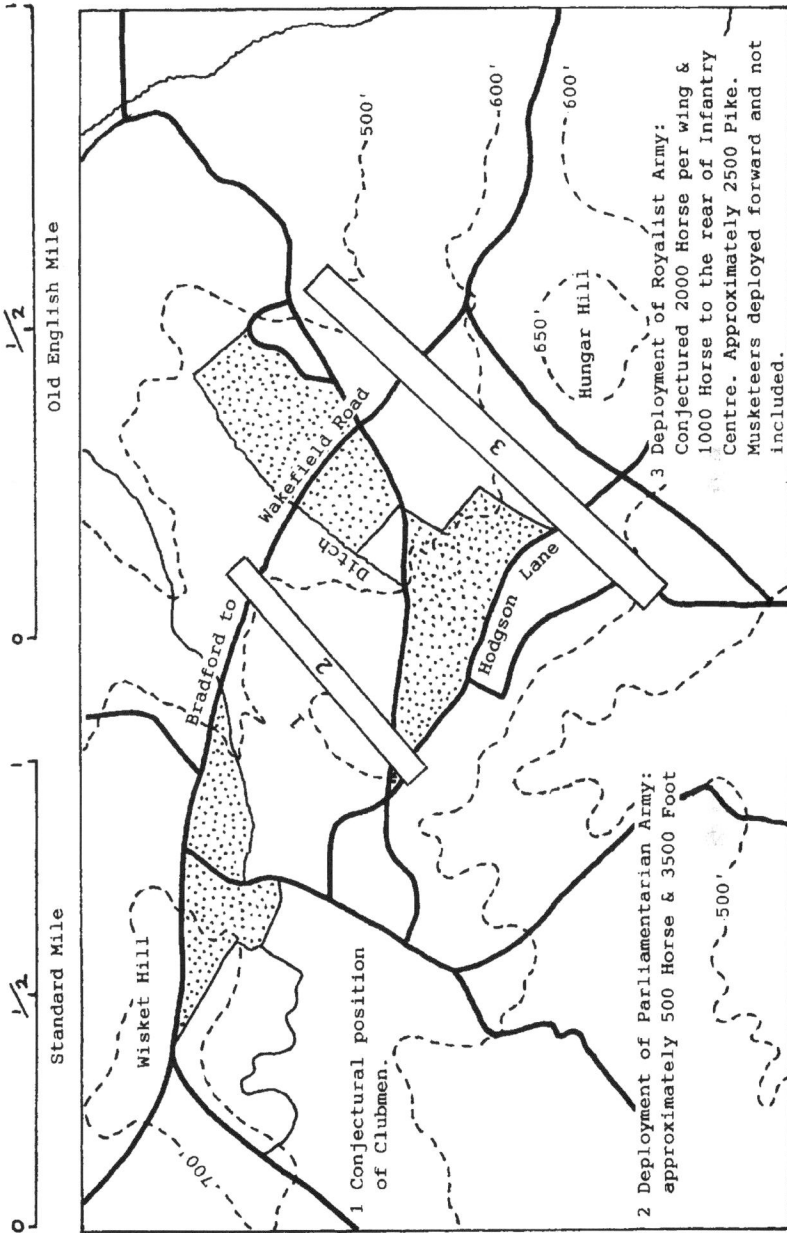

BATTLE LINES AND BATTALIA

1 Conjectural position of Clubmen.

2 Deployment of Parliamentarian Army: approximately 500 Horse & 3500 Foot

3 Deployment of Royalist Army: Conjectured 2000 Horse per wing & 1000 Horse to the rear of Infantry Centre. Approximately 2500 Pike. Musketeers deployed forward and not included.

Standard Mile

Old English Mile

Wisket Hill

Bradford to Wakefield Road

Ditch

Hodgson Lane

Hungar Hill

500'

600'

600'

650'

700'

500'

ridge. Continuing to the south of Hungar Hill the track then descended into a river valley which proceeded on a southerly course until it passed but a short distance to the west of Howley Hall. Though not perhaps an obvious route, the river valley may have been intended to cover the advance of the army until it was almost upon the Royalist camp. Lord Fairfax and his son were intimately acquainted with the landscape hereabouts. It was from Howley Hall in May 1643 that Sir Thomas had launched his daring night attack against the Royalist garrison at Wakefield. The Fairfaxes would naturally have planned their assault so as to maintain until the last possible moment the vital element upon which the whole enterprise so heavily depended - that of surprise. In addition, the manner in which the advance to Howley was abandoned, combined with the manoeuvre by which the Parliamentarian army deployed across 'Fairfax Hill', tends to support Hodgson Lane rather than the Bradford/Wakefield road.

If, as proposed here, it was planned from the outset to attack Howley Hall via Hodgson Lane, a substantial proportion of Lord Fairfax's army would already have entered the lane by the time the Parliamentarian forlorn hope had captured 'Fairfax Hill'. Sir Thomas Fairfax, in all probability stationed on the hill with Captain Mildmay's forlorn hope, reported that in response to the Royalists drawn up half a mile away on Adwalton Moor, the Parliamentarian army then deployed for battle:

> We being all up the Hill drew into Battalia Also. I commanded the Right Wing with about a 1000 Foot, & 5 Troops of Horse. Major Gen: Gyffard the Left Wing, which was about the same number. My Father commanded all in chiefe.[214]

Thomas Stockdale, riding with the body of the army in the company of Lord Fairfax, crucially added the following details:

> the van coming up fell upon the enemies on the left hand and the main battle upon those on the right hand..... the rear fell on in the middle.[215]

As the southern edge of 'Fairfax Hill' abuts onto Hodgson Lane it would have been a simple matter for the army to wheel left out of the lane and to advance in line of march northwards across the length of the hill. Though there may have been a hedge line dividing Hodgson Lane from the enclosures to the immediate north, the hill itself was almost entirely unenclosed. Once the hedge had been breached or a portion of it possibly removed, the deployment would have continued unhindered.

Therefore the van - consisting of the 1200 Leeds foot commanded by Major General Gifford - formed the left wing with, according to Fairfax, 5 troops of horse. Given that the total strength of the 10 troops of Yorkshire horse amounted to roughly 400 mounted men, Gifford probably commanded 200 horse. In addition, Fairfax's comment that Gifford led approximately 1000 foot broadly accords with known strength of the Leeds garrison. Stockdale then reported that the main battle formed the right, with the Bradford garrison taking a position in the centre of the line. The main battle consisted of the 1500 Lancashire foot plus the 500 Halifax infantry. Sir Thomas Fairfax, according to his own account, commanded 1000 foot and 5 troops of horse. Therefore the 2000 strong main battle divided into two equal divisions: 1000 foot under Sir Thomas Fairfax on the right, and 1000 foot in the centre. The seven Bradford companies, according to Stockdale, then completed the centre by taking up a position to the right of the Leeds foot. The formation was completed by the three troops of Lancashire horse who, presumably, formed a reserve with the Yorkshire Clubmen. Apart from the Bradford men having to march from the rear of the line to the centre, the army would have had to do no more than occupy the length of 'Fairfax Hill' in the formation in which it was initially drawn up. In order to secure the flanks the left wing would have deployed across the Bradford/Wakefield road as far as the northern edge of the battlefield ridge, while elements of Sir Thomas Fairfax's cavalry would have been stationed in Hodgson Lane and possibly on the remainder of the ridge to the south. The principal objective being firstly to occupy the elevated ground of 'Fairfax Hill', and secondly to take maximum advantage of the protection afforded by deployment across the full width of the battlefield ridge. The Clubmen - following to the rear of the regular army - probably assembled on the reverse slope of 'Fairfax Hill', just to the south east of the Tong/Drighlington township boundary. Finally the three troops of Lancashire horse most likely formed a mobile reserve to the immediate rear of the infantry centre, close perhaps to the position taken up by Lord Fairfax and Thomas Stockdale. It has been speculated that the Clubmen acted not only as an irregular source of manpower to bolster the Parliamentarian army, but more importantly perhaps, constituted the pike element in Lord Fairfax's infantry. If this were indeed the case it would make sense of the Royalist claim that the regular Parliamentarian foot consisted almost entirely of musketeers.[216] Unfortunately none of the sources - Parliamentarian or Royalist - make any reference to the position of the four pieces of cannon.

The front line of the Parliamentarian order of battle would therefore have consisted of approximately 3500 foot plus about 400 horse divided into two wings of 200 horse each. Deployed in normal 'order', a block of 600 foot in 6 ranks of 100 men each would occupy a frontage of 100 yards. The Parliamentarian foot consisted of the equivalent of six such blocks giving a total infantry frontage of approximately 600 yards. A block of 66 horse organized in normal 'order' of three ranks of 22 horses each would produce a frontage of 132ft. Each wing of cavalry consisted of the equivalent of three such blocks of horse. This would have produced a cavalry frontage of 132 yards on each wing. In total the battle line of horse and foot would have amounted to 864 yards - perhaps more than 900 yards if gaps between blocks were included.[217] This was in fact the approximate distance between the Bradford to Wakefield road on the Parliamentarian left flank and Hodgson Lane on the right flank. The extra yardage required to occupy the full width of the ridge would have been easily accomplished by either reducing the number of ranks in each block, thereby extending the frontage, or by bringing forward Clubmen to plug the gaps.

Royalist attempts to draw up Newcastle's forces on Adwalton Moor must have been pretty chaotic. Commanders leading the army in line of march would have received news of the substantial enemy force advancing towards them, while word of the skirmish for Wisket Hill would have spread rapidly through the ranks. The imperative at this point would have been to occupy the most advantageous terrain in the shortest possible time. That terrain was the crest of Hungar Hill. It would, however, have been immediately apparent to Royalist commanders arriving on the hill that the area of highest ground surrounding the summit was far too small to permit a proper deployment of the whole army. With Hungar Hill a command post, Royalist units at the head of the march, and those following close behind, were ordered from the Bradford/Wakefield road over the brow of Hungar Hill, to be marshalled into formation across the open expanse of the moorland ridge. As men continued to stream forward, cluttering the moor with horse and foot, those forces still in line of march on the Bradford/Wakefield road would have been compelled to deploy upon the falling ground to the north of the moor and below the level of the battlefield ridge. A substantial portion of the army were thus drawn up upon land that was not to witness combat of any description. Newcastle's forces were simply too numerous to permit the deployment of the entire army on the best available ground.

The terrain, however, was not the only difficulty to confront Newcastle. Almost as soon as the earl had begun to deploy his forces he was compelled to despatch troops westward to contest the enclosures lying between the Parliamentarian army occupying 'Fairfax Hill' and the Royalists drawing up on Adwalton Moor. Sir Henry Slingsby confirmed that Newcastle's musketeers were commanded forward, leaving the massed pike blocks to form the infantry centre of the Royalist battle line.[218] The account attributed to the earl implied that it may have taken two hours to properly draw up the foot and correctly place the artillery.[219] During this time battle was joined; initially for possession of the hedged enclosures and then for the moor itself. The course of the fighting was to push the Royalist battle line back towards the summit of Hungar Hill. To Newcastle and those charged with the ordering of the army it must have seemed as if they had neither control of events nor the means by which to reverse the tide of battle.

It has been demonstrated that the Parliamentarian army, with the manpower available to it, would have faced few problems in occupying the full width of the battlefield ridge. Using the same source as a basis for calculation it is possible to show how the Royalist army, as Adwalton Moor became congested with horse and foot, would have been forced to deploy men north of the Bradford/Wakefield road.[220]

It has been argued that Newcastle's forces, roughly 10,000 men in total, may have consisted of around 5000 horse and the same number of foot. It would have been normal practice to divide the cavalry into two wings of 2500 horse each. However, because space was somewhat limited, it is likely that Newcastle would have deployed a reserve of say 1000 horse upon Hungar Hill, directly to the rear of the infantry centre. This was a conventional tactic, and as such, a plausible arrangement regardless of other considerations. Each cavalry flank would therefore have numbered 2000 horse. A cavalry wing of this size would have been divided into two lines, with perhaps 1000 horse in each line. A block of 500 cavalry arranged in three ranks of 167 men and deployed in 'order' would have occupied a frontage of 333 yards. Without allowing for gaps two such blocks, forming the front line of the cavalry wing, would consume 666 yards of land. Two cavalry wings, each arranged in four 500 horse blocks with two blocks per line, would therefore occupy a total frontage of 1332 yards.

It has been suggested that of Newcastle's 5000 foot as few as 2000 may have been musketeers. However, for the sake of the exercise it will be assumed that the foot divided equally into 2500 shot and 2500 pike. During the course of the fighting the Royalist musketeers were commanded forward to defend the enclosures, leaving the pike to form the centre of the Royalist battle line. Therefore Newcastle's 2500 musketeers will be excluded from the calculation. A total of around two and a half thousand pike may have divided into four blocks of 600 men. Each block deployed in 'order', and consisting of six ranks of 100 men per rank, would have occupied a frontage of 100 yards. Therefore, without gaps, four such blocks would measure 400 yards in length. Add this to the projected cavalry wings of 666 yards each and the resulting frontage totals just under a standard mile at 1732 yards. This is an absolute minimum figure as it excludes all gaps between formations and Newcastle's entire musket compliment of approximately 2500 men. The width of the battlefield ridge at the point of Royalist deployment across the centre of Adwalton Moor was just over 1500 yards. The measurement is aligned with the old coal pits shown on the 1852 Ordnance Survey map of which the duchess of Newcastle had complained:

> no place was left to draw up my Lord's [left wing of] horse, but amongst old coal-pits.[221]

Thus it would have been impossible for Newcastle to cram the entire Royalist army, including musketeers, onto the moorland provided by the width of the battlefield ridge.

Fight for the Fields

Once the Parliamentarian army had drawn up in battalia across 'Fairfax Hill' the potency of the threat posed by Newcastle's cavalry became the principal concern of Lord Fairfax and Thomas Stockdale. In order to secure a more defensible position, an immediate attack was launched against the Royalist

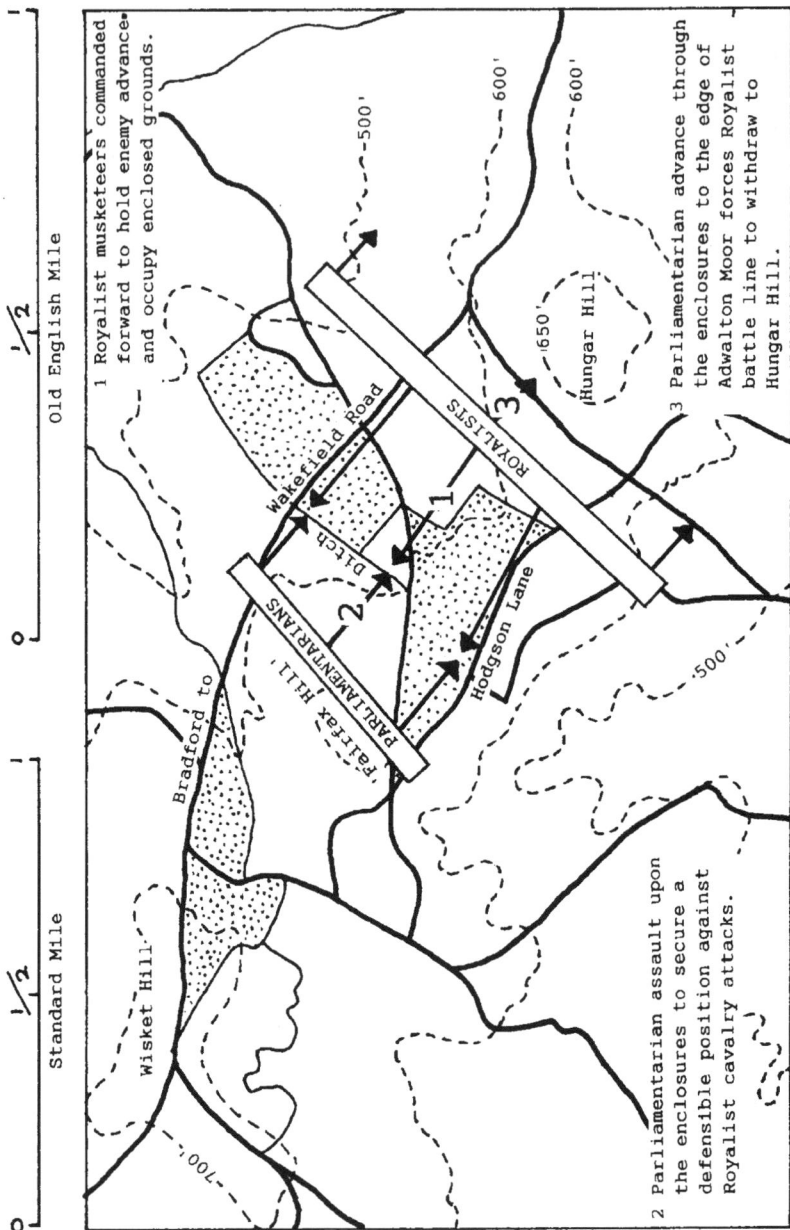

FIGHT FOR THE FIELDS

1 Royalist musketeers commanded forward to hold enemy advance and occupy enclosed grounds.

2 Parliamentarian assault upon the enclosures to secure a defensible position against Royalist cavalry attacks.

3 Parliamentarian advance through the enclosures to the edge of Adwalton Moor forces Royalist battle line to withdraw to Hungar Hill.

Standard Mile

Old English Mile

Wisket Hill

Bradford to

Fairfax Hill

PARLIAMENTARIANS

Ditch

Wakefield Road

Hodgson Lane

ROYALISTS

Hungar Hill

700'

500'

600'

600'

650'

500'

86

forces occupying the hedged enclosures standing between the Parliamentarians on 'Fairfax Hill' and Newcastle's main force on Adwalton Moor. Possession of the fields would provide Lord Fairfax with the protection his outnumbered forces required. This was probably the best the Parliamentarians could hope for, particularly as they now found themselves engaged in the kind of full-scale encounter they had always sought to avoid. The initial Royalist occupation of the enclosures had been intended to protect the deployment of Newcastle's army upon Adwalton Moor. As a consequence, it is difficult to properly determine the precise point at which the Royalist musketeers, commanded forward from Adwalton Moor, actually became involved in the fighting.

After stating that the Royalist forlorn hope had been evicted from 'Fairfax Hill' - and forced to retreat all the way back to Adwalton Moor - Sir Thomas Fairfax then described the deployment of his father's army and the subsequent Parliamentarian assault against the enclosures:

> We advanced through the enclosed Grounds till we came to the Moor, beating the Foot that laid in them, to their main Body .[222]

Fairfax's account implied that the Royalist forlorn hope was driven back to Adwalton Moor before, or as, fresh Royalist infantry were in the process of occupying the enclosures. Thomas Stockdale, by contrast, may have been suggesting that the Royalist forlorn hope was quickly supported by large detachments of Newcastle's horse and foot well before it was chased from 'Fairfax Hill':

> Upon Atherton Moor they [the Royalists] planted their ordnance and ordered their battalia, but they manned divers houses standing in the enclosed grounds betwixt Bradford and Atherton moor with musketeers, and sent out great parties of horse and foot by the lanes and enclosed grounds to give us fight.[223]

Sir Henry Slingsby's comment, noted above, that the Royalist forlorn hope was commanded by Newcastle to make a stand, probably on 'Fairfax Hill', supports the possibility that the position was reinforced *before* Captain Mildmay captured the hill. This would then make sense of Slingsby's chronology that from 'Fairfax Hill' the Royalist forces were gradually driven back, from hedge to hedge and house to house, onto Adwalton Moor. Alternatively it is possible that the Royalist horse and musketeers were deployed in the lanes and enclosures *following* the Parliamentarian capture of 'Fairfax Hill', but just in time to prevent the wholesale retreat of the Royalist forlorn hope to Adwalton Moor. Whatever the correct sequence of events, it is clear that the Royalist musketeers had occupied the enclosures by the time the Parliamentarian deployment across 'Fairfax Hill' had been completed. The Royalist forlorn hope either retreated to the enclosures *along* with the reinforcing musketeers, or were *joined* by the musketeers having first withdrawn to the hedges.

View looking south east from what was once Drighlington Common towards the line of the ditch and hedged enclosures. Adwalton Moor is situated beyond the houses lining the Whitehall Road (A58). This is the area through which the centre of the Parliamentarian line advanced following its formation into battalia upon 'Fairfax Hill'.

Thomas Stockdale's account also described Royalist horse and foot advancing by the lanes and enclosed grounds. Two of these lanes were certainly the Bradford/Wakefield road and Hodgson Lane, while a third may have been the track from Adwalton to Birkenshaw, which formed the northern perimeter of the hedged enclosures. Sir Henry Slingsby's report that all Royalist musketeers were deployed forward meant that the reinforcements numbered between 2000 and 2500 foot together with an unknown number of horse. If these forces arrived in time to join Clavering and Newcastle upon 'Fairfax Hill' one may wonder why the Royalists were unable to defend the hill for longer. The simple and most likely explanation is that they did not attempt to. With an uninterrupted view of the approaching Parliamentarian army, Newcastle and Clavering probably decided to let the enemy have a volley or two of shot before withdrawing to the relative security of the enclosures. They may have been concerned that the horse, if forced back, could have become trapped against the enclosures with no room to manoeuvre. Once the Royalist musketeers were positioned amongst the hedges, the horse almost certainly withdrew from the lanes to the moor. This would explain Sir Thomas Fairfax's recollection that the Parliamentarians then fought the enemy *foot* that had occupied the hedged enclosures.

The evidence suggests that the Parliamentarian assault upon the enclosures and the line of the hedged ditch was conducted on a broad front.

Thomas Stockdale described a concerted attack against Royalist forces that opposed both wings of the Parliamentarian army:

> and then the van coming up fell upon the enemies on the left hand and the main battle upon those of the right hand, and after some dispute beat the enemy both out of the houses they had manned and from the skirts of the moor to the height.[224]

The advance would have been led by Lord Fairfax's musketeers who, becoming involved in a protracted fire fight with Newcastle's musketeers, slowly dislodged the Royalists from the hedges and houses. With perhaps as many as 5000 musket armed foot fighting at close range, the resulting noise and smoke would have been particularly dramatic. Sir Henry Slingsby's comment that the Parliamentarian attack was notable for its fierceness reflects the urgency with which Lord Fairfax's army was compelled to assault the enclosures. In a contest of almost equal numbers of musketeers, the Parliamentarian success might to some extent be accounted for by a Royalist concern to occupy time. By slowly falling back towards the main Royalist position on Adwalton Moor, Newcastle's musketeers would have remained intact as a fighting force while allowing the bulk of the army to continue to deploy across the moor and beyond. The archaeological evidence described by Norrisson Scatcherd demonstrated that the fire fight was at its most intense within the enclosures. Given the number of musket armed foot engaged, one would expect just such a concentration of battlefield debris. To the north east, in the vicinity of the hedged ditch, the discovery of battlefield relics became noticeably more sporadic, petering out altogether towards the Bradford/Wakefield road. This would appear to indicate that although the Parliamentarian onslaught commenced on a broad front, as Thomas Stockdale described, it gradually became concentrated in and around the enclosures.

As a consequence of the inexorable progress of Lord Fairfax's musketeers through the enclosures, the Royalist army deployed upon Adwalton Moor was obliged to withdraw from its original position across the centre of the moor, to a new line on the north western slopes and summit of Hungar Hill. This realignment explains Stockdale's recollection, noted above, that the Royalists retreated 'from the skirts of the moor to the height'. As the Parliamentarian musketeers advanced through the enclosures, eventually driving the Royalist musketeers onto Adwalton Moor, Newcastle's left wing of horse would have found itself within a dangerously short range of Lord Fairfax's foot. By drawing back the entire line to Hungar Hill, Newcastle not only prevented the over exposure of his troops, but importantly enabled the horse to clear the coal pits. This repositioning, of the left wing of horse in particular, helps to explain the subsequent development of the fighting on the southern half of the moor.

Horses And Hedges: The Royalist Cavalry Offensive

Lord Fairfax's successful occupation of the enclosures and ditch not only altered the alignment of the Parliamentarian army, but also determined the manner in which Newcastle attempted to regain the initiative. The configuration of the enclosed fields, together with the location of the hedged ditch line, threw the Parliamentarian right wing, commanded by Sir Thomas Fairfax, to within 350 yards of the repositioned Royalist line. At the same time a distance of about half a standard mile had opened up between Major General Gifford's left wing, manning the line of the ditch, and the enemy forces directly opposite. The Parliamentarian line thus exhibited a zigzag appearance which, far from proving to be a handicap, materially assisted its subsequent defence. That the Parliamentarian army was thus deployed is supported firstly by the early 19th century investigations of Norrisson Scatcherd, and secondly by the duchess of Newcastle's insistence that the hedges and ditch constituted a significant obstacle to Royalist cavalry operations.[225]

With Lord Fairfax's army safely established in the enclosures and behind the ditch, Newcastle launched a cavalry assault against the closest and weakest point in the enemy's defences. Driven to retreat by the ferocity of the Parliamentarian onslaught, the Royalists were now desperate to move forward from what must have been their final fall-back position upon Hungar Hill. Sir Thomas Fairfax described how the Royalist horse then subjected those under his command to the severest pressure:

> Ten or 12 Troops of Horse charged us in the Right Wing. We kept the enclosure, placing our Musketeers in the hedges in the moor, which was good Advantage to us who had so few horse. There was a Gate, or open place to the Moor, where 5 or 6 might enter abreast. Here they strove to enter, and we to defend; But after some Dispute, those that entered the passe found sharpe entertainment; & those that were not yet entered, as hott welcome from the Musketeers that flanked them in the hedges. All, in the end, were forced to retreat, with the loss of one Coll: Howard, who commanded them.[226]

As Sir Thomas Fairfax commanded the Parliamentarian right, the Royalist horse drawn against him must therefore have formed part of the left flank of Newcastle's army. Having withdrawn to a position clear of the coal pits, amongst which they had originally deployed, Newcastle's cavalry were finally to join the fighting. However, the ground that now became available to them, combined with the target against which the attack was to be directed, meant that a mass charge of the entire cavalry wing was impossible. The north eastern half of Adwalton Moor, previously occupied by the Royalist pike blocks, now provided a path free of old coal workings by which the enclosures could be

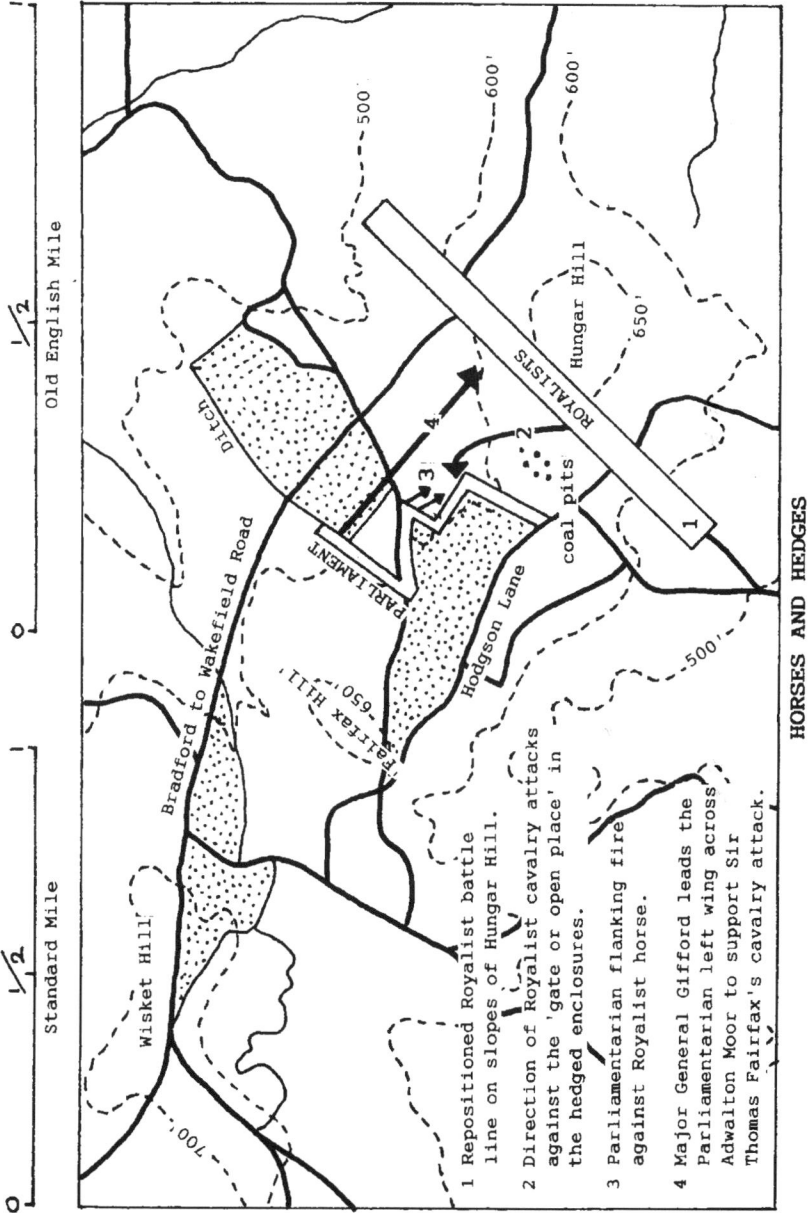

HORSES AND HEDGES

1 Repositioned Royalist battle line on slopes of Hungar Hill.

2 Direction of Royalist cavalry attacks against the 'gate or open place' in the hedged enclosures.

3 Parliamentarian flanking fire against Royalist horse.

4 Major General Gifford leads the Parliamentarian left wing across Adwalton Moor to support Sir Thomas Fairfax's cavalry attack.

91

attacked. The ten or twelve troops of Royalist cavalry described by Fairfax would have amounted to between 500 and 600 mounted men. This must have been close to the maximum number that could have passed swiftly to the north of the coal workings, while remaining clear of the Royalist pike drawn up to their immediate right on the slopes of Hungar Hill. In addition, as Sir Thomas recalled, the opening in the hedge line was sufficient only to admit 5 or 6 horse at a time. A mass onslaught of 2000 cavalry would therefore have been no more effective than a charge of 500 or 600 horse given the objective of the assault.

There are a couple of clues which suggest the probable location of this opening onto the moor. Firstly its position allowed a direct attack by forces operating to the north east of the disused coal workings, while secondly the opening was protected by Parliamentarian flank fire. The point at which the 1643 hedge line running north east from Hodgson Lane, with Adwalton Moor to its right hand side, turned 90° to the north west, provided a hedgerow boundary that could have been attacked from the moor as described. An opening here would have permitted flanking fire from further along the hedge line, as it once again turned through 90° to resume a north easterly direction close to the route of the modern A58 Whitehall Road (see accompanying map 'Horses and Hedges'). The funnelling of Newcastle's horse against a small objective such as this would have provided a huge target for the musketeers manning the hedges. The opening nevertheless proved to be a vulnerable point, the consequent fierceness of the fighting resulted in the death of the Royalist brigade commander Colonel Howard. Sir Thomas Fairfax may have attempted to defend the opening itself with pike or horse rather than vulnerable musketeers.

Having forced the enemy to withdraw, Fairfax then described a second and more desperate Royalist attempt to enter the enclosures:

> The Horse came down again and charged us, being about 13 or 14 Troops. We defended ourselves as before, but with much more Difficulty, many having gotten in among us; but were beaten off again, with losse; & Coll: Herne who commanded that party was Slaine. We pursued them to their Cannon.[227]

The targeting of the 'gate or open place' in this fashion indicated that its penetration and exploitation offered perhaps the only way in which Newcastle and James King could realistically dislodge the Parliamentarians from their defences. The fact that the Royalists launched two such attacks in quick succession, each delivered with considerable determination, would appear to demonstrate as much. Sir Thomas Fairfax's important recollection that 'The horse came *down* again' supports the argument outlined above that the Royalist battle line had by this juncture withdrawn to the slopes of Hungar Hill. 13 or 14 troops of Royalist horse would have totalled around 650 to 700 men, again indicating that a brigade of this size was the most practical formation in the circumstances. It is not clear whether the second attack was composed of fresh

View looking north west across Adwalton Moor from the Royalist battle line on the slopes of Hungar Hill. This is the point at which the left flank of horse ended and the infantry centre began. The large warehouse (centre left) marks the approximate spot at which the Royalist cavalry attempted to enter the enclosures by forcing the 'gate or open place'.

troops or consisted of cavalry that had participated in the first charge. However, given that Newcastle stationed around 2000 horse on the left flank, the probability is that the second assault was delivered by men who had not taken part in the first attack. The fighting, even more desperate and severe than before, once again claimed the life of a Royalist officer. The testimony of Sir Thomas Fairfax demonstrated just how close the second attack came to success. It is not difficult to envisage, in the confined and confused surroundings of the hedge line opening, how the fighting must have hung in the balance for what doubtless seemed an endless and exhausting period of time.

Continuing his account, Sir Thomas Fairfax went on to describe how his men had chased Newcastle's retreating cavalry across the moor to the Royalist gun line. The pursuing Parliamentarian force would have consisted of the five troops of Yorkshire horse under the command of Sir Thomas, who doubtless acting upon his own initiative, saw an opportunity to strike a decisive blow. Newcastle's cannon would have been deployed as part of the Royalist battle line, perhaps concentrated - given the likely direction of the Parliamentarian pursuit - in the general area of the infantry centre. The account attributed to the earl of Newcastle stated that the Parliamentarian advance, and the consequent Royalist withdrawal, had occupied roughly two hours. If, as appears likely, the fight for Wisket Hill had begun at about 9 o'clock, then the Royalists would have been driven back to Hungar Hill by around 11 o'clock. Though these estimated timings are clearly far from precise, the Royalist cavalry attacks, followed by Sir Thomas Fairfax's counterattack, must in all probability have taken place before noon.

The defeat of Newcastle's horse is perhaps both a convenient and appropriate point at which to introduce Sir Philip Monckton's cryptic yet intriguing reference to the battle. Monckton, a Royalist cavalry commander, made, according to his memoirs, an important contribution to the Royalist victory at Adwalton Moor:

> Sir Will: Throckmorton late Knight Marshall was Comissary General of the Horse to his Grace of Newcastle at the battle of Aderton Moore, of which Battle he hath often said that if I did not winn the day I saved it and that which I did was not by Chance but Conduct.[229]

As a senior commander in Newcastle's army, Sir William Throckmorton would have been acutely aware of just how close the Royalist came to defeat at Adwalton Moor. In such desperate circumstances any action that made a material difference to the outcome of the fighting was bound to leave a lasting impression. So what precisely could Monckton have done to earn Throckmorton's approbation? One possibility springs to mind. As a cavalry officer who 'saved the day' it would appear most likely that Monckton was stationed on the Royalist left flank. For it was this wing that launched the unsuccessful attacks against the enclosures. When the second assault was broken up and chased across the moor by Sir Thomas Fairfax, it is possible that 600 or so as yet unused Royalist horse, together with many or all of those that had survived the first attack, would have remained drawn up and in position upon Hungar Hill. In addition to these units the infantry centre, now bolstered by musketeers, would have been likewise endangered by the flight of the retreating Royalist cavalry. The possibility of a general panic spreading through Newcastle's battle line would therefore have been very real, and the consequences of such a panic potentially catastrophic. Perhaps it was here that Monckton, taking charge of the remaining left flank horse, held the troops in good order while his fleeing comrades swept past. If, as suggested here, Throckmorton was indeed referring to such conduct, then Monckton's prompt action and leadership, while not itself responsible for victory, might well have prevented a damaging spread of panic and ultimately a crushing defeat.

As Sir Thomas Fairfax declined to provide an account of events once his cavalry had reached the Royalist cannon, it must be assumed that the pursuit was halted and forced to draw back. The testimony of Thomas Stockdale however suggests that Fairfax, far from retreating, rallied his men in order to occupy a new position on the moor itself:

> our horse very bravely recovered part of the moor from the enemy, and maintained it...[230]

The likelihood is that Sir Thomas's cavalry, around 200 in total, would have been met by repeated volleys of musket fire. The Royalist musketeers, evicted from the enclosures, were probably drawn up in advance of the pike blocks already in position on the slopes of Hungar Hill. This would make sense of Sir Philip Warwick's description, discussed below, of the final stages of the battle.

With the Parliamentarians relatively secure in the enclosures and in occupation of at least a section of Adwalton Moor, the momentum appeared to belong to the Fairfaxes. Newcastle had bought sufficient time to deploy his forces - which was important - but had been compelled to give ground. The earl's subsequent attempts to regain the initiative had likewise been defeated, even the Royalist cannon had been subjected to a fleeting threat. The day hung in the balance.

The Critical Action

Despite Sir Thomas Fairfax's success on the Parliamentarian right wing, it was to be events on the Parliamentarian left that were ultimately to prove decisive. Although accounts of the fighting are complicated and confusing, it is nevertheless possible to unravel the process by which a controlled Royalist withdrawal became a crushing Royalist victory.

The initial progress of the Parliamentarian advance was readily conceded by the authors of the Royalist sources. Even the propaganda newsbook *Mercurius Aulicus* was prepared to admit that the Parliamentarian attack:

> was at first so strong and violent, that His Majesties Forces were fain to give ground untill they came within reach of their owne Canon.[231]

By contrast Thomas Stockdale, while recognizing the tenacity of Lord Fairfax's men, somewhat soberly continued his report by concentrating upon what was to become the battle's fatal error:

> Thus far we had a fair day, but the success of our men at the first drew them unawares to engage themselves too far upon the enemies, who having the advantage of the ground, and infinitely exceeded us in numbers,[232]

At first glance Stockdale's remarks might be interpreted as a criticism of Sir Thomas Fairfax's impetuous charge across the moor. However, subsequent events demonstrate that Stockdale was in fact bemoaning what turned out to be the ill judged advance of Lord Fairfax's left wing. Sir Thomas Fairfax's brief but revealing comment, inserted between his account of the first and second Royalist cavalry attacks, claimed that the Parliamentarian left wing:

> at the same time was engaged with the Enemys Foot. Ours gained ground of them.[233]

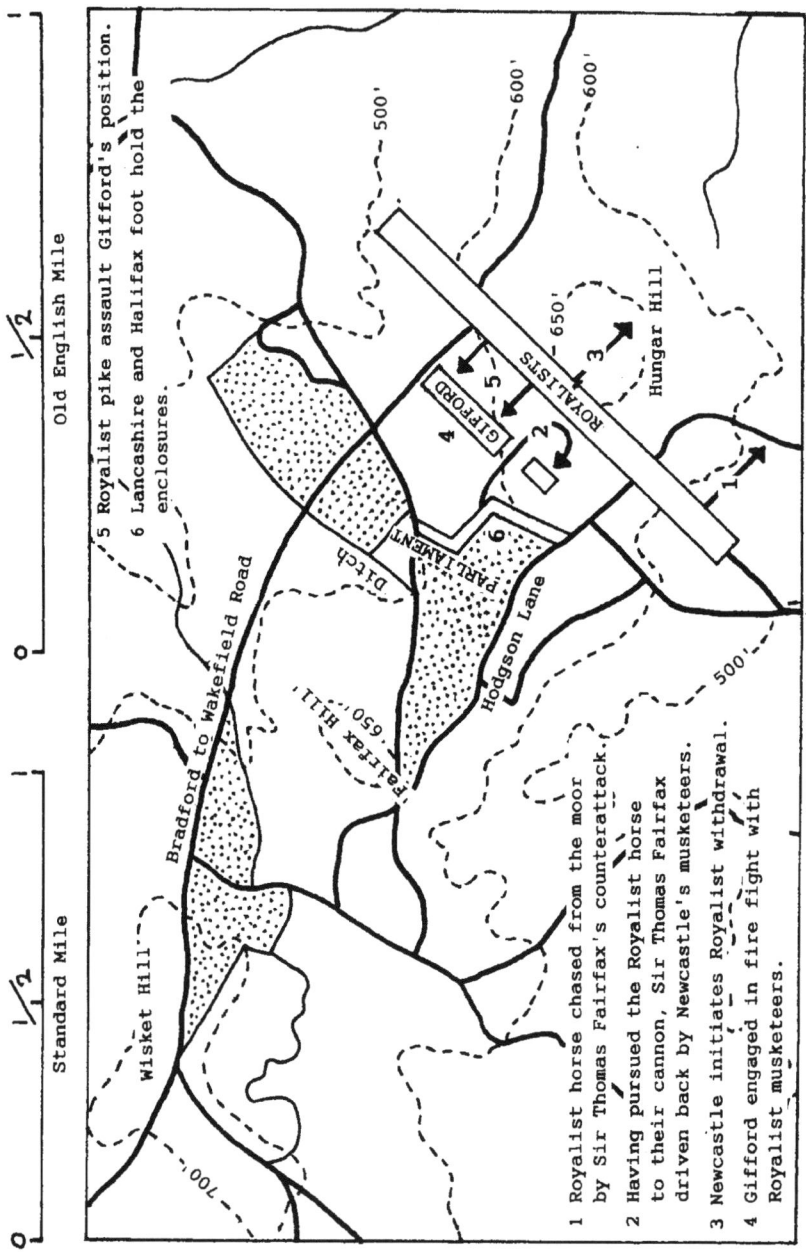

THE CRITICAL ACTION

1 Royalist horse chased from the moor by Sir Thomas Fairfax's counterattack.

2 Having pursued the Royalist horse to their cannon, Sir Thomas Fairfax driven back by Newcastle's musketeers.

3 Newcastle initiates Royalist withdrawal.

4 Gifford engaged in fire fight with Royalist musketeers.

5 Royalist pike assault Gifford's position.

6 Lancashire and Halifax foot hold the enclosures.

96

Fairfax continued by asserting that the result of his cavalry counterattack *and*:

> the Resolutions that our Soldiers shewed in the left wing, made the enemy think of Retreating. Orders were given for it, and some marched off the field.[234]

What appears to have happened is that Gifford, in command of the Parliamentarian left, successfully evicted the Royalists opposed to him from the line of the ditch. Here Gifford held his position, waiting upon events, while Newcastle launched his cavalry offensive against the enclosures on the Parliamentarian right. Gifford must have remained behind the ditch at this point for had his men ventured onto the moor they would have become easy prey for Newcastle's massed cavalry. Such a development, had it occurred, would surely have attracted the attention of both Royalist and Parliamentarian accounts. As it was, with the moor eventually cleared of Royalist horse, Gifford commanded his men forward in order to support Sir Thomas Fairfax's highly visible counterattack. This may explain Sir Thomas Fairfax's readiness to hold the cavalry on the moor. Gifford's foot, supported by his five troops of horse, advanced in good order to commence a fire fight with the Royalist musketeers of Newcastle's centre. Given the alignment of the rival armies, Gifford's advance would have pitted his men against the foot they had but recently forced to withdraw. Had not Gifford made such an attack it is difficult to believe that even Sir Thomas Fairfax would have remained unsupported in the middle of an open moor with only 200 horse at his disposal. It might also have been Gifford's intervention that prompted the controlled departure of some Royalist units observed by Fairfax. Alternatively the order to begin the withdrawal could have been issued as a direct consequence of the failed second Royalist cavalry assault. If, as seems likely, Newcastle was planning to vacate the field, the day must have by now appeared lost, both to the earl himself and to his senior commanders. Sir Thomas Fairfax, from his new station on the moor, would have been particularly well placed to observe any movement in the Royalist battle line. Indeed such movement would have bolstered further Fairfax's resolve to hold his ground. Had Newcastle intended to continue the battle he would surely have ordered a further cavalry attack against Sir Thomas Fairfax's small and exposed contingent of horse. Whatever the correct sequence of events, the Royalist withdrawal would have been entirely consistent with the cautious manner in which Newcastle and James King had prosecuted the Yorkshire campaign. Had events continued to unfold in this fashion, the Fairfaxes would have been left in possession of both the moor and a famous victory.

Sir Philip Warwick's account of the battle - almost certainly the result of a personal conversation with the earl of Newcastle - began by indirectly supporting Sir Thomas Fairfax's claim of an embryonic Royalist withdrawal:

> In the same year [1643] the Earl of Newcastle got an important victory over the Lord Fairfax at Adderton-moor; where-in this is memorable, that when the day

seemed lost on his [Newcastle's] side, and many of his horse and foot standing *doubtful and wavering* (author's italics)[235]

Though Warwick does not mention a withdrawal of forces, his comments would appear at the very least a tacit acknowledgement that one was probably about to begin. Given Newcastle's eventual triumph, the earl was arguably unlikely to concede to Warwick that he had commanded or was aware of a removal of Royalist forces from the field. Incredible though it may seem, it was to be this 'doubtful and wavering' army, in the process of leaving the moor, that in a short space of time was to regain control of events and rout an apparently victorious enemy.

The circumstances in which the battle was decided are remarkable, for it would appear that it was an act of near insubordination that finally turned the tables. Sir Thomas Fairfax, from his vantage point upon Adwalton Moor, stated that:

> While they [the Royalists] were in this wavering Condition, One Coll: Skirton, a wild & desperate man, desired his Gen: to let him charge once more, with a stand of pikes, with which he broke in upon our men; they not relieved by our Reserves, commanded by some ill affected officers, & chiefly, Major Gen: Gyffard, (who did not his part as he ought to have done) our men lost ground.[236]

Fairfax's description implies that this 'Coll: Skirton' demanded in the most vehement terms ('a wild and desperate man') a final opportunity to engage the enemy, an opportunity that the orders of his General (Newcastle) were about to deny him. Outraged to the point of desperation, 'Skirton' appears to have persuaded Newcastle, for it must be assumed that it was the earl, to allow the pike to advance. In an army bound essentially by the time honoured ties of social deference, this was indeed remarkable. As far as Sir Thomas was concerned, the intervention of a single Royalist officer had dramatically overturned events, to the extent that the vulnerability of the Parliamentarian position upon the open moor was exposed and exploited.

So who precisely was the remarkable 'Skirton'? Unfortunately his real identity remains an unsolved mystery. The extensive research of P.R.Newman has failed to uncover any reference to a Royalist colonel bearing the surname in question.[237] The duchess of Newcastle's account of Adwalton Moor, in narrowing down the likely candidates, provides a possible clue:

> At last the pikes of my Lord's army having had no employment all the day, were drawn against the enemy's left wing, and particularly those of *my Lord's own regiment.*[238] (author's italics)

This evidence has guided Stuart Reid to the tentative conclusion that Fairfax's 'Coll: Skirton' was in fact Postumous Kirton, a Royalist infantry colonel who is known to have commanded the earl of Newcastle's regiment of foot.[239] Such an identification would appear both logical and warranted. It was to be approximately thirty years before Sir Thomas Fairfax compiled his recollections of the Yorkshire war. It may well be imagined how, in attempting to recall the name of a particular individual, Fairfax's memory inadvertently failed him. However, in the absence of any corroborative evidence, the true identity of Sir Thomas' 'Coll: Skirton' must remain a doubtful and open question.

Remarkably the mystery of the Royalist pike attack does not end there. An alternative version of events has grown up around the supposed participation of the earl of Newcastle. The Royalist propaganda newsbook *Mercurius Aulicus*, dated Monday 3rd July 1643, proclaimed that at the critical point of the battle:

> he [Newcastle] presently alighted from his Horse, went himself to his Foot, and taking a Pike into his hand, bid them *follow him* assuring them, *not a man should goe further then he himself would lead them*, bidding them now *shew themselves for King Charles and their Countrey and by the help of God they would not leave one Rebel in the North*; wherby the Noble Earle so animated the whole Army that they charged with unexpressible courage, and so amazed the Rebels with the bravery of their coming on, that the Rebels soon fell into confusion, and were not brought againe into rank and order,[240]

A similarly dramatic account of Newcastle's gallantry at Adwalton Moor forms part of an official document by which the earl was elevated to the rank of marquis in October 1643. While the objectivity of the source material is perhaps open to question, there may well be something of substance in these reports. Newcastle, though cautious and inexperienced as a military commander, was nevertheless a courageous leader of men in the heat of battle, and was in fact to demonstrate a similar bravery at Marston Moor in July 1644. Sir Thomas Fairfax, closer to the action than any other eyewitness, save of course for Newcastle himself, conspicuously failed to record the earl's intervention. All that may safely be concluded here is that such an event, if indeed it did take place, would have been entirely consistent with what is known of Newcastle's character.

It is perhaps a pity that so much confusion should attend what turned out to be the turning point of the battle. That Newcastle was heavily involved is certain. Whether he personally led the pike attack is less so. It is conceivable that from the despair of having to reluctantly order the withdrawal of his forces, Newcastle became so enthused by the protestations of 'Skirton' that he readily took his men forward. In the earl's mind such conduct might protect his personal reputation, regardless of the outcome of the battle, from the hostility of many of those who served the King at court. Ultimately, it was to be personal considerations of this kind that prompted Newcastle's period in exile following the loss of the north at Marston Moor.

Whether it was Newcastle, 'Skirton', Kirton, or one as yet unidentified that led the Royalist pike advance, the outcome of the attack, by contrast, is well documented. Sir Philip Warwick's account provides what is perhaps the crucial detail:

> a stand or body of pikes, which being not usefull, where the two armies were stronliest engaged, *came up to the defence of their foot*, and charged by Fairfax's horse, repelling them, gave leisure to rally horse and foot, and by the credit thereof entirely defeated Fairfax's army,[241] (author's italics)

Significantly Warwick described the relative positions of the Royalist pike and musketeers. In order to relieve Newcastle's musketeers the pike had to be commanded forward, thereby confirming that the musketeers, as a consequence of their eviction from the enclosures, were in fact positioned ahead of the pike. Newcastle's musketeers had thus been able to present an uninterrupted wall of fire against the advance of the Parliamentarian left wing commanded by Gifford. As units of the Royalist army could be seen leaving the battlefield, one can imagine how Gifford's men would have probably advanced to within 50 yards of the enemy. They would doubtless have been encouraged by the absence of Royalist cavalry attacks and the continued presence of Sir Thomas Fairfax's horse to their right.

Gifford commanded the 1200 strong Leeds garrison together with five troops of Yorkshire cavalry. Stuart Reid has suggested that Gifford's 1200 foot may have been divided into two battalions; one led by Gifford himself and the other by Sir William Fairfax.[242] Sir William had in fact assisted Sr Thomas Fairfax in the capture of Wakefield. Gifford's advance across Adwalton Moor was probably supported by Lieutenant Colonel Forbes' seven companies of Bradford foot and perhaps a number of Clubmen. Forbes is known to have been taken prisoner during the retreat to Bradford, and so may well have involved his men in the fire fight on Adwalton Moor. In addition the Bradford companies were deployed in the centre of the Parliamentarian line, to the right of the Leeds garrison. It would have been natural enough for these men to follow their Leeds comrades into the thick of the action once Gifford had ordered the left forward.

The Royalist pike attack, when finally it came, was assured and unstoppable. Whether the onslaught was delivered by the entire Royalist pike force, or principally, as the duchess had intimated, by those of Newcastle's own regiment of foot, remains unclear. Yet so effective and successful an advance must surely have consisted of a considerable number of men. Gifford deployed something like 1700 horse and foot against Newcastle's centre, a force that could only have been defeated by a large and committed Royalist attack. Sir Philip Warwick described a failed Parliamentarian cavalry assault, doubtless intended as a final attempt to shatter the momentum of the pike advance before the shock of impact gave the Royalists a potentially decisive advantage. Though the Parliamentarian cavalry charge may have included both wings of the army, for all ten troops of Yorkshire horse were by this time drawn up on the moor, the assault was possibly the work of Gifford's cavalry. Throughout his account Warwick referred only to Lord Fairfax, thereby implying that 'Fairfax's horse' was that under the overall command of the Lord General, and therefore not necessarily a specific reference to those of the right wing led by Sir Thomas Fairfax. The Royalist musketeers, as they were joined by the advancing Royalist pike, most likely accompanied their comrades forward, wielding their muskets as improvised clubs. As a consequence Newcastle almost certainly held a numerical advantage at the point of contact, for the Royalists had perhaps 5000 musket and pike at their disposal. Given the urgency of the situation, it is difficult to believe that Newcastle would not have committed as many men as possible. Once the decision to attack had been taken and the order given, sheer weight of numbers would have become a critical and deciding factor.

Cannons and Cavalry: Royalist Victory

As previously noted, Sir Thomas Fairfax claimed that the Parliamentarian left wing had been compelled to give ground because, at the critical moment, Major General Gifford had failed to mobilize the reserve. The wording of Fairfax's account is significant. 'Our men lost ground' suggests that the initial impact was absorbed, and that though falling back the Parliamentarian left remained capable of further resistance. That Gifford's wing initially held together is supported by Sir Henry Slingsby's version of events:

> now the battle began to decline on the other part, so that their [the Parliamentarian] reserve was sent for.[243]

Here again the impression created is one of Parliamentarian difficulty, hence the need for reinforcement, rather than total crisis. It would appear that Gifford's line recoiled but was not immediately broken, thus allowing some sort of breathing space in which a hurried request for assistance could be made. The Parliamentarian reserve consisted almost entirely of Clubmen, some of whom may have attached themselves to Gifford's initial advance on to the moor. A number might also have responded to the call for reinforcements if the order had in fact been received before Gifford's wing disintegrated. What seems certain is that a command of some kind was given, but that the command was either issued too late or was simply overtaken by the speed of subsequent developments. Sir Thomas Fairfax's accusation that Gifford was at the very least culpable of a most reprehensible dereliction of duty will be examined in greater detail below.

A second 'conspiracy theory', that the Parliamentarian advance was intentionally undermined by a severe shortage of ammunition, was proposed by a resident of Bradford at the time of the battle. Joseph Lister claimed that a certain 'Major Jeffiries' had treacherously withheld vital supplies of ammunition, thereby compelling the Parliamentarian musketeers to slacken their

CANNONS AND CAVALRY

1 Advance of Royalist pike force
   Gifford to give ground.

2 As Gifford forced back, James
   King outflanks Parliamentarian
   left wing.

3 Outflanked, Gifford's wing and
   Clubmen brake and are routed –
   pursued to Bradford.

4 Royalist cannon fire forces Sir
   Thomas Fairfax back to the hedged
   enclosures. Royalist horse again
   attack the 'gate or open place'.

5 Receiving an order to retreat,
   Sir Thomas Fairfax stages a
   fighting withdrawal through the
   enclosures and along Warrens Lane
   to Halifax.

Standard Mile

Old English Mile

Wisket Hill

Bradford to Wakefield Road

Fairfax Hill

650'

700'

500'

600'

600'

650'

500'

GIFFORD

ROYALIST
FOOT

FAIRFAX

HORSE

KING

Hungar Hill

Warrens Lane

HORSE

102

James Nayler

rate of fire. This being perceived and expected by the Royalists, due to prior knowledge, was thus seized upon by the enemy pike who advanced with determination to total victory.[244] Lister, almost certainly reporting the most popular story in circulation immediately after Adwalton Moor, would have known many of the Clubmen who retreated to Bradford in the aftermath of battle. Wild and insupportable claims were an obvious and inevitable consequence of such a crushing military defeat. If Lord Fairfax's musketeers had indeed run short of ammunition, then it may simply have been the case that re-supply could not take place swiftly enough to prevent disaster, despite the best efforts of all concerned. It is perhaps a depressing but all too familiar story that in such desperate circumstances unfounded suspicions quickly attract a more than persuasive credibility.

At precisely the moment that Fairfax and Lister were claiming treachery for the non appearance of the reserve/ammunition, Lieutenant General James King, realizing that the Parliamentarian tide had begun to turn, launched an outflanking manoeuvre against the struggling Parliamentarian left. Thomas Stockdale reported that the Royalists:

> sent some regiments of horse and foot by a lane on the left hand to encompass our army, and fall on their rear, which forced us to retreat, and our men, being unacqainted with field service, would not be drawn off in any order, but instead of marching fell into running; the commanders did their best to stay them, but in vain, for away they went in disorder.[245]

Stockdale clearly believed that it was the Royalist flank attack that finally broke Gifford's men. Stockdale claimed that the Parliamentarians were forced to withdraw, implying that Gifford was attempting to maintain position up to this point, and that an active Parliamentarian resistance continued to take place. What is important to note is that the Parliamentarians began to *retreat*, indicating that Gifford had issued a command to that effect, thereby confirming Stockdale's additional observation that Gifford's officers, in complying with their commander's decision, had attempted to withdraw the men in good order. It may well be the case that the command to retreat was given before Lieutenant General King's forces actually made contact with the rear of the Parliamentarian left. The psychological impact of witnessing the Royalist encirclement, while already subject to severe pressure, would instinctively have provoked such a response. In addition, a withdrawal represented the soundest military option, particularly if the ditch and enclosures could be reached in marching order. In the circumstances a properly conducted retreat could well have saved Gifford's wing and with it the wider Parliamentarian position.

That Lieutenant General King's intervention turned Gifford's attempted resistance into a conscious withdrawal is supported by Sir Thomas Fairfax's recollection of events. Having noted that the Parliamentarians were forced to

View looking south west along Warrens Lane towards Oakwell Hall, the route by which Sir Thomas Fairfax staged a fighting retreat to Halifax.

give ground to the Royalist pike, Fairfax confirmed the difficulty of Gifford's situation:

> Which the enemy seeing, pursued their Advantage by bringing on fresh Troops [ie James King's horse and foot]. Ours being herewith discouraged, began to flee, and so were soone routed.[246]

Sir Thomas underlined the point that the advantage gained by Newcastle's pike became decisive upon the introduction of additional Royalist forces. What both Stockdale and Fairfax demonstrate is that the encircling of Gifford's position defied any rational Parliamentarian response. Within a short space of time the men, overtaken by blind panic, were running out of control, making whatever escape they could.

Though the sight of James King's horse and foot, probably proceeding at a trot rather than a gallop, prompted Gifford's retreat, there may have been an additional factor that helped to transform the retreat into rout. It has been noted that a number of Clubmen were already engaged upon the moor, either as a result of Gifford's initial advance or the call for reinforcements. The propaganda newsbook *Parliament Scout*, dated Thursday 29th June to Thursday 6th July 1643, in describing Lord Fairfax's defeat at Adwalton Moor, reported that the Parliamentarians had at first driven the Royalists from their positions:

but pursued them too far, and thereby gave the enemy opportunity to come in the rear of them, which the club-men perceiving, cryed out, they were betrayed, and fled.[247]

As irregular soldiers the Clubmen may not have deemed themselves to be bound by, or subject to, whatever passed for Parliamentarian military discipline at this point of the war. They were unpaid volunteers, and as such would have regarded their service as a personal matter. While Gifford's officers strove to hold the regular troops in good order, it is possible that the Clubmen were the first to break. Whether on the moor itself or attacked in a position behind Parliamentarian lines, their panic would have quickly communicated itself to Gifford's increasingly desperate men. Like a fire spreading out of control, the Parliamentarian left was quickly consumed by a blind and uncontrollable desire for self preservation. The total disintegration of the Clubmen may also help to explain Thomas Stockdale's somewhat bitter aside, noted above, that they were:

> fit to do execution upon a flying enemy, but unfit for other service, for I am sure they did us none.[248]

Sir Henry Slingsby's comment that Lieutenant General King commanded forward *'all the horse that remained'* may help to clarify the precise line of the flank attack.[249] It is simply not possible that Slingsby was referring to every single Royalist cavalryman still in position. The right wing of horse, deployed to the north of Adwalton Moor, below the level of the battlefield ridge, had yet to become involved in the fighting. In addition, remnants of the left wing also held station on the slopes of Hungar Hill. Slingsby was in fact referring to the cavalry that had been deployed behind the infantry centre, just to the north west of Hungar Hill summit. In the withdrawal ordered by Newcastle following the failed cavalry assaults upon the enclosures, units to the rear of the Royalist line would have been the first to depart. Amongst them a number of the centre horse. Slingsby was therefore making reference to those that *remained*, significantly drawn up close to Hungar Hill, precisely the position from which Newcastle and James King would have directed the battle. King simply took command of the mounted regiments immediately to hand, and followed by the foot not involved in the pike advance, was able to make swift progress across the northern edge of Adwalton Moor and along the Bradford to Wakefield road. The road would have provided relatively easy access to the rear of the Parliamentarian position, passing through the enclosures to either side and over the line of the ditch. If, as some reports claim, Newcastle was at this time upon the moor, at the head of his own regiment of foot, then it would naturally have fallen to James King to support the pike advance with all speed.

While the Royalist foot were driving Gifford's wing to retreat, probably at about the time James King was setting off to outflank the Parliamentarian left, the Royalists finally brought their cannon into action. The gunners had probably fled when Sir Thomas Fairfax's counterattack threatened to encompass their position, now however the sudden and unexpected change of fortune presented an opportunity to bring the ordnance to bear. The account attributed to the earl of Newcastle claimed that once the Royalist foot had been properly deployed and the cannon brought into play the Parliamentarian left was forced to retire within half-an-hour.[250] This might time the disintegration of Gifford's wing to around half past eleven or possibly noon. Certainly by early afternoon it would appear that the outcome of the battle was no longer in doubt. The account described how the cannon was directed against a body of Parliamentarian horse, an event recounted in greater detail by the duchess:

> At which very instant [ie the defeat of Gifford] my Lord [Newcastle] caused a shot or two to be made by his cannon against the body of the enemy's horse, drawn up within cannon shot, which took so good effect, that it disordered the enemy's troops.[251]

The body of Parliamentarian horse to which the duchess referred was in fact that commanded by Sir Thomas Fairfax. With the Royalist pike directed against Gifford's wing, Newcastle's cannon opened up against Fairfax's cavalry which had remained in position to the south of the pike advance. That Sir Thomas recalled the Royalist bombardment in some detail was due to a remarkable act of 'divine intervention' that directly connected the bombardment to the earlier struggle to defend the enclosures against Newcastle's horse:

> While we were engaged in the fight with the Horse that entered the gate, 4 Soldiers had stript *Coll: Herne* naked, as he laid dead on the ground (men still fighting round about him), & so dextrous were these villaines that they had done it, and mounted themselves again before we had beat them off. But after we had beaten them to their Ordinance (as I said) and now returning to our ground again, the Enemy discharged a piece of Cannon in our rear; The bullet fell into Capt: Copleys Troop, in which these 4 men were; Two of them were killed and some hurt, or marke remained on the rest, though dispersed into severall ranks of the Troop which was the more remarkable, We had not yet Martial Law among us, which gave me a good occasion to reprove it, by shewing the Soldiers the sinfulnesse of the Act, and how God would punish when man wanted power to do it.[252]

It would appear that the initial success of the Royalist pike onslaught, swiftly augmented by the introduction of the cannon, persuaded Fairfax that the open moor was no longer tenable. By withdrawing once again to the relative safety of the hedged enclosures, Sir Thomas doubtless reasoned that a rapidly deteriorating situation might well be saved. If the Parliamentarian position were to be stabilized, then Lord Fairfax might retain the option to extricate his men as a body, thereby retaining an army in being.

It is interesting to note that Captain Copley's troop of Parliamentarian horse included one James Nayler, a Yorkshireman who was subsequently to become a prominent leader of the early Quaker movement. Nayler, at the age of 25, had enlisted as a Corporal with Copley's cavalry the day before Sir Thomas Fairfax stormed Wakefield on 21st May 1643.[253] A.J.Hopper's research has confirmed that Christopher Copley was indeed one of Lord Fairfax's cavalry commanders at Adwalton Moor. The remaining nine troops of Yorkshire horse were led by Captain Lawrence Parsons, Sir Thomas Fairfax, Sir Henry Foulis, Sir Thomas Mauleverer, George Gill, John Asquith, John Bright, John Alured and Matthew Alured.[254]

Having returned to the enclosures Fairfax rejoined the Lancashire and Halifax foot who, it must be assumed, had remained among the hedges while Sir Thomas led the cavalry counterattack onto the moor. It is perhaps possible that a small number of infantry may have followed, but without any supporting reference the known evidence would suggest otherwise. Sir Thomas Fairfax continued his account by describing what turned out to be the final phase of the battle:

> The Horse also Charged us again. We not knowing what was done in the left wing, our men mentained their ground, till a command came for us to Retreat having scarce any way now to doe it; the enemy being almost round about us, and our way to Bradford cut off; But there was a lane in the field we were in, which led to Halifax, which, as a happy providence, brought us off without any great losse.[255]

The momentum of the battle had been completely reversed. With the earl of Newcastle and Lieutenant General King driving the Parliamentarian left to destruction, the Royalists launched a renewed cavalry assault upon the enclosures. The attack, undertaken by the left wing, would have included many of those horsemen who had earlier in the day failed to dislodge Fairfax's men. Attempting once again to force a passage through the 'gate or open place' they would have been met, as before, by volleys of Parliamentarian musket fire. Fairfax recalled that the position was successfully maintained until the arrival of an order to retreat. Though it is today difficult to recreate the lines of sight that would have existed across the 17th century battlefield terrain, it is certainly possible that from the enclosures Sir Thomas would have been unable to see precisely what was happening to Gifford's wing, particularly when one considers that the battlefield would have been covered with great clouds of drifting smoke. In addition those Parliamentarians defending the enclosures would have been far too busy fighting to properly comprehend developments beyond the danger of their immediate surroundings.

Confirmation that Sir Thomas Fairfax received a final command to withdraw was provided by Sir Henry Slingsby. Sir Henry described how the spectacle of Lord Fairfax's shattered left wing, pursued all the way back to Bradford by the main body of the Royalist army, prompted a belated attempt to save what was left of the army:

Stockdale who stood at my Lord Fairfax's elbow, adviseth my Lord not to hazard the rest, seeing all was lost, but to shift for himself: so that they were totally routed: and his excellency that night sat down before the town of Bradford.[256]

It was therefore upon Stockdale's judgement that Lord Fairfax despatched a messenger to his son. Thomas Stockdale's description of Lord Fairfax's eventual and probably despairing departure from the field provided an indication of just how precarious the Parliamentarian situation had become:

and with much importunity I persuaded the Lord General to retire, who stayed so long upon the field, until the enemies were got betwixt him and Bradford, yet he took byways and recovered the town.[257]

Having advanced to the field of battle from Bradford, it would have been Sir Thomas Fairfax's initial reaction to direct his retreat back towards the town. With the Halifax and Lancashire foot leading the way north west through the enclosures, Sir Thomas would have attempted to screen the infantry with his five troops of Yorkshire horse. However, it would have soon become apparent that the advance of Newcastle's foot had overtaken Fairfax's position among the hedges. To Sir Thomas' right, as he turned towards Bradford, the Royalist infantry could by now be observed marching over 'Fairfax Hill', an event confirmed by Sir Henry Slingsby:

and also the colours advancing in a thick body up the hill,[258]

To continue towards Bradford would have invited an additional attack from the Royalist forces ahead. The only solution was to find an alternative. Fortunately, a track to the left of the enclosures, which ran on a broadly parallel course to Hodgson Lane, provided Fairfax with an escape route to Warrens Lane and from there to Halifax. It may have been the case that the lane was well known to those of Fairfax's men who hailed from the town. In addition the sudden change of direction would have come as a relief to the Lancashire men, doubtless anxious to retrace their steps westward towards Manchester rather than Bradford. Though hard pressed throughout by Royalist cavalry, Sir Thomas managed to withdraw to Halifax in good order and with a minimum of casualties - a considerable achievement.

That Sir Thomas Fairfax's retreat led the Parliamentarian forces to Warrens Lane is strongly supported by local tradition and archaeological evidence. The track running parallel to Hodgson Lane, referred to above, which enabled Sir Thomas to escape the enclosures for Warrens Lane, lies in the immediate vicinity of the old Bradford to Wakefield railway line. John Riley Robinson described that in the 1870s local residents recalled how the construction of the line had unearthed considerable quantities of battlefield debris. Robinson also confirmed that the fighting had continued into Warrens

Lane, and that the discovery of military archaeology had been a frequent occurrence:

> One old resident, stooping beneath the weight of years, took great pains to point us out where, in Warrin's Lane, the fight had raged so fiercely, and where grape and canister shot, horse shoes of strange forms, and cannon balls, musketry balls, and other relics of the war have been frequently found.[259]

Norrison Scatcherd's early 19th century excursions to Adwalton Moor, noted earlier, also recorded the discovery of battlefield objects north of Warren's Lane. That the locality was the scene of heavy fighting cannot be doubted. Scatcherd's testimony extended to the moorland itself, reporting that swords and pikes had been discovered towards the Adwalton village side of the moor, precisely the area in which Major General Gifford's men had been repelled by the Royalist pike assault.[260]

And so by early afternoon the fighting upon Adwalton Moor battlefield had come to a close. Lord Fairfax's army, on the verge of a remarkable victory, had finally broken. Gifford's men, disordered beyond control, were pursued towards Bradford, while Sir Thomas Fairfax somehow guided the remainder to Halifax. It was left for Newcastle to press home his hard won and scarcely believable victory as best he might. The Royalists had set out that morning intent upon defeating the Fairfaxes by siege, unexpectedly Newcastle had achieved his principal objective in open battle. While the Royalists could look forward with an excited sense of anticipation to the consolidation of their newly won supremacy, more immediate concerns would have occupied the Fairfaxes. As Lord Fairfax and Sir Thomas scrambled away from the field of battle, their principal objective, apart from safety, must have been the salvage of some semblance of an army, and the occupation of a defensible position from which whatever might be saved could be rallied. Thus the bitter and largely unequal struggle that had begun with Newcastle's invasion of Yorkshire in December 1642 appeared to have been brought to a decisive conclusion. Seven months of desperate Parliamentarian resistance finally lay shattered upon a desolate ridge of West Riding moorland. The day would prove to be Newcastle's finest moment.

As was demonstrated in the introduction to this book, the far reaching repercussions of Adwalton Moor were not only to create a new balance of military power in the north of England. Adwalton Moor changed fundamentally the way in which Westminster was in future to prosecute the Parliamentarian war effort. As the afternoon of Friday 30th June 1643 gave way to evening, the dramatic news of Adwalton Moor had yet to reach London, but in the towns and villages of the West Riding, word would have spread rapidly. It is to events across Yorkshire, in the hours and days that followed, that attention is now directed.

CHAPTER 5

AFTERMATH AND CONCLUSION

Casualties

The dead, the wounded, and the captured - casualties are inevitably the most immediate consequence of any military action. And so it was at Adwalton Moor. The majority, as in many other battles of the period, occurred once the outcome of the fighting had been decided. While the vanquished ran for all they were worth, the victors pursued their helpless prey, killing and looting indiscriminately.

In accounting for the Parliamentarian defeat at Adwalton Moor, Joseph Lister - a 17th century native of Bradford - described how the triumphant Royalists had:

> put them to the route, and fell on hacking and hewing down the foot, many being slain, and as many as could escaped to Bradford, whither my Lord Fairfax got also.[261]

Lister was of course referring to the destruction of Major General Gifford's Leeds and Bradford infantry, as well as the Parliamentarian reserve of West Yorkshire Clubmen. Though it was the defeat of these men that decided the fate of the battle, Lister's vivid recollection serves to remind that the casualties at Adwalton Moor were divided into three. Firstly there were the Parliamentarian casualties sustained as a result of the rout and pursuit to Bradford; secondly there were the Parliamentarian casualties inflicted upon the Lancashire and Halifax men as they withdrew via Warrens Lane; and thirdly there were Newcastle's Royalist casualties, sustained during the course of the fighting before victory was finally secured. Estimates of numbers, as might be expected, varied greatly. However it is possible, despite the inevitable exaggeration of partisan accounts, to arrive at plausible conclusions.

The duchess of Newcastle claimed 700 Parliamentarians slain and a further 3000 taken prisoner. The account attributed to her husband, while somewhat less ambitious, still reported 500 dead and 1400 captured.[262] Each of these sources described the casualties to be a consequence of the flight for Bradford, thus confirming that those in question were indeed the soldiers and Clubmen under the command of Major General Gifford. It was noted above that the number of Parliamentarian soldiers ordered onto the moor by Gifford totalled around 1700 horse and foot. Even if as many as 1000 Clubmen are added to this figure, the Royalist casualty estimates - to say the very least - remain implausibly high. In stark contrast Sir Thomas Fairfax reported that:

> Of those that fled there were about 60 killed, & 300 taken prisoner.[263]

This would appear much more reasonable, particularly as Sir Thomas made no attempt to calculate the number of men who, having survived the rout, simply deserted the army and returned to their homes. Sir Thomas Fairfax, not involved in the retreat to Bradford, had therefore no personal interest in the distortion of what were believed to be the correct figures. In addition Thomas Stockdale, without providing totals, appeared to be more concerned with the great many that had been taken prisoner, or had deserted, than the number of Parliamentarian fatalities.[264] Lord Fairfax's Yorkshire army consisted of fewer than 2500 men. Even if one were only to subtract from that Sir Thomas' more moderate estimates of dead and wounded, plus an unknown but presumably significant quantity of deserters, the consequences, as Stockdale suggested, would indeed have been serious. On balance therefore, taking into account the strength of Gifford's wing, it would appear reasonable to accord a greater weight to the testimony provided by Sir Thomas Fairfax.

Thomas Stockdale stated that Sir Thomas successfully withdrew most of the main battle to Halifax.[265] Thus the 2000 or so Lancashire and Halifax men survived largely in tact. Sir Thomas himself recalled that casualties were remarkably few:

> But there was a lane in the field we were in, which led to Halifax, which, as a happy providence, brought us off without any great losse, saving one *Capt: Talbott* & 12 more which were slaine in this last encounter[266]

Thomas Stockdale confirmed the death of Talbot and added that Lieutenant Colonel Forbes, the commander of the seven companies of Bradford foot, had also been taken prisoner. The capture of Forbes, as noted above, lends weight to the view that the Bradford men were part of the ill-fated force that followed Gifford onto Adwalton Moor.

Royalist accounts of Newcastle's casualties, while conceding a significant number of wounded, admitted to surprisingly few dead:

> We had many soldiers hurt, two colonels of horse slain, Heron and Howard, and some officers hurt, as Colonel Throckmorton, Colonel Carnaby, Captain Maison, all recoverable, and not above twenty common soldiers slain.[267]

The injuries sustained by Colonel Throckmorton and Colonel Carnaby are interesting. As both were colonels of horse the probability is that they saw action with either Newcastle's centre or left flank cavalry. Throckmorton would

View looking north west, of the former Crown Point Hotel situated on the Whitehall Road (A58) in Drighlington. The land to the rear of the hotel is said to be the site of a mass burial.

therefore have been in a reasonable position to observe at first hand the distinguished conduct, discussed above, of Sir Philip Monckton.

Though perhaps remarkable, the Royalist claim of a considerable but unknown number of wounded, combined with a surprisingly small total of fatalities - around twenty in an army of at least 10000 - is nevertheless suggestive of precisely the type of battle that the Royalists were in fact compelled to fight. For two hours or thereabouts Newcastle gave ground in exchange for time. At no point during the fighting was a 'last stand' contemplated, even when forced to withdraw to what was to become the final Royalist position upon the moorland 'heights' of Hungar Hill. The dramatic intervention of Newcastle's pike, had it proved unsuccessful, would have amounted to no more than a brief interlude in the earl's controlled and continuing withdrawal from the field of battle. Had that advance stalled, the pike would have withdrawn, Lieutenant General King would have remained upon Hungar Hill, and the Royalist cannon would not have opened fire. The preservation of the Royalist army remained an inviolable tenet throughout the battle, hence the conspicuous absence of the large number of dead that might well have been expected had Newcastle ordered the defence of a fixed field position. Victory at any cost was never an option. Thus while hundreds of Royalist soldiers were quite possibly wounded at Adwalton Moor, a figure of only twenty dead in an army totalling 10000 plus is not nearly as unlikely as one might suppose.

One of the many local traditions associated with Adwalton Moor concerns the location of a mass grave. James Parker, writing in the first decade of the 20th century, reported that:

> The killed and those that died from their wounds were buried near to the wood adjoining Crown Point Grounds, on the other side of the Leeds and Whitehall Road at Drighlington.[268]

The private residence that was once the Crown Point Hotel stands on the north western side of the modern A58 (Whitehall Road) within the village of Drighlington. The land to the rear of the old hotel - the 'Crown Point Grounds' - leads to a wooded area of old coal workings known in the 19th century as the 'Pit Hole Plantation'. It was presumably to this wood, now used as pasture, that Parker was referring. This, interestingly, is the area in which Gifford's retreat from Adwalton Moor became a wholesale rout. As far as the author is aware the authenticity of Parker's claim has not to date been tested by archaeological investigation.[269]

The Retreat to Hull

The four or five days that followed Adwalton Moor quickly determined the way in which the outcome of the fighting was to be imposed upon the Yorkshire war. While the shock waves of battle rapidly engulfed the whole of the county - from the Lancashire border in the west to the port of Hull in the east - Thomas Stockdale's eyewitness account of the fighting was carried safely to Westminster. Though the grave implications of Stockdale's report were to be responsible for the urgent formulation and implementation of a new Parliamentarian strategy of war, it was the frantic pace of events in Yorkshire that determined the extent to which the victorious Royalists would capitalize upon their newly won advantage. An examination of the primary sources demonstrates that the broad chronology of early July 1643 is easily followed and understood. However, while the general development of the situation in Yorkshire is readily apparent, the discrete detail of day to day events is much more difficult to discern. Though each of the eyewitness and contemporary sources contribute important evidence, it is only a close and combined reading that permits a properly intelligible account.

Newcastle's siege of Bradford, an inevitable consequence of Adwalton Moor, prompted the Parliamentarian evacuation of the West Riding and the perilous but ultimately successful retreat of the Fairfaxes to Hull. Both siege and escape are deserving of a full and detailed examination in their own right. However, by concentrating upon a day to day chronology, the reader may better appreciate the relationship of events, and consequently the process by which the fighting at Adwalton Moor produced a much altered map of Yorkshire.[270]

Friday 30th June

Having reached the temporary sanctuary of Bradford during the afternoon of the 30th, it would gradually have become apparent to Lord Fairfax and Thomas Stockdale that Sir Thomas and the main battle had abandoned their attempt to reach the town. Given that Sir Thomas' wing consisted in part of the Halifax men, it must have appeared fairly certain that that was where the younger Fairfax would now be found. While Lord Fairfax and his officers assessed what remained of Gifford's men, it was agreed that Thomas Stockdale should make for Halifax as soon as possible. Anxious to discover precisely what had happened to Sir Thomas Fairfax, the move for Halifax also afforded Stockdale the opportunity to despatch word to Westminster before a Royalist blockade of Bradford could become effective. On arrival at Halifax, Stockdale was informed that the Lancashire men, save for 20 horse and 200 foot, steadfastly refused further service and had departed for Manchester. At least Sir Thomas and the Halifax troops remained intact, determined to continue the struggle.

The earl of Newcastle, arriving before Bradford the same evening, established his quarters to the south of the town at Bowling Hall. The earl planned to position his ordnance the following morning, thereafter to commence a prolonged bombardment. The larger field pieces were difficult to transport and position quickly - realistically a siege couldn't begin to take effect until Saturday morning at the earliest.

Saturday 1st July

Thomas Stockdale's arrival at Halifax on Friday evening meant that Sir Thomas Fairfax was quickly appraised of the desperate situation in Bradford. Sir Thomas characteristically decided to reinforce his father with all speed. Together with the Yorkshire forces that had been successfully withdrawn from Adwalton Moor to Halifax, Sir Thomas managed to get into Bradford during Saturday morning, well before Newcastle was in a position to completely envelop the town.

Once the Royalists had deployed their ordnance upon the hills overlooking Bradford from the south, the bombardment and siege could finally commence. Lord Fairfax and his son faced an impossible situation. Possessing neither the men nor the supplies to withstand a blockade, the Fairfaxes had little prospect of relief. The one remaining Parliamentarian garrison at Hull, due to the hostility of the governor Sir John Hotham, had already declared a refusal to help. However, when all appeared lost, news arrived of the arrest of Hotham on suspicion of treachery. The fortified and impregnable port of Hull was thus placed at the disposal of the Fairfaxes, thereby offering a place of sanctuary should the Parliamentarian position in the West Riding become untenable.

Thomas Stockdale, in a hurried postscript, described how news of

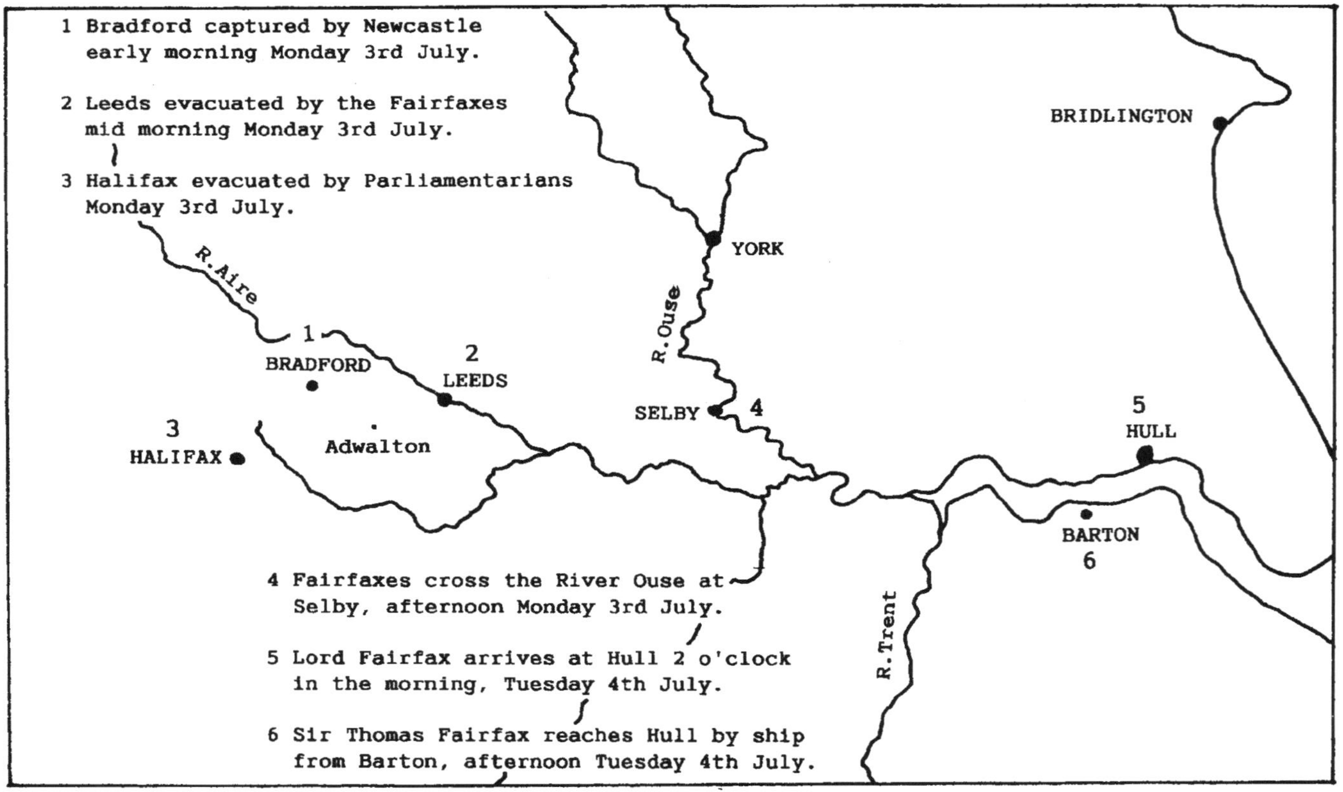
1 Bradford captured by Newcastle early morning Monday 3rd July.
2 Leeds evacuated by the Fairfaxes mid morning Monday 3rd July.
3 Halifax evacuated by Parliamentarians Monday 3rd July.
R.Aire
1
BRADFORD
2
LEEDS
3
HALIFAX
Adwalton
YORK
R.Ouse
SELBY
4
BRIDLINGTON
5
HULL
BARTON
6
R.Trent
4 Fairfaxes cross the River Ouse at Selby, afternoon Monday 3rd July.
5 Lord Fairfax arrives at Hull 2 o'clock in the morning, Tuesday 4th July.
6 Sir Thomas Fairfax reaches Hull by ship from Barton, afternoon Tuesday 4th July.

RETREAT TO HULL

Newcastle's bombardment of Bradford had been brought to Halifax just as he was completing his letter to Westminster. The Royalists had taken possession of several houses just outside the defences and were threatening to break into Bradford itself. Despite fierce Parliamentarian resistance, it was clear that the position was beginning to crumble. It was decided therefore that Lord Fairfax should that night make for Leeds, leaving his son to defend Bradford with 800 foot and 60 horse. Given the deteriorating situation, Sir Thomas must have been aware that his role was in fact to cover his father's escape, rather than to hang onto the town at all costs. The only real refuge was clearly Hull. Unless the Fairfaxes were prepared to abandon Bradford altogether, the inescapable reality was that, in addition to the capture of the town, they themselves would soon fall victim to Newcastle's siege.

Sunday 2nd July

After the bombardment of Saturday, Newcastle offered a cease-fire in order to negotiate the surrender of the town. In the absence of Lord Fairfax - who was by this time at Leeds - Sir Thomas agreed to the earl's request in the hope that the inhabitants of Bradford might be saved by some honourable agreement. Newcastle may have been concerned to prevent the unnecessary and inevitable bloodshed that would have resulted from fierce hand to hand street fighting. In addition the earl may have considered the offer to negotiate to be no more than that required of a Christian gentleman on the Sabbath.

As the talking dragged on throughout the day, Sir Thomas became increasingly convinced that the negotiations were in fact no more than a smoke screen by which the Royalists were masking preparations for a final assault. By nightfall Newcastle's men had closed in on both ends of the town, only heavy fighting repulsed two concerted Royalist attacks. With the truce shattered it was clear that the Parliamentarian position was now hopeless. Fairfax and his senior officers therefore took the unavoidable decision to evacuate Bradford before daybreak brought the inevitable fall of the town.

Monday 3rd July

In the early hours of Monday morning, shortly before dawn, the Parliamentarian horse and foot, by taking separate routes, attempted to fight their way through the blockade to Leeds. In the face of overwhelming odds the infantry advance stalled and the majority were forced back into Bradford. The cavalry, fairing little better, were soon routed and captured by units of Royalist horse. Of the Parliamentarian infantry, 80 somehow reached Leeds, while only six cavalrymen - including Sir Thomas Fairfax, Sir Henry Foulis, and Major General Gifford - successfully managed to escape. Captain Mudd, who had taken part in the initial skirmish for Wisket Hill, died in the attempted breakout while Sir Thomas' wife was also taken prisoner.

After daybreak Newcastle's forces entered Bradford unopposed, taking around 300 Parliamentarian foot captive. The citizens were fearful of bloody revenge for the manner in which the Royalist attack upon the town of 18th December 1642 had been brutally repulsed. Newcastle however ordered that quarter should be given and all were unexpectedly spared. The earl's decision, according to a well known local tradition, was prompted by a disturbed night's sleep in which a ghostly apparition had warned that the inhabitants of Bradford should be mercifully treated.

Sir Thomas and his bedraggled companions arrived in Leeds early on Monday morning. Within two hours a Council of War had decided that as Royalist forces would shortly encircle the town, the only option was to make for Hull. Lord Fairfax and Sir Thomas, accompanied by three or four troops of horse, 200 dragoons and 300 foot, managed to get as far a Selby without further incident. Meanwhile Royalist prisoners in Leeds broke out of gaol, taking possession of the arms and ammunition that the Fairfaxes had been compelled to leave behind.

At Selby Sir Thomas and his father were attacked by Royalist cavalry from the nearby garrison at Cawood Castle. After fierce street fighting Sir Thomas, despite a serious wound, drove the enemy to retreat, thus permitting the bulk of the small Parliamentarian force to cross the Ouse by boat. Due to overcrowding however some men were drowned, leaving the horses to swim the river as best they could.

Upon receiving news that Leeds had been occupied by escaped Royalist prisoners, Newcastle despatched reinforcements to secure the town. Later the same day the earl was informed of the Parliamentarian evacuation of Halifax, while the small garrison defending Lord Fairfax's house at Denton was also captured.

Once across the Ouse Lord Fairfax made for Hull. Sir Thomas, following at a distance with a detachment of horse, was continually harried from all directions by Royalist patrols.

Tuesday 4th July

Lord Fairfax's contingent, having crossed the Ouse ahead of Sir Thomas' party, forged ahead without delay. Making good progress across the level terrain of the East Riding, the Lord General finally reached the safety of Hull at around 2 o'clock on Tuesday morning.

Sir Thomas meanwhile had become engaged in a desperate race to evade capture. Having left his young daughter in the temporary safety of an isolated house in the vicinity of the River Trent, Sir Thomas sent to Hull a messenger requesting a passage across the Humber from the north Lincolnshire ferry town of Barton. In a final attempt to escape the enemy, it appears that Sir Thomas once more crossed the Ouse - thus opening a route to the south bank of the Humber. With fewer than 100 horse remaining, and pursued relentlessly by

Royalist cavalry, Sir Thomas reached Barton in time to board for Hull, under the welcome protection of the ship's guns. It was a narrow and important escape, the significance of which - as will be discussed below - has been generally overlooked.

Wednesday 5th July

Though the Fairfaxes, with what remained of their decimated forces, had reached the safety of Hull, all of Yorkshire now lay in Royalist hands. This in effect meant that the north had fallen to Newcastle - a long awaited strategic breakthrough of enormous significance. Hundreds of miles away at Westminster, Thomas Stockdale's letter, having reached the capital from Halifax, was read to a deeply shocked Parliament. While Lords and Commons urgently set in train the process by which the Scots would enter the war, Sir Philip Warwick described the territorial impact of Adwalton Moor:

> This victory made the Earle seem Lord of the North; for from Berwick to Newcastle, and from Newcastle to Newark, all was the King's, and the cheife Nobility and Gentry engaged in his army, and several towns and castles garrison'd for him; particularly the town of Newcastle, the city of York, and the Earle of Newcastle's own house, Welbeck; the Lord Frenchevill's house, Staley; and the Earle of Chesterfield's, Shelford; and that most important garrison, Newark.[271]

Conclusion

It has been a principal purpose of this book to establish a clear and unequivocal case for the elevation of Adwalton Moor to the status of major Civil War event. It is the contention of the present writer that the real significance of the battle has been overlooked, and that as a consequence, there has been a real failure to properly understand the influence of Adwalton Moor beyond the theatre of operations in which the battle was fought.

It has been demonstrated in the introduction to this book that the magnitude of the Parliamentarian defeat at Adwalton Moor altered the direction of the English Civil War. The battle compelled Westminster to forge a military and religious alliance with Scotland, creating a new balance of power in which armed Royalism in the north of England was destroyed. This book has sought to recognize, for the first time since Clarendon, the direct relationship between the Scottish alliance and the battle of Adwalton Moor. A relationship, it has therefore been argued, that establishes Adwalton Moor as one of the Civil War's principal battles. As a consequence it is appropriate to reconstruct the battle itself in the kind of detail that signals and underlines the importance of the fighting.

The overriding impression of Adwalton Moor is one in which, to borrow an old and much used cliché, victory was snatched from the jaws of defeat. It took a surprising and unexpected turn of events to alter the course and outcome of the battle. As has been demonstrated, the determination of the Parliamentarian army had persuaded the Royalists to order a tactical withdrawal, apparently leaving the field and the honour of the day to the Fairfaxes. Yet within the space of perhaps thirty or so minutes the situation had changed beyond recognition; half of the Parliamentarian army had broken and were fleeing for Bradford, while the remaining half had begun a fighting withdrawal towards Halifax. In attempting to account for this Parliamentarian disaster, within the context of the battle narrative itself, the views of Thomas Stockdale and Sir Thomas Fairfax have briefly been touched upon. Stockdale *appeared* to blame the impetuous advance of Gifford's wing, while Fairfax went as far as to accuse Gifford of treachery. Thus it has long been the case that Major General Gifford has shouldered the blame for defeat at Adwalton Moor. However, it is in fact much more likely that Gifford was simply a scapegoat, and that the accusations against him no more than a smoke screen to cover - in the bitter aftermath of defeat - a dispute about the leadership of the Parliamentarian army.

Thomas Stockdale's account of Adwalton Moor, written within hours of the battle, is charged with the frustrations and bitterness of a cruel and decisive defeat. Stockdale's description of the fighting in fact contained a fairly unambiguous assertion that Lord Fairfax himself was principally to blame. In reporting the composition of the Parliamentarian army, Stockdale had bluntly commented:

> The horse were commanded by Sir Thomas Fairfax, who should have led the main battle, if the Lord General could have been persuaded to absent himself.[272]

Thus it would appear that an attempt had been made, in advance of the planned attack upon Howley Hall, to encourage Lord Fairfax to relinquish overall command in favour of his son. While Stockdale's caustic aside may simply indicate a dissatisfaction with Lord Fairfax's performance at Adwalton Moor, it nevertheless hints at a wider discontent that may have been simmering for some time. Stockdale's contrast of the ill advised advance of the outnumbered Parliamentarian left onto Adwalton Moor, with the success of Sir Thomas Fairfax's retreat to Halifax, reads as a subtle justification for his earlier imputation of Lord Fairfax's military competence. Stockdale's frustration was born of the knowledge that the battle had all but been won. Had the Parliamentarians remained within their defensive positions, Newcastle would have completed the Royalist withdrawal, thus leaving Lord Fairfax's army intact. Though the intended attack upon Howley Hall had been overtaken by events, the fighting of Adwalton Moor had almost driven Newcastle from the field. While the Parliamentarians couldn't hope to destroy the entire Royalist army, the assault upon Howley Hall had been intended to disrupt once again

Newcastle's Yorkshire campaign. This was very nearly achieved at Adwalton Moor. Had Newcastle withdrawn, the Royalists would have been compelled to rethink their strategy, while the resulting breathing space would have presented a further opportunity to reinforce Lord Fairfax's army.

Having come agonizingly close to success, Stockdale may have felt it his duty to apportion blame in the interests of the future Parliamentarian war effort. Stockdale clearly felt that Sir Thomas Fairfax, had he taken command, would have that day won a famous victory. It may also have been the case that these disagreements and consequent irritations continued unabated during the battle itself. Stockdale's impatience with the Lord General was highlighted by the difficulty with which Stockdale finally persuaded the old lord to vacate the field. Thomas Stockdale certainly believed that the manner in which the battle had been lost thoroughly justified the attempt to relieve the Lord General of overall command.

While it is certainly possible to empathise with Stockdale, it is perhaps unfair to level too much criticism at Lord Fairfax. Though Ferdinando's generalship may well have left something to be desired, particularly at what turned out to be the critical point in the fighting, the realities of 17th century warfare provide mitigating circumstances. The Parliamentarian line of battle extended for almost three quarters of a mile, as the army pushed forward the right wing advanced further than the left. In the noise, confusion and smoke of 17th century combat, it would gradually have become impossible to retain overall control of events. Decisions were naturally delegated by the practicalities of warfare to colonels and, in some cases, to captains. As battle progressed fighting tended to become more and more localized until one side or the other forced an advantage that could be exploited. Lord Fairfax was probably completely unaware that Major General Gifford intended to order an advance onto Adwalton Moor. Indeed, Gifford himself almost certainly took the decision quickly, intending to support and capitalize upon Sir Thomas Fairfax's success, a success that had only just become apparent to Gifford's wing of the battlefield. It is worth remembering that the manner in which the Fairfaxes had thus far prosecuted the war had depended to a large extent upon risk and daring. As noted above, this was a point readily conceded by Clarendon. The Fairfaxes were quite clearly in a desperate situation; they and their men were consequently prepared to take desperate action. Having taken that desperate action - action that appeared to have prompted a Royalist retreat - could any 17th century commander have realistically legislated for the turn of events that was to decide the outcome of Adwalton Moor? Sir Philip Warwick - quoted earlier but worth repeating – emphasized that:

> where-in this is *memorable*, that when the day seemed lost on his side [Newcastle's], and many of his horse and foot standing *doubtful and wavering*....[273] [Author's italics].

surely confirms the point that the wholly unpredictable is always likely to tilt the balance one way or the other.

While Thomas Stockdale implied that military incompetence had defeated the Parliamentarian army, Sir Thomas Fairfax and Joseph Lister appeared convinced that treachery had in fact provided the Royalists with victory. Sir Thomas Fairfax, without the slightest equivocation, not only pinned the blame for Adwalton Moor on Gifford, but also accused the Major General of treacherously delaying the planned attack on Howley Hall. Fairfax claimed that his father had directed Gifford to prepare the army to march at 4 o'clock in the morning, but that Gifford had so delayed the ordering of the men that the Royalists had somehow been provided with both prior notice and time to prepare their positions. Sir Thomas continued by accusing unnamed officers of intentionally failing to mobilize the Parliamentarian reserve, and Gifford himself of an unspecified dereliction of duty. Broadly similar charges were made by Joseph Lister, a puritan inhabitant of Bradford at the time of the battle:

> But there was one Major Jeffiries, keeper of the ammunition, who proving treacherous, and withholding it from the Parliament's men, who called for it, and could get none, were forced to slacken their firing; which the enemy perceiving, and probably had private notice from the traitor,[274]

Lister's 'Major Jeffiries' might have been a confused reference to Major General Gifford or one of the unnamed officers accused by Sir Thomas Fairfax. Whatever the true identity of 'Jeffiries' the notion that the Parliamentarian army was undone by treachery appears to have enjoyed some currency in the aftermath of defeat.

In order to make sense of Fairfax's claims it is necessary to consider the wider context of the Yorkshire war. Though Thomas Stockdale complained that the Royalist army had received intelligence of Parliamentarian intentions, it was Sir Thomas Fairfax who insinuated that the breaching of security was the work of a traitor. Yet there is nothing in Gifford's conduct, either before or after Adwalton Moor, to suggest that the Major General's commitment to the Parliamentarian cause was in any way questionable. On the day of the battle Lord Fairfax's march to Howley had been delayed by a considerable and possibly decisive margin. Once the fighting had begun it was the exposure of Gifford's wing that effectively defeated the Parliamentarian army. The common denominator in each of these occurrences was, of course, Major General Gifford. However given Gifford's character and general conduct before, during and after Adwalton Moor, it would appear reasonable to suspect an alternative explanation for Sir Thomas' accusations; particularly when one considers Sir Henry Slingsby's observation that the earl of Newcastle had remained completely unaware of any Parliamentarian plan to assault Howley Hall.

Throughout the Battle of Adwalton Moor Sir Thomas Fairfax characteristically led his men from the front. Whether defending or attacking, Sir Thomas was always to be found amid the fiercest fighting. Fairfax knew just how close the Parliamentarian army had come to victory, and in this he shared Stockdale's frustration. However Sir Thomas, apparently convinced that betrayal had led to defeat, was unable - or perhaps unwilling - to entertain the possibility that responsibility for the disaster might lie elsewhere. As an experienced soldier and commander, Fairfax would have fully understood the critical role of a General. It is, one suspects, almost inconceivable that at some point Sir Thomas did not reflect upon his father's leadership at Adwalton Moor. But even if Fairfax secretly shared Stockdale's opinion of the Lord General, it would naturally have been unthinkable to break the bonds of family loyalty by blaming his father. The Fairfaxes had proudly, if reluctantly, taken up the Parliamentarian cause in 1642 - by the middle of 1643 they had in essence become Parliamentarianism in Yorkshire. Deserted, as they doubtless saw it, by Sir Hugh Cholmley and then the Hothams, the Fairfaxes became increasingly reliant upon their own counsel and each other. In a war that was to become famous for dividing brother from brother and father from son, Ferdinando and Thomas stood side by side. In such circumstances it is perhaps understandable that Sir Thomas should attempt to explain a *family* defeat by laying blame elsewhere.

From the Royalist perspective the euphoria of victory was immediately diluted by the dramatic escape of the Fairfaxes to Hull. Though Adwalton Moor finally provided Newcastle with the breakthrough he so desperately required, the Royalist failure to apprehend the Lord General and his son ensured that the war in Yorkshire would effectively continue unresolved. Without the enterprise and daring of Ferdinando, and particularly Sir Thomas, it is questionable whether the Parliamentarian forces remaining within the walls of Hull would have posed the kind of threat that was to prompt the outright refusal of Newcastle's Yorkshire commanders to move south while the town remained in Fairfax hands. It would have been a credible military option, had the Fairfaxes been apprehended, for Newcastle to mask the port while the bulk of the Royalist army marched through Lincolnshire towards the counties of the Eastern Association.

Consequent Royalist irritation is evident in the accounts of both the duchess of Newcastle and Sir Henry Slingsby. Despite explicit orders to mobilize Royalist cavalry units at York, the Fairfaxes, upon reaching Selby, were able to hold off the unsupported horse from Cawood garrison while making good their escape. The duchess complained that:

> though my Lord, knowing they [the Fairfaxes] would make their escape thither [Hull], as having no other place of refuge to resort to, sent a letter to York to the Governor of that city, to stop them in their passage; yet by neglect of the post, it coming not timely enough to his hands, his design was frustrated.[275]

Sir Henry Slingsby related much the same story, placing particular emphasis upon the importance of intercepting the Fairfaxes before they crossed the Ouse at Selby:

> when this was known to my Lord of Newcastle that my Lord of Fairfax was making with all speed for Hull, he sends after him, & his orders to York, to make out all the horse they could to stop him at Selby; but as orders are ill obey'd & slowly taken, they come to late; yet some of our horse jumps with him at Selby, & in the Town skirmages, but we are put to retreat.[276]

The implications of this Royalist failure have generally been overshadowed by the story of the escape itself. Anyone familiar with the Civil War in Yorkshire is almost certain to be acquainted with Sir Thomas' daring and breathless race for freedom. Accounts of the northern campaign often fail to appreciate the significance of this missed opportunity. Given the subsequent role of Sir Thomas in the Yorkshire campaign of 1643/1644 and the wider conflict in 1645, his removal from events would surely have produced a radically different war.

There remains one particular aspect of the battle of Adwalton Moor which requires further comment and perhaps clarification. It will be recalled that the deployment of the Royalist army is here argued to have extended beyond the ridge upon which the battle was fought, thereby excluding from combat those Royalist units so positioned. The width of Adwalton Moor was simply insufficient to allow upon it the cavalry of Newcastle's right flank. Instead the horse were forced to deploy below the level of the ridge, on the falling ground to the north of the moor, from where they would have been unable to follow events on the battlefield itself. One may reasonably wonder why so large a component of Newcastle's army was not commanded into action at some opportune moment. The answer must be, at least as far as the Royalists were concerned, that no such opportune moment presented itself during the course of the fighting. Firstly, there was no space on the ridge for an additional 2000 horse - at any time in the battle. Even when Royalist cavalry deployed on the left flank were chased across the moor by Sir Thomas Fairfax, their immediate replacement in the line of battle, had it been required, would have been undertaken by the mounted regiments positioned to the rear of Newcastle's infantry centre. At this point in the battle the decision had been taken to withdraw forces rather than reposition them. Secondly, the terrain in which they were deployed did not permit the free movement of cavalry. Thirdly, the predominant Royalist requirement for much of the battle was in fact musket armed foot. Finally, the failure of two determined Royalist cavalry assaults upon the heavily defended enclosures convinced Newcastle and Lieutenant General James King that the preservation and good order of remaining forces was paramount.

Though the 2000 or so horse of the Royalist right flank stood by while events unfolded out of sight upon the battlefield ridge, their exclusion from combat did not leave Newcastle short of manpower. The Royalist's committed in the region of 8000 men to the fighting of Adwalton Moor, a force that represented a two to one superiority in troop numbers. What Newcastle lacked was infantry firepower - though ultimately it was to be infantry muscle power, at push of pike, that turned the tide of battle. Adwalton Moor serves to underline the research of P.R.Newman, referred to earlier, that the Royalist preponderance in mounted men constituted a fundamental military weakness. It was this deficiency in musket armed foot that forced Newcastle to give ground, and it was only after the failure of the horse to make any headway that the remaining pike were introduced, and that against the better judgement of the senior commanders. Had it not been for the illusive 'Skirton', one would today be discussing the extent to which a serious imbalance of Royalist forces at Adwalton Moor had contributed to Lord Fairfax's remarkable victory.

Though historians have often been critical of Newcastle's performance as a military commander, Adwalton Moor nevertheless remains the most significant of the earl's martial achievements. The King, in grateful recognition, bestowed the title of marquis, while in the Royalist capital of Oxford, public celebrations proclaimed Newcastle's great victory in the north:

> This newes as it was entertained with Belles and Bonfires, so a *true* Thanksgiving for it was appointed on the Thursday following to be held in all the principall Churches of *Oxford*, which was performed accordingly.[277]

A more private celebration was recorded by Jane Cavendish, the earl's eldest daughter. Born to Newcastle's first wife Elizabeth Howard (nee Basset) in 1622, Jane developed, like her father before her, a passion for poetry. Aged 21 at the time of Adwalton Moor, Jane composed a deeply felt verse of thanks to commemorate her father's safe deliverance from the field of battle:

On the 30th June, to God

> This day I will my thankes sure now declare
> By Sermons, Bounties of each harty prayer
> To thee great God who gave thy bounty large
> Saveing my ffather from the Enemies charge
> Not onely soe, but made him victour leade
> Chargeing his Enemies wth linckes of lead
> To let them now thy workes plaine see
> Sayeing my little flock shall Conquerers bee
> And it was true ffairfax was then more great
> But yet Newcastle made him sure retreat.
> Therefore Ile keepe this thy victory's day
> If not in publique, by some private way
> In spite of Rebells, who thy Lawes deface
> And blott the footesteps of thy sonns blood trace
> Thus will my soules devotion to thee send
> And all my life in thankes a votery spend.[278]

Though more than 350 years have elapsed since the events of the English Civil War changed the course of British history, the Civil War itself remains a battlefield over which fighting continues to this day. Historians, engaged in a perpetual war of words, have of course devoted enormous energy to many aspects of the Great Rebellion, particularly the origins and causes of the political breakdown that resulted in internecine conflict. In addition, the passions aroused in the 17th century are today physically apparent in the large numbers of English Civil War re-enactors, more numerous than for any other period of the nation's past. And finally, several Civil War battlefield sites are once again the scene of conflict as developers and conservationists struggle to determine the future of these historic landscapes. This, sadly, is an issue of particularly pressing relevance for Adwalton Moor.

In 1995 English Heritage published its *Register of Historic Battlefields*. Though the register identified over forty sites of national importance, the document itself carried with it no powers of statutory protection. The register is only permitted to function as a guide and adjunct to the normal planning process, thus leaving historic battlefield sites in the domain of, and subject to, development applications. At the time of writing a section of Adwalton Moor battlefield is itself subject to such an application. The success or otherwise of the campaign to preserve the site will depend to a considerable extent upon the degree to which the land in question can be shown to have been part of the wider battlefield. While there are grounds for optimism, it remains the case that the true extent of Adwalton Moor battlefield has yet to be 'scientifically' established. The lack of an extensive and systematic archaeological survey means that grey areas around the periphery of the site will continue to fall prey to piecemeal development. A great deal of the battlefield has already been lost, but much of real value remains, sufficient to provide a more comprehensive understanding of precisely what took place on Friday 30th June 1643.

The recovery of archaeological evidence would clearly serve to strengthen the hand of those fighting to preserve that which remains of Adwalton Moor battlefield. The land over which our ancestors fought, for either the earl of Newcastle or Lord General Ferdinando Fairfax, still retains many of its historic secrets. Archaeology may yet provide the ammunition that produces victory in what is in effect a second battle of Adwalton Moor. The battle of 30th June 1643 changed the course of the English Civil War, it is to be hoped that the second battle may hasten the day when the protection of the law is extended to include the soil upon which the nation's history was made.

APPENDIX

New Archaeological Evidence

The recovery, during April 2003, of battlefield debris in Drighlington village by West Yorkshire Archaeological Services provides further supporting evidence for the interpretation of the battle given in chapter four.

The demolition of 163 Moorside Road enabled a metal detecting survey to be undertaken ahead of proposed redevelopment work. Moorside Road runs along the north western fringe of Hungar Hill, linking the site of old Adwalton village with the south east corner of modern Adwalton Moor. The road, it was argued in chapter four, marks the approximate line of the final Royalist position upon the slopes of Hungar Hill. Therefore, the site of 163 Moorside Road, which would have been occupied in 1643 by part of Newcastle's infantry centre, is clearly interesting and important.

The metal detecting survey recovered twelve small finds, including six musket balls, one pistol round, and three metal buttons - precisely the kind of evidence indicative of 17th century military activity. In chapter four it was argued that the site would have formed part of the Royalist line attacked by Major General Gifford's Leeds and Bradford infantry, an assertion lent additional weight as a consequence.

Given the success of this particular survey, it is to be hoped that any future demolition work at Adwalton Moor battlefield would be accompanied by similar archaeological investigation.

NOTES

Introduction

1. Clarendon, *History of the Rebellion*, ed W Macray (Oxford, 1888), Vol.VIII, p89.
2. S R Gardiner, *History of the Great Civil War 1642-1649* (London, 1901), Vol I 1642-1644, p175 & p178.
3. J H Hexter, *The Reign of King Pym* (London, 1941), p134.
4. C V Wedgwood, *The King's War 1641-1647* (London, 1958), p239.
5. A Woolrych, *Battles of the English Civil War* (London, 1961), pp49-50.
6. J Jones, 'The War in the North. The Northern Parliamentary Army in the English Civil War 1642-1645' (Ontario D Phil., 1991), p123.
7. P Haythornthwaite, *The English Civil War 1642-1651. An Illustrated Military History* (London, 1994), p68
8. M Bennett, *The English Civil War* (London, 1995), p46.
9. L. Kaplan, 'Steps to War: the Scots and Parliament 1642-1643', *Journal of British Studies*, Vol. IX No.2 (May 1970), pp60-61.
10. *Journal of the House of Commons* (JHC), Vol.3, 1642-1644, p155.
11. Historical Manuscripts Commission (HMC), Portland Mss., Vol. 1, p718.
12. JHC, Vol.3, p155.
13. *Journal of the House of Lords* (JHL), Vol.6, 1643-1644, p122.
14. British Library Thomason Tract (BLTT) E59 (12).
15. Clarendon, *Rebellion*, Vol. VII, p135.
16. Gardiner, *Great Civil War*, p67.
17. See, for example, Haythornthwaite, *English Civil War,* p59; Bennett, *English Civil War* p44; PR Newman, *Atlas of the English Civil War* (London, 1985), p25 & p39.
18. *Life of William Cavendish Duke of Newcastle*, ed CH Firth (London, 1906), p29n.
19. *Ibid.*, p26.
20. *English Historical Review*, Vol. II (January, 1887), p172.
21. *Life of William Cavendish*, ppx-xi.
22. *Ibid.*,p29.
23. Clarendon, *Rebellion,* Vol. VII, p177 & Vol. VIII, p86.
24. *Life of William Cavendish,* p29n.
25. *Dictionary of National Biography* (DNB), (London, 1899), p437.
26. *Life of William Cavendish,* p29n.
27. *Ibid.*, pp29-30.
28. Clarendon, *Rebellion*, Vol. VII, p177.
29. *Life of William Cavendish*, p29n.
30. *Ibid.*, pxi.
31. PR Newman, *The Old Service* (Manchester, 1993), pp263-264.
32. Clarendon, *Rebellion*, Vol. VIII, p86.

33. See, for example, *The Civil Wars. A Military History of England, Scotland, and Ireland 1638-1660,* ed. J Kenyon & J Ohlmeyer (Oxford, 1998).

34. The process given here by which the English Parliament and the Scottish Presbyterians became religious and military allies is based on the published research of Lawrence Kaplan (for full reference see note 9 above).

35. Kaplan, *Journal of British Studies,* pp54-56.

36. *Ibid.,* p57.

37. York Minster Library, C.W.T. 43-03-11, "Saye & Sele William Fiennes, Viscount - The Queens Proceedings in Yorkshire"(1643), p3.

38. Kaplan, *Journal of British Studies,* p61.

39. *Ibid.,* p60.

40. J R Robinson, 'The Battle of Adwalton Moor', *North of England Tractates* No. 20 (1887), p3.

Chapter One

41. Thomas Lord Fairfax, 'A Short Memorial of the Northern Actions During The War There, From The Year 1642 Till 1644', *Yorkshire Archaeological Journal* (YAJ), Vol. VIII (1884), pp213-214.

42. CR Markham, *Life of the Great Lord Fairfax* (London, 1870), p392-394.

43. YAJ, Vol. VIII , p199-200.

44. Markham, *Lord Fairfax*, p392.

45. H M C, Portland Mss., Vol. I, pp717-719.

46. A Hopper, *'The Readiness of the People': The Formation and Emergence of the Army of the Fairfaxes, 1642-1643,* (York, 1997), pp7-10.

47. *The Diary of Sir Henry Slingsby*, ed.Rev D Parsons (London, 1836), pp96-97.

48. The provenance of the Nalson collection is more fully discussed in HMC, Portland Mss., Vol. I, ppiii-vi.

49. For an analysis of the earl's military prowess at Adwalton Moor see chapter four.

50. *Life of William Cavendish,* pp24-25.

51. PR Newman comments, 'The entire memoir reads like an apology on Newcastle's behalf, drawn up from his reminiscences and a few available documents'. PR Newman, *Marston Moor, 2 July 1644: The Sources and the Site* (York, 1978), p9.

52. *Life of William Cavendish*, pxliii & pxlvii.

53. *Ibid.,* pix.

54. *Ibid.,* pvii.

55. *Ibid.,* Appendix XI, pp215-217.

56. *Ibid.,* p215.

57. CR Markham provided a brief explanation. Markham, *op.cit.,* p103.

58. *The Diary of Sir Henry Slingsby*, pp96-97.

59. DNB, p376.

60. Clarendon, *Rebellion*, Vol. XV, p100.

61. For example: JT Cliffe, *The Yorkshire Gentry: from the Reformation to the Civil War,* (London, 1969).

62. GR Smith, *Without Touch of Dishonour. The Life and Death of Sir Henry Slingsby 1602-1658.* (Kineton, 1968), p33.

63. *Ibid.*

64. PR Newman, 'The Royalist Army in Northern England 1642-5' (York D Phil., 1978), p191.

65. J Jones, 'The War in the North. The Northern Parliamentary Army in the English Civil War 1642-5' (Ontario D Phil., 1991), p105-106.

66. Brown's comments occur in section 3.6 of a document prepared by English Heritage for a now aborted public enquiry into the proposed development, since withdrawn, of part of the present day battlefield site.

67. *Diary of Sir Henry Slingsby*, p95.

68. J Rushworth, *Historical Collections*, (London, 1721), Vol. V, p279.

69. DNB, p419.

70. PR Newman, *Companion to the English Civil Wars* (Oxford, 1990), p134.

71. DNB, p419-420.

72. *Ibid.*, p420.

73. *Ibid.*, p422.

74. Cited in RC Richardson, *The Debate on the English Revolution Revisited* (London, 1977), p17.

75. Rushworth, *Collections*, Vol. V, p279.

76. Sir Philip Warwick, *Memoires of the Reign of King Charles I* (London, 1701), pp257-258.

77. DNB, p437.

78. *Ibid.*, pp438-439.

79. BLTT E59 (12).

80. BLTT E60 (18).

81. Gardiner, *Great Civil War,* pvi.

82. BLTT E59 (21).

83. D Cooke, *The Forgotten Battle: The Battle of Adwalton Moor* (Heckmondwike, 1996).

84. N Scatcherd, *The History of Morley* (Leeds, 1830), pp272-281.

85. J James, *The History and Topography of Bradford* (London, 1841), pp138-139.

86. J James, *Continuation and Additions to the History of Bradford and its Parish* (Bradford, 1866), pp62-64.

87. Markham, *Lord Fairfax*, pp103-107.

88. Robinson, *North of England Tractates*, p3

89. E Lamplough, *Yorkshire Battles* (Hull, 1891), pp192-195.

90. J Parker, *Illustrated Rambles from Hipperholme to Tong, Bradford, Percy Lund* (1904), pp297-300.

91. H P Kendall, 'Local Incidents in the Civil War', *Transactions of the Halifax Antiquarian Society* (1909), pp26-28.

92. A H Burne & P Young, *The Great Civil War. A Military History of the First Civil War 1642-1646* (London, 1959), pp60-63.

93. P Young & R Holmes, *The English Civil War. A Military History of the Three Civil Wars* (London, 1974), pp111-113.

94. For P R Newman's treatment of Adwalton Moor see, Newman, 'Royalist Army', pp184-192.

95. I E Broadhead, *Yorkshire Battlefields* (London, 1989), pp146-149.

96. M Bennett, *Traveller's Guide to the Battlefields of the English Civil War* (Exeter, 1990), pp58-64.

97. For J Jones treatment of Adwalton Moor see, Jones, 'War in the North', pp106-117.

98. English Heritage, *Battlefield Report: Adwalton Moor 1643* (London, 1995).

99. English Heritage, *British Battles* (London, 1996) pp114-115.

100. Cooke, *Forgotten Battle*.

101. S Reid, *All The King's Armies* (Staplehurst, 1998). For Reid's treatment of Adwalton Moor see pp76-79.

Chapter Two

102. The most famous portrait of the earl of Newcastle is that given by Clarendon. Despite praise for his 'invincible courage', it is difficult not to conclude that Clarendon believed Newcastle to be an unwise choice as Northern General. Clarendon, *Rebellion*, Vol. VIII, pp85-88. For a twentieth century assessment of Newcastle as General of the Northern Royalist army and Colonel of his own regiment, see Newman, *Old Service*, particularly pp.79-80 & 261-266.

103. *Life of William Cavendish*, pp12-13.

104. *Ibid.,* p13.

105. Clarendon, *Rebellion*, Vol. VIII, p84.

106. For a facsimile reprint of the declaration by which Newcastle announced and justified both the invasion of Yorkshire and the recruitment of Catholics, accompanied by a commentary on the preceding negotiations, see S Reid, *A Declaration made by the Earl of Newcastle* (Leigh-on-Sea, 1983).

107. *Victoria County History of Yorkshire* (VCHY), (London, 1913), Vol. III, p421.

108. *Lucy Hutchinson: Memoirs of the Life of Colonel Hutchinson*, ed. J Sutherland (London, 1973), p79.

109. AJ Hopper, ''Fitted for Desperation': Honour and Treachery in Parliament's Yorkshire Command, 1642-1643', *History*, Vol. 86, No282 (April, 2001), pp138-154.

110. Clarendon, *Rebellion*, Vol. VII, p121n.

111. *Ibid.*, Vol. VIII, p84.

112. Jones, 'The War in the North', pp100-101.

113. *Life of William Cavendish*, ppix-x.

114. For a detailed analysis of the way in which the Fairfaxes prosecuted the Yorkshire Parliamentarian war effort up to the Battle of Adwalton Moor, see Hopper, *"Readiness of the People."*

115. VCHY, Vol. III, P421.

116. C Russell, *The Crisis of Parliaments 1509-1660* (Oxford, 1971), p355.

117. Reid, *All The King's Armies*, p71-72.

118. *Life of William Cavendish*, px.

119. DNB, pp135-136.

120. G Trease, *Portrait of a Cavalier* (London, 1979), pp103-104.

121. *Ibid.*, pp106-107.

122. Markham, *Lord Fairfax*, p95.

123. *Life of William Cavendish*, p20, n4.

124. VCHY, Vol. III, pp422-423.

125. Gardiner, *Great Civil War*, p159.

126. BLTT E59 (1), E59 (21).

127. Trease, *Cavalier*, p116.

128. A Baker, *A Battlefield Atlas of the English Civil War* (London, 1986), p19.

129. *Diary of Sir Henry Slingsby*, p95.

130. Cromwell estimated the Queen's army to be '1200 horse and 3000 foot'. Historic Manuscripts Commission, 7th Report, Appendix, pp551-552.

131. Hopper, *"Readiness of the People"*, p16.

132. VCHY, Vol. III, p423.

133. The course of the fighting at Howley and the terms under which the Hall was besieged remain an issue of contention. See Markham, *Lord Fairfax*, pp102-103; Newman, 'Royalist Army', pp182-183; Jones, 'The War in the North', pp102-103.

134. Sir Thomas Fairfax described the town as 'a very untenable place'. YAJ Vol. VIII, p213.

135. HMC, Portland Mss., Vol. I, p718.

136. YAJ, Vol. VIII, p213.

137. *Ibid.*

138. *Life of William Cavendish*, p24.

139. *Diary of Sir Henry Slingsby*, pp95-96.

140. *Life of William Cavendish*, p215.

141. *Ibid.*

Chapter 3

142. Scatcherd, *History of Morley*, p276.

143. Captain John Hodgson, 'Memoirs', *Bradford Antiquary* (1903), p142.

144. *A Map of the Mannour or Lordship of Tong in the West Riding of the County of York; Surveyed for Sir George Tempest by John Dickinson 1725*, West Yorkshire Archive Service (Bradford), MS 9/2.

145. Joh(a)n Rosworm, 'Good Service Hitherto Ill Rewarded', *Ormerod Tracts*, (1844), Ch XI, p228.

146. James, *The History and Topography of Bradford*, p138.

147. YAJ, Vol. VIII, p213.

148. English Heritage, *Battlefield Report: Adwalton Moor*, p4.

149. HMC, Portland Mss., Vol. I, p717.

150. Scatcherd, *History of Morley*, p272.

151. West Yorkshire Archive Service (Wakefield), *Township of Drighlington Tithe Map 1848*, D5/3/46.

152. Dr A Brown, *Proof of Evidence. Application for Planning Permission by Prince's Ltd and Commercial Developments Ltd on Land Adjacent to Cross Lane, Hodgson Lane and the A650 Drighlington By-Pass*, Bradford (1998), 3.10.

153. R Muir, *The Countryside Encyclopaedia* (London, 1988), p201.

154. N Pevsner, *Yorkshire The West Riding* (Harmondsworth, 1967), p187.

155. HMC, Portland Mss., Vol. I, p717.

156. English Heritage, *Battlefield Report: Adwalton Moor*, p2

157. Scatcherd, *History of Morley*, p277.

158. Parker, *Illustrated Rambles*, p297.

159. Scatcherd, *History of Morley*, p276.

160. YAJ, Vol. VIII, p214.

161. HMC, Portland Mss., Vol. I, p717.

162. *Ibid*.

163. YAJ, Vol. VIII, p213.

164. *Life of William Cavendish*, p24.

165. *Ibid*., Appendix XI, p215.

166. *Map of East Bierley, 1599, Savile of Rufford Collection*, Nottinghamshire Record Office (Nottingham), DDSR 1/6/45. I am indebted to Glenn Foard for drawing my attention to this vital piece of evidence.

167. West Yorkshire Archive Service (Bradford), MS 9/2.

168. Kendall, *Halifax Antiquarian Society*, p8.

169. West Yorkshire Archaeological Service, *Land at Cross Lane, Drighlington, Bradford West Yorkshire. Archaeological Assessment* (June 1998, Report No 608), 4.3.4.

170. Scatcherd, *History of Morley*, p276.

171. *Ibid.*, p278.

172. West Yorkshire Archive Service (Wakefield), D5/3/46.

173. HMC, Portland Mss., Vol.I, p718.

174. Scatcherd, *History of Morley*, p272.

175. Yorkshire Archaeological Society (Leeds), MD 5/15.

176. *Life of William Cavendish*, pp24-25.
177. VCHY, Vol. II, p355.
178. *Life of William Cavendish*, Appendix XI, p216.

Chapter 4

179. HMC, Portland Mss., Vol. I, p717.
180. BLTT E59(1).
181. YAJ, Vol. VIII, p213.
182. Jones, 'The War in the North', pp52-53.
183. Reid, *All the King's Armies*, p81.
184. *Ibid.*, p77.
185. Jones, 'The War in the North', p106.
186. HMC, Portland Mss., Vol. I, p717.
187. *Life of William Cavendish*, p20n.
188. HMC, 7th Report, Appendix, pp551-552.
189. A full strength cavalry troop could have numbered 80 horse. However, under strength units averaging 50 horse per troop would give a total of 4000.
190. P R Newman, 'The 1663 List of Indigent Royalist Officers considered as a primary source for the study of the Royalist Army', *Historical Journal*, Vol. 30 No4 (1987), pp885-904.
191. YAJ, Vol. VIII, p213.
192. *Life of William Cavendish*, p24.
193. Reid, *All the King's Armies*, p5.
194. *Life of William Cavendish*, p215.
195. *The Civil Wars, A Military History of England Scotland and Ireland 1638-1660*, ed J Kenyon and J Ohimeyer (Oxford, 1998), p209.
196. Philipp J C Elliot-Wright, *Brassey's History of Uniforms, English Civil War* (London, 1997), p49.
197. *Life of William Cavendish*, p25.
198. C Carlton, *Going to the Wars* (London, 1992), p126.
199. BLTT E59(11).
200. Markham, *Lord Fairfax*, p103.
201. YAJ, Vol. VIII, p213.
202. HMC, Portland Mss., Vol. I, p717.
203. *The Diary of Sir Henry Slingsby*, p96.
204. HMC, Portland Mss., Vol. I, p717.
205. Reid, *All the King's Armies*, p77.
206. *Ibid*.
207. S Peachey, *The Mechanics of Infantry Combat* (Bristol, 1992), p9.
208. YAJ, Vol. VIII, p213.
209. *Diary of Sir Henry Slingsby*, p96.
210. P R Newman, *Royalist Officers in England and Wales 1642-1660* (London, 1981), p73.

211. HMC, Portland Mss., Vol. I, p718.

212. West Yorkshire Archaeological Service, *Land at Cross Lane, Drighlington Bradford, West Yorkshire: Archaeological Test Pitting* (September 1999, Report No 737) 5.5.

213. *Life of William Cavendish*, pp215-216.

214. YAJ, Vol. VIII, p213.

215. HMC, Portland Mss., Vol. I, p718.

216. D Evans, 'The Army of Lord Fairdinando Fairfax 1642-1645', *English Civil War Times*, No.55, p16.

217. C Hollick, 'Frontages', *The Battlefields Trust News*, Vol.2, No5 (November 1993), p10.

218. *The Diary of Sir Henry Slingsby*, p96.

219. *Life of William Cavendish*, p216.

220. Hollick, *'Frontages',* p10.

221. *Life of William Cavendish*, p24.

222. YAJ, Vol. VIII, p213.

223. HMC, Portland Mss., Vol. I, p717.

224. *Ibid.*, p718.

225. Scatcherd, *History of Morley*, pp276-278; *Life of William Cavendish*, pp24-25

226. YAJ, Vol. VIII, p213.

227. *Ibid*.

228. *Life of William Cavendish*, p216.

229. *The Monckton Papers*, ed E Peacock (Philobiblon Society,1884), pp14-15.

230. HMC, Portland Mss., Vol. I, p718.

231. BLTT E60(18).

232. HMC, Portland Mss., Vol. I, p718.

233. YAJ, Vol. VIII, p213.

234. *Ibid.*, p214.

235. Warwick, *Memoires of King Charles I*, p257.

236. YAJ, Vol. VIII, p214.

237. Newman, *Royalist Officers*.

238. *Life of William Cavendish*, p25.

239. S Reid, 'The Earl of Newcastle's Regiment of Foot', *English Civil War Times*, No.53, p18.

240. BLTT E60(18); A Collins, *Historical Collections of the Noble Families of Cavendish* etc (London,1752), p31.

241. Warwick, *Memoires of King Charles I*, p257

242. Reid, *All The King's Armies*, p77.

243. *Diary of Sir Henry Slingsby*, p96.

244. *The Autobiography of Joseph Lister*, ed. T Wright (London, 1842), p19.

245. HMC, Portland Mss., Vol. I, p718.

246. YAJ, Vol. VIII, p214.

247. BLTT E59(12).

248. HMC, Portland Mss., Vol. I, p717.

249. *Diary of Sir Henry Slingsby*, p96.

250. *Life of William Cavendish*, p216.

251. *Ibid*., p25.

252. YAJ, Vol. VIII, pp213-214.

253. D Neelon, 'James Nayler in the English Civil Wars', *Quaker Studies*, 6/1 (2001), pp12-13.

254. Hopper, *"Readiness of the People"*, p16.

255. YAJ, Vol. VIII, p214.

256. *Diary of Sir Henry Slingsby*, p97.

257. HMC, Portland Mss., Vol. I, p718.

258. *Diary of Sir Henry Slingsby*, p96.

259. Robinson, *North of England Tractates*, p7.

260. Scatcherd, *History of Morley*, p278.

Aftermath and Conclusion

261. *Autobiography of Joseph Lister*, p19.

262. *Life of William Cavendish*, p25 & p216.

263. YAJ, Vol. VIII, p214.

264. HMC, Portland Mss., Vol. I, p718.

265. *Ibid.*

266. YAJ, Vol. VIII, p214.

267. *Life of William Cavendish*, p216.

268. Parker, *Illustrated Rambles*, p297.

269. I am indebted to Ron Barnes, Drighlington local historian and former headmaster, for information concerning the Crown Point Hotel and its associated grounds.

270. The Royalist siege of Bradford and the Parliamentarian retreat to Hull are here based upon the accounts of Thomas Stockdale, Sir Thomas Fairfax, John Rushworth, Joseph Lister, Sir Henry Slingsby, the earl of Newcastle, and the duchess of Newcastle.

271. Warwick, *Memoires of King Charles I*, p258.

272. HMC, Portland Mss.Vol. I, p718.

273. Warwick, *Memoires of King Charles I*, p257.

274. *Autobiography of Joseph Lister*, p19.

275. *Life of William Cavendish*, p26.

276. *Diary of Sir Henry Slingsby*, p97.

277. BLTT E60(18).

278. Osborn Ms b233 f39, Beinecke Library, Yale University.

BIBLIOGRAPHY

Primary Printed Sources

A Declaration made by the Earl of Newcastle, ed.S Reid (Leigh-on-Sea). British Library Thomason Tracts.

Cavendish M, *Life of Willaim Cavendish*, ed. CH Firth (London, 1906).

Clarendon's *History of the Rebellion*, ed. WD Macray (Oxford, 1888).

Collins A, *Historical Collections of the Noble Families of Cavendish...* (London, 1752).

Hodgson Captain J, 'Memoirs', *Bradford Antiquary* (1903).

Journal of the House of Commons 1642-1644, Vol. 3.

Journal of the House of Lords 1643-1644, Vol. 6.

Lucy Hutchinson: Memoires of the Life of Colonel Hutchinson, ed. J Sutherland (London, 1973).

Roseworme J, *Good Service Hitherto Ill Rewarded*, Ormerod Tracts (1844?), ch XI

Rushworth J, *Historical Collections* (London, 1721), Vol V.

The Autobiography of Joseph Lister, ed. T Wright (London, 1842).

The Diary of Sir Henry Slingsby, ed. D Parsons (London, 1836).

Thomas Lord Fairfax, 'A Short Memorial of the Northern Actions During The War There, From The Year 1642 Till 1644', *Yorkshire Archaeological Journal* Vol. VIII (1884).

Thomas Stockdale to William Lenthal, Historical Manuscripts Commission, Portland Mss., Vol. I, pp 717-719.

Warwick, Sir Philip, *Memoires of the Reign of King Charles I* (London, 1701).

Secondary Sources

Aston M, *Interpreting the Landscape* (London, 1985).

Baker A, *A Battlefield Atlas of the English Civil War* (London, 1986).

Bennett M, *The English Civil War* (London, 1995).

Brown, Dr A, *Proof of Evidence. Application for Planning Permission by Prince's Ltd and Commercial Developments Ltd on Land Adjacent to Cross Lane, Hodgson Lane and the A650 Drighlington By-Pass* (Bradford, 1988).

Carlton C, *Going to the Wars* (London, 1992).

Cooke D, *The Forgotten Battle: The Battle of Adwalton Moor* (Heckmondwike, 1996).

Dictionary of National Biography (London, 1899).

Elliot-Wright P J C, *Brassey's History of Uniforms, English Civil War* (London, 1997).

English Heritage Battlefield Report, *Adwalton Moor 1643* (London, 1995).

Gardiner S R, *History of the Great War 1642-1649* (London, 1901), Vol. I 1642-1644.

Haythornthwaite P, *The English Civil War 1642-1651. An Illustrated Military History* (London, 1994).

Hexter J H, *The Reign of King Pym* (London, 1941).

Hopper A J, *'The Readiness of the People'* (University of York, 1997).

James J, *The History and Topography of Bradford* (London, 1841).

Jones J, 'The War in the North. The Northern Parliamentary Army in the English Civil War 1642-1645' (Ontario PhD,1991).

Kenyon J & Ohlmeyer J, *The Civil Wars* (Oxford, 1998).

Markham C R, *Life of the Great Lord Fairfax* (London, 1870).

Muir R, *The Countryside Encyclopaedia* (London, 1988).

Newman P R, *Marston Moor, 2 July 1644: The Sources and the Site* (York, 1978).

Newman P R, *Royalist Officers in England and Wales 1642-1660* (London, 1981).

Newman P R, 'The 1663 List of Indigent Royalist Officers considered as a primary source for the study of the Royalist Army' *Historical Journal*, Vol. 30, No 4 (1987)

Newman P R, 'The Royalist Army in Northern England 1642-1645' (York PhD, 1978).

Parker J, *Illustrated rambles from Hipperholme to Tong* (Bradford, 1904).

Reid S, *Gunpowder Triumphant* (Leigh-on-Sea, 1987).

Reid S, *All The King's Armies* (Staplehurst, 1998).

Scatcherd N, *History of Morley* (Leeds, 1830).

Smith G R, *Without Touch of Dishonour* (Kineton, 1968).

Trease G, *Portrait of a Cavalier* (London, 1979).

Turton A & Peachey S, *Armies of the First English Civil War 1642-1646* (Bristol, 1993).

Victoria County History of Yorkshire (London, 1912), Vol. II & III.

Wedgwood C V, *The King's War* (London, 1958).

West Yorkshire Archaeological Services (Wakefield), *Land at Cross Lane, Drighlington, Bradford, West Yorkshire Archaeological Assessment* (June 1998), Report No 608.

West Yorkshire Archaeological Services (Wakefield), *Land at Cross Lane, Drighlington, Bradford, West Yorkshire Archaeological Test Pitting* (September 1999), Report No 737.

Woolrych A, *Battles of the English Civil War* (London, 1961).

Young P & Holmes R, *The English Civil War: A Military History of the Three Civil Wars 1642-1651* (London, 1974).

INDEX

Turnham Green [1642], viii,xiv

Vane, Sir Henry, xx-xxi

Wakefield, 28-29,32-34,36,71,82,100,108
Wakefield-Tong Lane End Turnpike Trust, 46
Waller, Colonel Sir William, xi,xxi
Warburton, J., 41,45-46,49-50
Warwick, Sir Philip, xvi-xvii,11,95,97-98,100-101,119,121
Wedgwood, C.V., xi
Welbeck Abbey, 4
West Yorkshire Archaeological Services, 127
Western Association, xi
Westminster, x,xiv,xxi,10,23,71,110,114-115,117,119
Wetherby, 23,25-26,28
Wharfe, River, 26
Willoughby of Parham, Francis Lord, xv
Woolrych, A., xi

Yarm Bridge, skirmish [1643], 29,31
York, xiv-xv,7,10,12,23,25-26,28-29,31-33,36,68,119,123-124
Yorkshire Battlefields Society, 18
Yorkshire Coalfield, 60
Young, Brigadier Peter, 16-17